T0291167

Praise for *America as No. 3*

'How the US and China adjust to their new positions in the world is the big question of our time. It will affect all our lives — from the climate emergency to the likelihood of global war. Hugh Peyman puts economics at the heart of this unfolding story. This is a refreshing and important change from the more common political and military analyses because the economic re-arrangement is startling.

Peyman provides a very readable account of this economic 'reality' and why it needs to inform international politics.'

Professor of Political Economy at King's College,
London, Shaun Hargreaves Heap

'Hugh Peyman is a seasoned witness of China's manufacturing prowess as Factory of the World. Get insights from a researcher who sees things from the top down and bottom up. A compelling read for global investors.'

Singapore Sovereign Wealth Fund GIC former CIO,
PIMCO Adviser and Avanda Co-Founder, Ng Kok Song

"All investors must pay attention to Hugh Peyman's elephant in the room, as a New New World is born. Most timely."

Blue Ocean Technologies Chairman, former State Street
Global Advisors Vice Chairman and GE Asset Management
Public Equities CIO, Ralph Layman

'Hugh Peyman is a rare foreigner who knows China from the ground up. The West must get used to the idea that West may no longer be best.'

Former Hong Kong Securities and Futures Commission Chairman,
Chief Adviser China Banking and Insurance Regulatory Commission and
South China Morning Post columnist, Andrew Sheng

Praise for *China's Change*

Winner of the 2018 Sharjah International Non-Fiction Prize.

'I strongly recommend China's Change. *All countries are looking for new solutions. How to get a new perspective?* China's Change *is a new perspective.* China's Change *is unique. For a foreigner to go into deep and long-term analysis of China, especially using traditional philosophy to understand China, is hard to come by.*'

"China's Father of Economic Reform",
Vice Minister of China's State Commission for Restructuring the
Economic System, Professor Gao Shangquan

'Far from seeing China through a Western prism — and consistently getting it wrong — Hugh Peyman understands China like few others.'

Author of When China Rules the World, Martin Jacques

'Hegel looked down on China until he read the Yi Jing (Book of Change). For a Westerner to dig out the Yi Jing *again, linking it to its impact on China's great change is very meaningful.* China's Change *has many facets. Not just on economics but culture, systems and governance. This is a big strong work.*'

Jean Monnet Chair Professor, Institute of International Affairs
Director, Renmin University, Wang Yiwei

'Through the extraordinary array of people he has known and met over 40 years, Hugh Peyman tells the story of today's China in a way never been done before.'

BBC Director-General, Tony Hall

'All travellers to China, whether on business, holiday or study, should take this book.'

Banyan Tree Resorts Founder, Singapore Management University Trustees Chairman, Ho Kwon Ping

'A very valuable book: makes cogent arguments with a lot of valid, interesting and provocative statements that will help people to think about China.'

Pulitzer Prize winner, Ian Johnson

'I was particularly drawn in by "what is China getting right?"'

Financial Times Global China Editor, James Kynge

'Hugh Peyman belongs to the realistic camp. What gives the book credibility is his 40 years' experience following China and particularly two decades living there.'

Anglo American Group China Chief Representative, William Fu

'A wholly original approach to understanding present-day China. It is difficult to do justice to the exceptionally wide-ranging scope.'

The Society of Professional Economists, Ian Harwood

'China's Change is a great way to discover how China has evolved from a static, command economy to one driven by entrepreneurs. Punctures the biggest myths about the Chinese economy. A great read.'

Matthews Asia Investment Strategist, former US diplomat, Andy Rothman

'Peyman has a flair for making the difficult to grasp and conceptualise into something accessible. What impressed me the most was how well written it is. Fascinating.'

Chatham House Editor, Mike Tsang

America as No.3

Get Real About China, India and the Rest

America as No.3

Get Real About China, India and the Rest

HUGH PEYMAN

NEW JERSEY · LONDON · SINGAPORE · BEIJING · SHANGHAI · HONG KONG · TAIPEI · CHENNAI · TOKYO

Published by

World Scientific Publishing Co. Pte. Ltd.

5 Toh Tuck Link, Singapore 596224

USA office: 27 Warren Street, Suite 401-402, Hackensack, NJ 07601

UK office: 57 Shelton Street, Covent Garden, London WC2H 9HE

Library of Congress Control Number: 2023941997

British Library Cataloguing-in-Publication Data
A catalogue record for this book is available from the British Library.

AMERICA AS NO.3
Get Real About China, India and the Rest

ISBN 978-981-127-316-2 (hardcover)
ISBN 978-981-128-351-2 (softcover)
ISBN 978-981-127-317-9 (ebook for institutions)
ISBN 978-981-127-318-6 (ebook for individuals)

For any available supplementary material, please visit
https://www.worldscientific.com/worldscibooks/10.1142/13329#t=suppl

Desk Editor: Venkatesh Sandhya

Typeset by Stallion Press
Email: enquiries@stallionpress.com

Printed in Singapore

For Matthew, Radhika, Mia and Ethan

Contents

Preface

Why write *America as No. 3: Get Real About China, India and the Rest*? The answer is simple. A once-in-a-century change in the world's economic order is underway. Yet few in the West grasp what that means or how to manage the new era.

America as No. 3 is not pro- or anti- anyone. It is a wake-up call. As Professor of Political Economy at King's College, London Shaun Hargreaves Heap says, "How the US and China adjust to their new positions in the world is the big question of our time. It will affect all our lives; and why it needs to inform international politics."

The title *America as No. 3* is not designed to lure readers with a false premise. It is the clear-cut conclusion of years of extensive research by the world's most highly regarded economic institution, the Organisation for Economic Co-operation and Development (OECD). With a staff of 2,100 and an annual budget of almost 400 million euros, professional economists widely consider the OECD to be the world's most credible long-term forecaster.

For a decade, OECD forecasts have anticipated the eventual US loss of top status. It is too obvious to ignore. Yet it is very largely missing from the general narrative about the West and the Rest. Instead, a US-led New World Order 2.0 is the US media talk or simply called a US-China Trade War to cover a range of conflicts.

Reality points to a very different new order, as yet unnamed. The new economic order is driven by two main facts. First, economics: the Rest's past rising education levels, economic development and reform significantly boost productivity. Second, demography: China and India are both four times bigger than the US. Indonesia's population will be only a little less than the US. The gaps cannot be ignored any longer, they are too telling.

The OECD forecasts that economically America will no longer be No. 1; and not even No. 2 by 2047. India will be. America will simply be No. 3. In fact, by the Purchasing Power Parity (PPP) measure, which the OECD and most economists use to compare economies' GDPs, China is already No. 1: ahead of the US in 2023 by 27%.

The other leading global institution, the International Monetary Fund (IMF), calculates that China and India alone will generate half the world's 2023 GDP growth: Asia 70%. Between 2023 and 2028, the IMF sees China and India contributing some 35% to world growth: 22.6% and 12.9% respectively. The US will follow with 11.3%, Indonesia 3.6%, Japan 1.8%, Brazil 1.7%, Russia and Germany 1.6%. The UK and France will only manage 1.5% each.

So why not tap into this powerful trend by being on good terms with the higher-growth economies? Particularly when considering the very likely future shape and leadership of the world economy, Is this a case of hubris, ignorance or incompetence, justified by US Exceptionalism; and prevented by vested interests?

Now is a bit late to close the stable door, not at least without a very large price tag. Economic momentum is so strong behind China, India and the Rest that any attempt to stop it in its tracks would be blown away. Not just by economics but by demographics. The West will very soon comprise only 10% of the world's population, the Rest 90%. This is a New New World. No longer is America the all-powerful New World.

That does not mean that the average American will be worse off than the average Chinese any time soon, not even this century. Indeed, the OECD sees the average American in 2050 much wealthier than the average Chinese. So why is there all the fuss and vitriol?

The brutal reality is that power transitions rarely go smoothly. Incumbents usually resist challenges. Rising economic powers can increasingly fund greater technological advances and military budgets. In a nuclear era, what could be more alarming? War could go nuclear; and that could speed the world to a very swift end.

All sides need to address this before it is too late. Denial or demonisation of competitors only makes matters worse. As does widespread ignorance about the much older ancient civilisations that want to emulate China. From India to Indonesia, Nigeria to Egypt, Turkiye and Iran, all aspire to increase their security and often regain previous regional eminence. Economics collides with geography and history that shape geopolitics.

A New New World is forming, likely to replace two centuries of Western dominance. The US is no longer the New World. Population numbers dictate that the West is only 10%, the Rest 90%.

No. 1, blinded by pre-eminence, is slow to see its power ebb. Even if it does, adjusting to the New New World is hard. Understanding the dynamics is difficult. Key elements may differ, especially if from another culture, history and value system. In the West there are many King Canutes: all in denial about the defining trend of the 21st century.

Friction grows relentlessly between the entrenched power, the US, and the first rising power, China. Increasingly, US domestic problems become intractable. Competence is questioned: government credibility and social cohesion suffer. The same problems recur, arising from the need for jobs and votes. Abroad tensions build.

Previously, "Other" countries did not matter. They were large but very poor. Now their economies punch closer to their demographic weight, providing some of the world's fastest economic growth. The West can benefit from it but only by changing course. This is a time for cooperation, not confrontation and containment.

That is easier said than done, even though they will still lag far behind the West in per capita income: average Americans are five times richer than average Chinese. That is not going to change significantly, even within several decades. So why ratchet up tension? Why indeed?

This is all about America remaining Top Dog. Not being the largest economy is unacceptable — and not just to many Americans but some in Asia too. Powerful vested interests benefit from Western dominance. That has to change if the West is to benefit from the economic rise of China, India and the Rest. How though?

Accept that mega-trend; and get on with the rest of the century. There are so many existential global challenges that threaten everyone, from climate change to cyber space. It seems so obvious, yet that is easy to write, much harder to do. Over simplistic solutions abound, threatening the planet's very existence.

Many in the US talk of decoupling China from the global economy. Economically, in theory, it could happen. Two or more groups could form: less efficient but one-day workable. That though is not the real danger. The greatest danger lies in the many turbulent years beforehand. Splitting apart the recently more inter-connected world economy will not be seamless or painless: indeed, quite the opposite.

Global systems cannot be switched on or off like a light. Decoupling could blow a fuse. A Great Depression could result, as it did in the 1930s: ended only by world war. Unintended self-harm is the real China Threat: the US harming itself and allies during the separation.

How robust will be political and financial systems or societies? What of heavily export-dependent economies, such as in Southeast Asia, principal targets like China or mature Western economies, unable to handle internal stresses or military overreach, such as the US and EU? All would be badly affected.

COVID and Afghanistan have raised the overlooked question of Western competence. Not just of governments but societies too. How will either respond to a fast changing world of which they understand far too little?

America as No. 3 pulls together the many strands of this transition. So far US-China friction has been analysed mostly from one perspective, be it politics, economics or security. One-dimensional approaches have a major drawback: each only covers part of the story in any depth. Compounding the error, most analyses have greater knowledge of one country than another. A single discipline perspective cannot integrate the three areas of politics, economics and security. It misses the critical linkages and relative weights between them.

I am a generalist by background, synthesising different elements into one picture and overall conclusion. My education, as well as a life in journalism and finance, taught me the great importance of intellectual rigour, balance and accuracy: a search for reality, not ideological conviction. I write not from an ideological perspective but from an economic one.

I first visited China in 1978: Shanghai has been home since 2002. I first worked in the US in 1972, at an eye-opening Oklahoman textile factory. Even Oklahomans called small town Tishomingo Little Dixie: a throwback to the pre-Civil War slave-owning South, which after its defeat saw many of the poorest Whites migrate westwards, including into the land of the Chickasaws. Afterwards, I travelled from coast to coast seeing many other Americas.

For three decades, I visited the US two or three times a year to discuss Asian investment prospects with fund managers. I visited Washington annually to gauge political currents, international policy and think tank interpretations. Eight years at Wall Street's leading firm Merrill Lynch, heading research into Asia from Korea to India, rounded off this great education. The seeds of the book were sown many years ago as the Acknowledgements recount.

Knowing first hand Americans' kind hospitality and generosity, I feel I should speak out. I believe their country has miscalculated badly and is moving unnecessarily in a very dangerous direction overseas. The same has happened in my native England.

America as No. 3 is written for them as well as for Matthew, Radhika and especially Mia and Ethan. Theirs will be a very different world. Greater uncertainty will exist, with dramatically reduced chances for the West to enjoy peace and prosperity, unless it reverses the collision course with China, India and the Rest.

Hopefully their generations will face up much better and more honestly than ours to reality. By cutting through delusion, denial and amnesia they can find global solutions to existential problems. With common sense, they can recharge all batteries.

New voices must be heard on China, for that to occur. Instead of Western thinking being held hostage by outdated Cold War ideology, new perspectives are essential to find solutions.

Listen to business people and economists, notably development economists. Not solely to security specialists, politicians and their media echo chambers that have captured the Western narrative. Usually lacking any grounding in real world money, current Western policy makers often have little-to-no China expertise, certainly not compared with those in business.

Would any Westerner with a heart problem go to a psychologist or a heart specialist? The answer is obvious. Similarly, why go to security advisers, stuck largely with Cold War or Russian backgrounds, lacking extensive on-the-ground China experience or even grasp of basic economics (two major knowledge gaps)?

Go to the many non-ideological Western entrepreneurs, managers and development economists who have "lived in country" for years. Handling it every day, they know how China works: its imperfections, startling changes and ambitions.

Yet those who can help most are left out of the mainstream discussion. Their informed voices must be heard before it is too late. *America as No. 3* draws heavily on their expertise, encountered during my two decades of living and researching in China. This may be the last chance.

Ubud, Bali, April 2023
hughpeyman@research-works.com

Prologue

The Last Chance

A single fact stilled the room. The world's Tech industry came to the annual jamboree in its usual boisterous New Year spirits, keen to see the hottest gizmos and hear the latest star-gazing claims. Vegas 2023 was no different until an expert delivered his short message.

China is making electric vehicles (EVs) 10,000 euro cheaper than Europe. He added, these are "good vehicles".

This was even more sobering than recent claims, swirling around, of how much cheaper Elon Musk could make the Tesla 3 in Shanghai than in America. That could be typical Musk bluster but this was about the whole small EV industry; and everyone knew that the US was even more expensive than Europe.

The fact made its way around the world on the news wires, yet received no Sputnik moment reaction that greeted the 1957 alarm. This time, America seemed silent, having run out of words and ideas. All attention was on the House of Representatives shenanigans and the latest COVID variant, not on the future of the world economy or the connected issue of world peace. The implications are obvious. It even brings into question the long-term viability of much US manufacturing, unless robots are the future.

With EVs the future of motoring, the world's largest manufacturing sector, looks as if it will no longer be dominated by the West. This would be for the first time since cars were invented. Eyes blinked, some may have watered.

The Western public was already anxious about national competitiveness. President Joe Biden had warned of "extreme competition" with China but surely not quite so quickly. Presumably Biden had meant America would be extremely competitive and not its chosen rival China. Was this game over before it had really begun?

The great symbolic significance was not to be missed. A car is the most expensive thing households buy, apart from a home. This was a body blow to auto-mad Americans and Europeans proud of their long engineering tradition: a most unwelcome indicator of the future.

At CES in Las Vegas, the "Most Influential Tech Event in the World", Patrick Koller, Chief Executive of Fovia, a major global auto components maker, stated China's 10,000 euro advantage as a fact: not an opinion, a fact. The century-old French-German firm knows China well.

China's advantage is no business secret. UK-based business intelligence firm JATO in 2022 spelled out the bald trends. Prices of such European cars had risen to euro 55,821 from euro 48,942 in 2015, while the average price in the US had risen to $63,864 from $53,038. In China, prices since 2015 had more than *halved* to euro 31,829 from euro 66,819: challenging mathematics.

China has become the Workshop of the World. This means that concentration and proximity of manufacturing drives down production costs and increases specialisation, spurring greater efficiency. Britain had this in the 19th century. Harvard's Michael Porter calls it the "cluster effect": eagerly sought.

How China achieved this is the heart of the book and will be detailed later. Here, it can best be summarized by five things – scale, competition, entrepreneurship, innovation and how China works, especially using traditional philosophy in governance and strategy (Chapters 5-8, notably *Sources of Dynamism* and *Strong Buttresses*).

I first looked at China's "renewable" green industries some 15-20 years ago. There was very little for investors to see. However there was one positive indicator. Since 1995, China's spending on Research & Development (R&D) has continued to rise significantly.

Well before China became the Workshop of the World, the government had produced a very long-term policy on R&D. A quarter of a century later it is still on track. That was promising for any economy; and especially for any new industry. In actual terms, as a percentage of GDP, China's spending has quintupled to 2.55% in 2022, the seventh year running of double-digit growth.

My colleagues and I saw in 2009 a young Siasun in Shenyang making very basic robots. In 2010, we examined BYD's EV prototype in Shenzhen, just seven years after making its first car. The battery was huge, the car small and its prospects unclear. Still, BYD was not named Build Your Dreams for nothing: it would follow its dream. Ambition was clear, changing its name to BYD broadcasted its intention to emulate VW, BMW and GM.

Today, Siasun's robots are used in outer space. BYD's EV sales, in (OEM unbranded) plug-in electric cars, comfortably lead Elon Musk's Tesla in China. One year ago BYD ranked fourth with 7.7% market share. Now it has a rising 17.3%.

With the exception of hydro, where China was already a world leader, China's renewable industries were insignificant. In the early days of non-fossil new energy, Chinese firms lagged far behind American leaders like GE or Denmark's Vestas in wind power; and numerous Western new players in solar. In other forms of green technology it was the same.

Signs of the Times

Without realising it, four decades before China's EV take off, I witnessed the origins of the first US-China trade dispute of the modern era. Along with a score of other guinea pig Western tourists, assembled by China Travel Services in Hong Kong to test China's travel industry in October 1978, I was puzzled.

Why did several places we visited, even industrial plants, highlight their mushrooms? In dank, dark cellars, even a cave, people in southern China's early winter were growing mushrooms. In fact, their eyes lit up when discussing them: clearly there was opportunity, money and something we did not understand.

Only a few months later the *Asian Wall Street Journal* gave the answer. So many in China were growing mushrooms that US growers complained about China dumping tinned mushrooms. Why? Presumably the hunt for scarce foreign exchange sparked the first trade dispute I can remember. This occurred even before China's Reform and Opening Up was announced. Not a big story but it was new: genuine news. Something was happening at China Speed.

Enterprising people were making the most of what they had, which often was very little. In this case, unused labour, plenty of spare time, dark, dank spaces and damp. Where they could find or create it, urban China was going back to work after years of disruption.

I could not imagine that 45 years later China would help alleviate world food shortages and dampen rising food prices from Japan to the US, Malaysia to Africa and Europe. In Shenzhen, alongside some world high-technology leaders, freight forwarders' offices were very busy.

Canned mushrooms were joined by tomatoes, seafood, ready-to-eat meals, corn and bamboo shoots in a $6.9 billion canned food export industry that in 2022 grew 22%. Small, compared with total China exports of $3.59 trillion, it illustrates a big fact. China never discards experience or knowledge, it just adds another layer to it; and numerous more layers on top of that. As writer Amy Tan put it, "nothing is ever completely thrown away...That is the Chinese aesthetic and also its spirit." (Chapter 21: *Understanding In a New Era*). Knowledge accumulates, finding new uses.

I certainly could not imagine that China would become the Workshop of the World. Let alone lead in industries that did not exist when China's historic economic recovery began.

Yet by 2022, some 80% of the world's solar panels and wind equipment were produced in China, half of all EV batteries. China is now only second to the US in nuclear energy; and produces half the world's new energy vehicles, with about 30% from its own makers, together with another 20% from foreign marques.

I still find such transformation stunning. Hard to believe but all data confirm it. Such memories resurface from my very first visit to the mainland at the dawn of China's dramatic economic recovery, when Shenzen was still a "fishing village" of 30,000 people in 1978 not today's nearly 18 million. A quarter of century later firms like BYD and Siasun provide clues to how this "night- and -day transformation" was achieved. Countless other company visits to China strengthened my conviction that the OECD is right about the future of the world economy and the likelihood of America as No. 3 by 2050.

Around the time Charlie Munger and Warren Buffet in 2008 bought Berkshire Hathaway's stake in BYD, I asked the battery-cum-carmaker about expansion. The new focus was electric vehicles, I learned: the target market the US, specifically California.

Why not China, I asked? There was no national battery charging system, nor likely to be, was the answer. I suggested that with state control of the energy sector China would find that easy to do. No, California would be much easier, I was told. State support there already existed. The US was the leader; and a much bigger market.

Today the tables have turned. China has 10 times more charging stations than the US, according to StockApps.com. More revealing still, 41% are fast-charging stations compared with only 19% in the US. Is that China speed or US indecision and incompetence? Whichever, it underlines the critical difference.

By 2025, Shanghai expects more than half its new cars to be fully electric. Some 80% of buses and taxis will be new energy vehicles. 760,000 charging stations will criss-cross the city: a hydrogen refueling network is growing. Shanghai is not alone. Beijing is equally ambitious. Shenzhen, home to BYD and many IT/electronic businesses, has developed pilot schemes and policies since 2009. These have now borne fruit. By 2025, Shenzhen expects to have one million new EVs.

China battery makers are led no more by BYD, though it still makes 15%. The new leader is a company I had never heard of until 2018. Founded in 2011, Fujian's CATL made 35% of world EV batteries in 2022 and plans Europe's largest $7 billion EV battery plant. This follows a $5 billion battery recycling plant in central China; and a $6 billion investment in battery manufacturing and related mining in Southeast Asia's largest economy Indonesia. Ford and Tesla talk with CATL about plants in the US.

The China Cost

The China Price caught world attention in the early 2000s. Ignoring the explanation of migrants working long hours for low wages, this was good news for the West. The China Price provided much cheaper goods to offset stagnant real wages, enabling many consumers to maintain living standards: a free gift.

What caught my attention was something else: the China Cost. Major global firms noticed it too. Mining giant BHP, already well established in China, set up a local procurement department in 2007. This sourced cheaper but equally good materials and equipment for operations worldwide. In six years it became an $800 million business.

William Fu, who was in charge, recalls that, "cost savings ranged from 50% to 30%. Lead times were much shorter than elsewhere." He added though that, "This cost advantage was eroded by increased labour, safety and compliance cost. However China's development in quality improvement and R&D investment enhanced the overall value, moving firms up the value-added curve where they maintained a cost advantage in overseas markets".

Cost advantages may persist longer in rapidly changing new industries like EVs than traditional ones. Probably because so much happens all at once that others simply cannot keep up with copying.

Dramatic confirmation of lower prices came from a very small but most telling example. After designing a new office in China, complete with European-standard finishing and costs, more than a decade ago a leading global firm did an experiment. Its next expansion set up a dummy company, with a Chinese name and no apparent connection to its foreign, well-heeled self. This duly advertised for contractors to work on its new office.

Specifications were identical to the previous office, down to the exact brand of paint for the reception desk. Instantly, quotes came in. The best was priced 30% lower than when the advertiser was clearly a foreign firm. Evidently, there was a local price and one for foreigners: what the market would bear. Presumably it would have disappeared over time as new foreign firms "wised up" to what was happening in China. Yet it seems the China advantage, now shared with foreign joint-venture partners in China, has persisted. How did this happen?

Marcus Shütz, formerly with Volkswagen (VW) and now a foreign consultant with long, direct experience of China's auto sector, explained about EVs. "Not much innovation is needed to build an EV (except for the battery and software) and *that's what Chinese firms are good at,*" he noted. What keeps them fit and honest is keen competition. There are more than 450 EV firms registered in China, all driving down costs; and/or increasing innovation and value.

Dr Schütz could have added that China has the world's most adventurous consumers who love novelty, fun and help shape new products. Who else would have called its European sedan Funky Cat? Great Wall Motors' (renamed GWM) ORA did - in staid Europe: Funky Cat.

Patrick Koller put down the "overwhelming cost" advantage to "lower research and development (R&D) costs, lower levels of capital spending and lower labour costs than rivals in Europe." That may seem straightforward but it is not. First, what are R&D and capital spending? Business schools and economists have precise Western definitions, yet these may not elsewhere capture on-the-ground realities or an enterprise's essence.

None would have imagined what I saw when BYD was in its infancy. Miles behind foreign competitors, it only competed at the low-end of the China market, where there were no foreign brands.

The car body on the conveyor belt coming towards us was a startling sight. I saw not one, two or even three figures working on each moving shell but seven. I counted again. It was seven, and there was a bizarre killer fact. Two workers did not even have their feet on the ground. One crouched inside the car, fixing something on the back seat, the other was splayed, face down, over the car roof working on the windscreen underneath as the body moved along.

When I raised this with a manager, as tactfully as I could, he explained what I had never considered. To save on capital, BYD broke down each task into its basic units. Then it analysed what could be done manually and what absolutely needed scarce capital.

I was reminded of this highly innovative approach when I read remarks by Bruce Aylward, head of the World Health Organisation (WHO) mission to China in 2020. He described what he saw in the early days of COVID. The approach was the same, if the word disease is replaced by the word manufacturing.

"China did not approach the new disease with an old strategy. It developed its own approach and extraordinarily has turned around the disease with strategies that most of the world did not think would work," Aylward stated (Chapter 12). There are non-Western ways that work, contrary to much Western thinking that presumes it knows best.

"This was probably the most ambitious, agile and aggressive disease containment effort in history." Aylward told reporters. China had taken, "an old approach, then turbo-charged it with modern science in ways unimaginable even a few years before."

In the West, he continued, "People repeatedly throw up their hands [in horror and surrender. Whereas] China says *this is what we have*. Get out the old ones [measures]. *Adapt, innovate*".

That is exactly what BYD did in its early days: adapt and innovate. The spirit has remained with it and all others now challenging the West with products that have an "overwhelming cost" advantage. The best don't waste resources. They figure out every small thing and prepare thoroughly.

No wonder, "Chinese automakers, for the first time, feel ready to establish themselves globally," said veteran US China auto consultant Michael Dunne in 2022. They are not mocked for poor quality, as Japanese and South Koreans were. Chinese makers have used China's extensive electronics hardware and software knowledge to establish a good reputation domestically with the world's most demanding consumers. These force innovation, especially in the car's interior: the experience.

They impress not only Chinese customers but also foreign auto makers. Now Europeans led by Germans, and Americans too, see China as the world's future vehicle centre. China has the talent pool and industrial ecology to support it.

Over time Chinese firms will capture the high brand premium prices that accrue to world leaders. For now they are content to have the breakthrough advantage of a much lower EV production cost. The next phase, as Huawei in phones is starting to enjoy, is premium pricing that secures much more of the value created. This was the lesson from Apple's great success. Don't just make the product, create and own the intellectual property.

Premium pricing is happening increasingly across the board; and around the world. In Indonesia, I have come across two very ordinary examples: swimming goggles and computer mice. The local supermarket carries two brands of goggles. Both are Chinese. The superior one, which has lasted well after two years of constant use, sells at a 100% mark up to the cheap version; and has earned its premium. More impressive still is Altec Lansing.

When a young monkey stole my mouse (one of the hazards of writing in Bali) I needed a replacement, fast. I knew the BBC (Bali Bintang Company) had the best computer accessories range in Ubud, so went there. Sure enough, the Chinese entry model was half the price of the mouse from world famous Philips.

What I had not expected was that another Chinese mouse was selling for only 5% less than the premium Dutch mouse. I recognised the brand's name. A gadget-freak friend had raved about Altec speakers. These he swore had better sound, were half the size and cost half the price of European competitors: better.

Altec was a US company founded in 1927 that went bankrupt. A Tel Aviv headquartered private equity group Infinity, with operations throughout China, backed by the China Development Bank, bought Altec in 2012. This was repositioned as Altec Lansing, stressing Altec's long history and pedigree, while delivering high-quality technology with unbeatable value.

This was less than a dollar cheaper than the Philips mouse but more stylish. I had never thought a mouse could be stylish. Soft creamy white is Altec's colour, not dull black: its shape, not clunky, as if made for large Caucasian hands. This is sleek, with a gentle, elegant downward slope, designed with smaller Asian hands in mind, just as Korea's Samsung did with the breakthrough clamshell phone two decades ago.

Effectively the Chinese-driven Altec earns a 100% premium to entry cost products; and on the back of a mouse that still says Made in China. The mouse works perfectly; and, being not in shiny black, is less attractive to monkeys. With the best, there is always something a little bit extra!

This brings us to a potential shift in global business and hence geopolitics.

Markets

Scale: China has 1.4 billion people and rising incomes. Yet it has so much more than that to punch globally well above its 18% demographic weight. China, with its curiosity about the new, owns about half the world's EVs.

More to the point for foreign firms, VW, the world's largest car maker, already generates 40% of its worldwide sales in China; and even more importantly half its profit. In 2022, it announced a further $2.3 billion investment there. Not in manufacturing but in a 60%-owned software company to develop assisted and self-driving car technology.

China is already a bigger auto market for Audi than Europe or North America. Audi's CEO announced another $2.3 billion investment, when accompanying German Chancellor Olaf Scholz to Beijing to shore up deteriorating German-China ties. Europe's largest economy's head was followed by Charles Michel President of the European Council on a similar mission.

All this comes after BMW moved EV production of the iconic Mini from the UK, some to China. In 2022 it opened a $2 billion battery plant in China, while investing a further $1.4 billion in another. Shenyang is now BMW's largest production base, employing 28,000 people: more than any in Germany. Home appliance maker Bosch is investing $1 billion in Chinese auto components. The list goes on: a billion here, hundreds of millions there….That is Germany, with a clear eye on the future.

Domestic politics, protectionism and trade restrictions have stymied China expansion in the US, despite significant American auto investment in China needing more outlets back home. Maybe Detroit's descendants think protection against European, Japanese and Korean EV makers is sufficient to offset this loss: may be, may be not. It will certainly come at a rarely mentioned significantly higher cost to the US economy and consumers, with harmful implications for price inflation, taxes and interest rates.

Europe has taken another view. It has given an initial green light to Chinese-made EVs: not the threat of decoupling. Foreign firms make some 40% of China's EVs so it is in their interest that markets stay open. China has become the world's second largest car exporter. Who knew that?

So far, China has made a good start in Europe. Countering perceptions that China makes low quality goods, some have already earned five-star safety ratings from European regulators. Germany's largest car rental firm Sixt has placed a multi-year order for 100,000 BYD EVs. Testing Europe's waters earlier were China's NIO, Xpeng and Li, along with the more established Geely and Great Wall.

China now makes almost 6% of Europe's EVs, according to French consultant Inovev. A steep rise is seen since Chinese brands make more affordable models. Wall Street's Jefferies expects the EU EV market to reach 3.9 million, almost 33% of all autos sold by 2025, 75% by 2030 and 95% in 2035, if helped by government policy. EVs are the future; and far faster than many can imagine.

JATO described the Chinese approach in its home market as emphasising five things: affordability, plentiful models that dwarf European offerings, tech savvy vehicles, designs led by consumer data and insight and strong appeal to young consumers. "It is difficult to envisage how the above elements, when applied strategically to the European market, would not appeal to mass consumers. So perhaps when it comes to global EV domination, it is more a question of how long it will take Chinese EVs to successfully enter the European market, rather than a case of whether they will succeed," JATO concluded in 2020.

One last telling example of China's growing global strength is another relatively new industry. China has led world industrial robot production for eight years. The International Federation for Robotics (IFR) says China produced 52% of the world's industrial robots in 2021. That should not surprise, China is the Workshop of the World. What is startling has been the pace of using robots itself.

In just three years, China's installed industrial robotic population has doubled. Over the past 10 years, robots per 10,000 workers have risen to 300 from only 13. China now ranks ninth globally for robots per worker. China aims to be a world leader in robots and industrial automation by 2025. No one in the industry is betting against it.

Diginomica's Chris Middleton, commenting on the IFR 2021 report said it showed, "Asia [China, Japan and South Korea] is automating fast to maintain its status as the world's low-cost manufacturing venue [N.B. no more about cheap labour]. Parts of Europe are catching up, and the US – while doing well – is losing ground to China in terms of modernising its factories."

All Middleton could say about the UK was that it had, "made so little progress that it was largely absent" from the report, despite robotics being a "central pillar" of the UK's 2017 Industrial Strategy. That is the scale of Britain's poor governance and lack of detailed long-term thinking: rank incompetence.

Industrial robots are only part of the story. Service robots provide much opportunity from commercial cleaning to elderly care. With China's urban working-age population plateauing before declining, with an aging population and rising health bills, service robots are another Next Big Thing.

Misunderstanding or Not Knowing

All this success is too often ignored – or unknown. Some foreign commentators now have a new concern about a "Collapsing China". Enforcement of anti-monopoly [anti-trust] measures, which were first put on the books in 2008 – so no one should be surprised – will kill China's innovation and "animal spirits", they claim. Obviously they have never read David Bonavia.

The leading China-Watcher of his generation Bonavia (Chapter 6: *Sources of Dynamism*) wrote in 1980 of the Chinese, "Their civilisation is based on the most forthrightly materialistic value in the history of mankind... The trick is to find how things work, and manipulate them for a better life." How things work includes how government regulations work.

Hardly a communist ideologue, Bonavia, a Double First in Chinese and Russian from Cambridge, knew China in ways that current journalists do not. He knew well its history, ancient and modern, its philosophy, politics and above all its people. Indeed he knew it much better than many academics who now comment on China in the Western media and advise governments. He knew that Chinese pragmatism would adapt as China transformed to a new phase.

The first most prominent innovators in China's economic reform era were Alibaba and Tencent. They saw the seemingly infinite potential of the internet; and captured it. They designed business models to fit China's market in the new economy, which, when scaled up could go global.

The second group, little different in age, is much more proficient in technical knowledge of traditional industries. These can be recast and transformed by science. One entrepreneur is Wang Chuanfu of BYD, another is Robin Zeng of CATL. The first is a former government research chemist, the other a physics PhD from China's elite Academy of Sciences. Other Wangs and Zengs populate China's industrial landscape.

For every giant whale wounded by anti-monopoly legislation, there are scores of invigorated, incentivised sharks just waiting to become whales, to adapt Michael Enright's description of China's corporate food chain from whales to sharks to piranhas. Ruthless piranhas in hot pursuit chase everything, with keen nostrils for profit, razor sharp teeth to tear into prey and no respect for reputations. All larger life is kept on its toes, again driving down costs.

There are still plenty of successful examples to inspire students and start-ups so as to keep competition strong, costs low. They will not be demotivated by anti-monopoly/pro-competition legislation, which differs little from what US President Roosevelt introduced in the 1930s. True Chinese entrepreneurs will simply adapt: their eyes on opportunity not obstacles, ever alert to working around barriers.

So much seems to be happening so quickly in the world's largest manufacturing economy. That is its significance of course; and the cause for alarm among the unprepared. In truth, China's private sector renaissance has been underway for a quarter of a century or more, yet its gathering momentum and growing force are still underappreciated or not known at all.

Geopolitics

Such dramatic shifts beg one question. How should the US and Europe respond? The US and German governments have taken very different approaches.

Chancellor Olaf Scholz broke ranks with Washington's desire to block China's economic progress. In November 2022, he told Xi Jinping that Germany would not decouple. Quite the opposite, it intends for German companies to develop with Chinese firms, in China and abroad. The world's largest chemicals producer BASF began to build its first mega plant outside Europe in Guangdong: total investment almost $10 billion. This indicates that it is not just in renewable industries that China's strength is showing.

Full implications of all this have yet to be seen but could well be a turning point in economics and geopolitics. First, by punching a large hole in the US plan to co-opt and coerce its allies to halt China's manufacturing rise by decoupling.

Second, this has restored the triangular competitive relationship between the three high-end manufacturing centres – the US, Germany and China. They compete for reasons of business not ideology. Maintaining this equilibrium is what Germany sought when in 2011 it developed the Industry 4.0 strategy.

All three are economic rivals. That seems to have been lost on Washington with its military-intelligence binary thinking. The US will be outnumbered in the triangle and in changing frameworks unless it adapts before it is too late. The real threat for the US is decoupling *itself* from the world economy: self harm, unintended isolationism.

The Last Chance

A Clash of Civilisations is not inevitable, yet danger mounts the longer the West ignores its top economic forecaster. In 2023, the OECD sees China's economy as 27% bigger than the US: by mid-century 70%. India too will be larger, leaving America as No. 3. (Table 1. Real GDP on Purchasing Power Parity Basis: *Economic Power Shift 2020–2060E*). Time to Get Real: listen to economists and business.

Three giant shocks lurk right ahead for the West: economic, demographic and competence. 90% of the world's population will soon be non-Western; and no more accepting exclusion from global decision making. After COVID, Afghanistan and domestic turmoil, many even question Western competence to get things right or done, let alone avoid nuclear destruction.

Economic size, not military might, is what counts among Great Powers. As leading military historian Paul Kennedy wrote, military strength is, "inextricably intertwined with economic power and technological progress". This need not threaten the West if understood and managed properly. Indeed, it would mitigate the real existential threats, from the environment to war. Otherwise nuclear conflict creeps ever closer: Kissinger's "Armageddon-like clash". The Doomsday Clock is only 90 seconds from midnight and global catastrophe.

A New New World with growing muscle and some different ideas is emerging, probably spearheaded by an expanding BRICS. How can the West best respond? The book proposes a Biden-Xi Grand Bargain, as Nixon struck with Mao. Grasp what Yin and Yang offer, as opposites can support each other for lasting mutual benefit. Take it. This could be the last chance.

Thesis

Chapter 1

Forecasts From the OECD and History

By 2050 China's GDP will be 70% larger than the US on a purchasing power parity (PPP) basis. India will be 4% bigger than the US.

OECD Forecast January 2023

The Chateau de la Muette, on the edge of the Bois de Boulogne in Paris, is a most unlikely place from which to shock the world. Steeped in history, the once famous chateau has faded into obscurity. No more remembered as a 16th century royal hunting lodge, famous for the world's first manned flight in 1783 ('the Mongolfier brothers' hot air balloon) or where France's last king Louis XVI spent with Marie Antoinette the happiest days of his life, before in 1793 meeting the guillotine.

Yet, now it merits a prominent place in 21st century history. For the chateau houses the OECD, which in 2014 issued what some Westerners might consider the 21st century's most subversive document. That is, if they knew of its existence. In fact, only a few phlegmatic economists even noticed. Buried deep under the dust of more immediately disturbing economic news and complex problems for the West, the title of *Real GDP long-term forecast to 2060 or latest available Source: Long-term baseline projections, No. 95 (Edition 2014)* doesn't quite have the same zing as *Pivot to Asia*.

However, the underlying economic fundamentals march on regardless: their consequences ever greater. For the West they will have plenty of

3

sting, especially the longer politicians and publics ignore the profound fundamental economic changes already well underway.

Meticulous monthly calculations detail the *relative* economic decline of the West and the *re-emergence* of the Rest: the pecking order. This should not surprise anyone, given the vast disparity in population sizes. However, it has rattled Western nerves. First China and India, then others among the world's oldest societies, are on course to regain their economic muscle.

The OECD Numbers

Numbers, history and geography count. Undeniable to those that will see, a watershed has been reached. Population size and rising education levels are so powerful; millennia of history provide today's decision-makers with many lessons in philosophy, statecraft and governance, while geographic proximity trumps distance.

Far from being a bunch of radical economists, the OECD is as respectable as it gets: dedicated to democracy and the market economy. Where it stands out is objectivity: free of distortion or wishful thinking. A primary goal is to help governments shape economic policy by understanding and predicting long-term global trends.

With 38 of the world's richest economies as members, an annual budget of almost euro 400 million and a secretariat with 2,100 staff, other professional economists regard highly the OECD for its long-term economic data and analysis. Unfortunately, non-economists do not. Few have ever heard of the OECD or read its reports, let alone dug into its data. They certainly ignore inconvenient facts. One is the different ways of using Real Gross Domestic Product (GDP).

At first sight, the West has an unassailable economic lead. This has been true for all our lives, indeed ever since our great grandparents' time. Not a fact to ignore. In 2017, OECD members comprised a seemingly well-entrenched 62.2% of global GDP.

Yet, that is not how most professional economists compare GDPs between countries. The OECD, like the International Monetary Fund (IMF) and the World Bank, as well as many academics, prefers to use Real GDP measured in US dollars at constant prices and Purchasing Power Parities (PPPs).

There is good reason. GDP (Appendices: *GDP and PPP*) expressed in PPP terms provides a much better answer to the key question of what each economy can provide in quantities of goods and services from the same unit of GDP (Table 1. Real GDP on Purchasing Power Parity Basis: *Economic Power Shift 2020–2060E*). By this measure, OECD members accounted for only 42.8% of world GDP not 62.2%.

Seemingly unaware of this, US Secretary of State Antony Blinken makes much of NATO's GDP being almost double that of China and Russia combined. Only days before Russia invaded Ukraine, Blinken confidently told the Munich Security Conference that NATO members had 45% of world GDP, while China and Russia only had 23%: implying a formidable advantage in any coming conflict not just with Russia but also China.

To be polite, Blinken made a basic schoolboy error. Accepted at face value by his audience of politicians and security advisers, it went unchallenged by the media. This is very dangerous for long-term Western security, let alone world peace. For Blinken ignored Sunzi's central advice, two and a half millennia old, to "know one's enemy and know one's self", to avoid potentially disastrous consequences.

Non-economists, from politicians to military planners, security advisers to journalists, should learn. With intellectual honesty, they must take seriously the OECD's *Real GDP long-term forecast to 2060, etc.*, even with its dull, overlong title.

Otherwise, non-economist narratives will push the West ever further into an unnecessary and potentially world-ending confrontation: not just with China but with the rest of the non-Western world. Too large to confront, the Rest comprises 90% of the world's population.

The recently powerless become, collectively, powerful. Other ancient civilisations, like previous regional powers in Indonesia, Nigeria, Egypt and Turkiye, wish to emulate China. They have the population numbers to compete and influence. The largest nine alone account for almost 60% of 2050's projected world population whereas the US will have 379 million, only 3.9%, the EU 440 million, some 4.5%. Even with all its Caucasian allies, the West won't reach 1 billion or 10% (Table 8: *Top 20 Populations 2050*).

This is not about rights and wrongs. It is all about economics and raw power: unchallengeable numbers. Values and rule interpretations can be debated endlessly but are a diversion, wasting time while the clock ticks down towards ever greater and more frequent disasters. Large numbers matter.

America being dethroned as the world's pre-eminent economy is not a new idea. Nothing has changed in history. One empire has always been replaced by another: 'twas ever thus. When people say, "it will be different this time", old timers and financial market veterans merely smile: it never is. Cycles persist as the concept of Yin and Yang holds (Chapter 20: *What Can the West Learn From Itself and China?*). Some economists and military historians have been pointing to this likelihood for almost half a century.

In the next two decades, the OECD forecasts China's GDP on a PPP basis will surge ahead of the US by accumulating $7.1 trillion ($7,100 billion) more than the US in the 2020s and $6.6 trillion in the 2030s (Table 1: *Economic Power Shift 2020–2060E*). China's advantage will only slow significantly in the 2040s and 2050s but will still average more than an extra $3 trillion each decade. That is $3,000 billion, real money.

This will continue to provide China with a handy edge over the US when it comes to government and military budgets. For context, by 2060, the

OECD forecasts US GDP on a PPP basis to be US$36.5 trillion, while China reaches $62.1 trillion, 70% more. India will be $42.2 trillion, some 16% more.

A further two decades, let alone three or four, are a very long time for the West to feel the rising heat from China, made worse by an accelerating India and the Rest. Conflict is possible, even likely, unless the downward spiral in US–China relations is reversed.

Less and less room exists for either side to manoeuvre. That is the growing problem. Especially as domestic US politics demand that "Something Must Be Done About China". Five years of trade tariffs and sanctions have not worked, including the start of decoupling. Indeed, China's trade surplus runs at record levels. Yet more of the same is proposed, old wine in new bottles: only the labels have changed.

Respecting the numbers, a fundamental rethink is required. That is why it is critical to find a way out of this *cul de sac* before it is too late. President Nixon and Chairman Mao did in 1972, crafting an accord that lasted four decades. Now it is for Biden and Xi to do the same to avoid the ultimate conflict.

History

History has its own version of the future. Most intriguing is *Fate of Empires,* a 1976 essay by Lieutenant-General and military scholar Sir John Glubb (Chapter 4: *The Power Equation and Decline of Empires).* This showed that empires last on average for 250 years: always more than 200 and never more than 300 years. That is quite an arresting fact. Chinese historiography has a similar idea. No dynasty lasts more than three centuries.

Very relevant today, the US and most of the West are in Glubb's sixth and final phase of empire, The Age of Decadence, a time of institutional decay. This all sounds familiar: divided societies whose political systems cannot make effective, timely decisions, as revealed by COVID deaths and mounting domestic problems.

A decade after Glubb, military historian Paul Kennedy stirred up a hornets' nest with *The Rise and Fall of the Great Powers*. President Ronald Reagan's Secretary of State George Shultz even went specially to allied capitals to denounce and deny it: a history book. It must have touched a raw nerve or the truth.

Kennedy made two all-important observations:(1)Military strength "is inextricably intertwined with economic power and technological progress". Put simply, economics mostly determines the size of military budgets and technological advance, which in turn are largely responsible for the outcome in war and hence power. (2)The US is on a disastrous path to financial overreach. It is only a question of time before this mattered. That time is now arriving.

Informed by five millennia of known history, China saw this coming. China has been preparing for decades, even long before screening in 2006 a wholly Chinese-made TV series about rising and falling powers. This prime-time 12-part documentary showed how the West became powerful through political and economic reform. Interviews included with historian Paul Kennedy, along with leading Western economists and world politicians. It also laid out global imperial history.

History's lesson is simple. Empires are replaced. These include regional empires such as the Ottoman, Russian, Austro-Hungarian and USSR. There is no reason why this cycle will cease, especially when China and India demographically are both more than four times the size of the US — just as America was four times larger than the UK. Numbers count.

Leading global firms, especially from Europe and Japan, knew four decades ago that the greatest long-term economic potential now lay outside the West. Global corporate giants saw that the post-World War II economic recovery expansion had run out of steam. They adjusted their long-term plans accordingly.

Increasingly profit would have to come from large population countries with rising education levels and productivity. These could drive incomes and hence market growth. This pointed to the less developed parts of Asia, most notably China, which had just begun to emerge from nearly four decades of isolation.

Companies have had no reason to be disappointed. China has helped give some of them world leadership. These include Volkswagen, Daimler-Benz, Toyota, BASF and ABB. Not that US firms could complain either. Honeywell, GE and Cummins have achieved the same. Since China joined the World Trade Organisation in 2001, US trade with China grew 500%: with other trading partners only 100%.

Rediscovering the economic history of China and India should be no surprise. For all but 200 of the last 2,000 years, China or India have been the world's leading economy, according to economic historian Angus Maddison. With considerably larger populations than the West, the Asian twins look set to do so again. Elsewhere, other populous countries will wish to regain their regional status: in Latin America, Africa, Asia and the Middle East.

Moving to Shanghai in 2002, I was asked why I was leaving Singapore after two enjoyable decades in Southeast Asia. My only answer was "to see the future".

I had watched before this Asian movie. Would China climb the economic ladder as Japan, South Korea, Taiwan, Hong Kong and Singapore had? Or would China stumble and collapse?

China's economic development has more than met my expectations. It has though been underestimated or even denied by Western sceptics, some hoping for its collapse. Such advance triggers Western fears.

Now the West heads rapidly towards a point of no return with China, barely without a murmur of dissent. As with global warming, first, there will be much more frequent stress before the final reckoning: time to rethink the future.

Yet only over-simplistic solutions are offered. Nero fiddling while Rome burns comes to mind. Binary choices miss nuance and collide with complexity. This is an emergency, yet, unlike with the climate, no one talks of a China, India and the Rest Emergency. Only of the need to impose Western values "for the global good", as if this were right or even possible today.

Britain and the rest of the West justified 19th and 20th centuries imperialism this way: the White Man's Burden, which was later wittily dubbed the Black Man's Burden. US neo-conservatives (neo-cons), Republicans and Democrats alike, as well as supposedly liberal Europeans, have taken up the same justification in the 21st. None have proven successful, past or present. The US is still embroiled in "forever wars": only their complexity and risk has risen.

Such a conclusion might well anger those who think they are on the side of the angels. Bear with me. After four decades living in Asia, watching China's economic comeback or "rise", as the ahistoric account calls it, the West is unmistakably and needlessly on a collision course with China, India and the Rest. All have the same 21st century ambition. To escape poverty, enjoy security and be recognised as befits their size: to be included and respected.

My China perspective comes from four decades of providing analysis and forecasts to global investors. Risk managers require one thing: results, accurate results. This is never always achieved but an attempt must be made. Analysis is based on facts: some much more important than others.

Financial markets demand one thing, reality or at least plausible perceptions of it. Participants must face facts, provide hard evidence: not hypothetical conjecture or clever sound bites. This is not a game. Like history, markets are ruthless in their judgment and eventually extract their due from faulty analysis.

Delusion, blaming others or simply sticking one's head in the sand like an ostrich is no solution. Yet many leaders do just that. As an investment strategist, I always take a long-term view, including of economic fundamentals. That way tries to see what others may have missed and act before it is too late.

This is all the more pressing because a cottage industry has emerged attacking the assumption of China's economy becoming larger than that of the US. The IMF and World Bank forecasts have been dismissed, though no one has taken on the OECD yet: a much harder task given its reputation among professional economists, though that may eventually happen. As the Chinese saying puts it, the loudest voices are from attention seekers, or, as English has it, empty vessels make the most noise.

Some holy cows and assumptions have to be slaughtered. Most Western and Western-educated or influenced Asian readers may have to adjust their thinking. Even many of those who believe China's economy could overtake the US think it will not happen any time soon.

Get Real: it is happening right now and by the OECD's calculations has already happened. Even if it is underway, many believe the US has ways to block China. This is wishful and very dangerous thinking, as *America as No. 3* will show.

I would not do this if I lacked the evidence from direct experience, travelling to all but one of China's provinces, municipalities or autonomous regions. I have read the *Coming War with China* in the late 1990s and the *Coming Collapse of China* in 2001. For decades now they have been proven wrong.

China has momentum. It will not stop or be stopped overnight. Of course, as its economy matures growth will slow, as it has, but China is still growing considerably faster than the West. This is particularly true in China's economically laggard inland areas where more than 60% of people live.

The naysayers deny or cannot see that three giant shocks lurk right ahead for the West — economic, demographic and competence. A New

New World is emerging, very likely the forerunner of a more balanced multipolar world. Like Yin and Yang, opposites can support each other, making each stronger and everything around them more stable.

It's The Economy, Stupid as Bill Clinton would say or as Paul Kennedy did say, military strength "is inextricably intertwined with economic power and technological progress". From on-the-ground observation, especially from two decades in China, using both Western and Asian sources, *America as No. 3* pulls together many strands that one-topic specialist books, usually by academics or politicians, fail to do.

As detailed in this chapter, the West's pre-eminent economics research organisation the OECD has spelt it out. China is already No. 1 in GDP PPP terms, leading the US by 27%. In 2050, China will be 70% larger, India 4%. Yet few in the West listen or want to know: a great mistake.

A Clash of Civilisations between China and the West is not inevitable but is ever closer. A nuclear winter need not fall but could. First, the West must grasp the facts; and learn China's strengths, as well as Western limitations. A Biden-Xi Grand Bargain like Nixon made with Mao is the obvious solution (Chapter 2: *US Foreign Policy, China's Economy and a Nixon-Mao Rerun*). US foreign policy and the three great shocks tee-up the book's core sections of the *Economic* and *Geopolitical Contests*.

Competence, as a phenomenon, deserves much more consideration after Afghanistan and COVID. The reasons are examined in *Western Failings*, starting with politics and society before looking in-depth at the media's role, which has enabled the decline.

Finally, *What Now*? What can be done to reverse the worsening outlook that has nuclear or cyber war as its finale? To avoid this, what could be done?

Chapter 2

US Foreign Policy, China's Economy and a Nixon–Mao Rerun

We simply cannot afford to leave China forever outside the family of nations, there...is no place on this small planet for a billion of its potentially most able people to live in angry isolation.

Richard Nixon, *Foreign Affairs*, 1967

Code named "Marco Polo", the secret mission could not have started more dramatically. Midway through the official banquet, the US National Security Adviser fell ill, succumbing to the combined summer heat of Vietnam, Thailand and India. Before leaving hastily, Pakistan's President announced his guest would rest in the cool of a hill station: no more would be seen of him that weekend.

Only a few miles away, on the outskirts of the capital, a Pakistani plane, engines at the ready, waited in the dark of night. In a plot worthy of John Le Carré, Tom Clancy or Frederick Forsyth, China Global Television Network (CGTN) recalled in 2019 what happened that night in Islamabad.

"Waiting on board were three [very senior] Chinese diplomats and an interpreter...but they weren't sure whether Kissinger would turn up. Hours passed in waiting. Finally, at 4 a.m. in the morning, two military vehicles drove onto the runway and stopped right next to the plane. Kissinger stepped out, a scarf and sunglasses covering his face, and got on the plane".

The presidential palace banquet drama was staged in 1971 by Henry Kissinger and President Yahya Khan, the chief intermediary in this making of history. Kissinger needed time to execute "Marco Polo", away from prying eyes. He disappeared into the night, undetected. Next stop, known to very, very few, was Beijing, on the other side of Asia's Iron Curtain. Kissinger, three experts and two secret service agents were to be the first American officials to visit China since 1949's revolution.

CGTN continued, "Around midday July 8, the plane landed in Beijing... In a few hours, he [Kissinger] would meet with Chinese Premier Zhou Enlai. They would have six sessions, clearing the path for an official meeting between Mao and Nixon. Together, two of the greatest political minds of the last century would not only end a decades-long feud, but completely change the political landscape of the Asia-Pacific region".

A good start was made but a long journey lay ahead, full of twists and turns for half a century. That is the past. The foreign policy shift Nixon and Kissinger engineered ended more than a decade ago. The US has now entered uncharted and increasingly dangerous waters.

US Foreign Policy

US foreign policy has changed fundamentally since Kissinger's realism. "Coevolution" between the US and China is no more. The Republican Party's moderate wing, internationalist not isolationist, pro-free trade not protectionist, has virtually evaporated. Democrats, driven more by domestic concerns, never had such a clear cut policy.

Since the Cold War's start, vested interests have steadily gained influence over US foreign policy and budgets. This is pretty standard organisational behaviour. Turf wars are the mask to grab individual benefits. Today's vested interests are neither new nor shrinking violets.

Despite being the last president to have commanded the US in war, Dwight D. Eisenhower felt the vested interests' wrath in 1958 when, as a small-government Republican, he sought military budget cuts. Fighting back, the US Air Force greatly exaggerated Soviet missile numbers, spreading them through the media. Democratic presidential candidate John F. Kennedy took the fake data to claim an alarming US future gap with Soviet capabilities.

This was subsequently proven to be a big lie. The USSR only had three such advanced missiles at the time. However the "Missile Gap" was widely swallowed, helping Kennedy narrowly win the 1960 election. In his final address to the nation, Eisenhower warned of the danger of what he called the military-industrial complex dictating policy to government; and vested interests manipulating politicians.

Their hold on government has only tightened. Half a century later, President Obama surrounded himself with more retired generals in senior positions than many presidents before him, says former US State Department official Ronan Farrow. Arms sales to foreign governments more than doubled under Obama. All this made "the world less safe and prosperous" in Farrow's words.

"For decades, the Pentagon and the CIA had bypassed the US civilian foreign policy systems", he noted. The militarisation of foreign policy in Afghanistan was what veteran diplomat and ostensibly Obama's representative on Afghanistan Richard Holbrooke called pure "mil-think". Another tag would be "mil-int-think": military-intelligence-thinking.

In *War on Peace: The End of Diplomacy and the Decline of American Influence* (2018), Farrow described a, "story of a life saving discipline torn apart by political cowardice": stinging words political cowardice. Watching, "the decline play out, with disastrous results for America", Farrow saw, "modern alliances in every corner of the earth, forged by soldiers and spies, and the costs of those relationships for the United States": experienced civilian diplomats replaced by soldiers and spies.

With the spirit of Sir John Glubb nodding in agreement (Chapter 4: *The Power Equation and Decline of Empires*) Farrow wrote, "we were witnessing the destruction of those institutions, with little thought given to engineering modern replacements". This was a very different approach from that of Kissinger who, "tended towards the general and the philosophical. Tactics, he felt, had triumphed over strategy and fast reaction over historicised decision-making".

Europe-raised Kissinger said the US, "is eternally preoccupied with solving whatever problems emerge at the moment....One great American myth is that you can always try something new". Obama's administration was fixated on innovation. In Kissinger's words, "to try something new [whereas he] wanted to apply lessons from the past and think of foreign policy as a historical process".

Increasingly the younger generation of European politicians and their advisers followed their American cousins in the search for novelty. Think tanks mushroomed, doors revolved round and round between government and the outside world. These sustained the careers of a new class of securocrat whose shiny new ideas promised to deliver the quick knock-out punch.

Biden's China policy has sent very mixed messages: squaring a circle is impossible. One side says one thing, another something else. The question is who to trust?

Chief diplomat Antony Blinken talks about "genocide" in Xinjiang and standing "robustly" by Taiwan. The US military, directly contravening the 1979 US agreement with China, has not reduced arms sales to Taiwan, by a long way, and has secretly stationed troops in Taiwan.

In Asia, this sounds like "White Man speaks with forked tongue", in Western cowboy movie lingo: more simply, good cop, bad cop. This does not make for good policy or trust: indeed, for some, trust is bankrupt. What brought us to this point?

China's Economy Overtaking the US

The answer lies in economic size. Military strength, military historian Paul Kennedy observed, "is inextricably intertwined with economic power and technological progress". Everyone from the Pentagon to the RAND Corporation think tank, along with seemingly every US securocrat in between, would agree when thinking of America as the clear, undisputed No. 1. What though when it isn't?

Tensions rise as China's economic heft nears America's. The previous chapter and appendix explain the correct way to compare economies by using GDP on the basis of Purchasing Power Parity (PPP). However, politicians and the media largely use just GDP, though even this only gives the US another eight years or so at the top. In PPP terms it is not even a question. China's economy is already No. 1; and more than 27% bigger than the US.

To many non-economists, GDP equates with power, dominance and military budgets. Yet, even by this short-hand measure, a major power transition looks to be underway. Based on the latest International Monetary Fund (IMF) forecasts up to 2027, China's GDP could overtake the US by 2030. From there the gap will widen relentlessly: a great shock to some; and a growing obsessive fear for others.

The real shocker will be that by 2050, on a PPP basis, China's GDP will be 70% larger than the US's. By 2060, non-OECD countries will be three of the world's four largest economies (China, India and Indonesia) and seven of the top 10. Indonesia will be more than half that of the Euro area's 17 countries combined ($12.3 trillion versus $23 trillion). The OECD forecasts the others will be Turkiye, Brazil, Mexico and Russia, with Japan and Germany ranked sixth and seventh.

There is further bad news for America. US military supremacy is not eternal. Even US military strategists do not believe that. Commercially, Huawei, the symbol of American's adversary, has not been killed and buried. The firm's next incarnation in game changing photonic chips and 6G will be an even bigger shock than its leadership in 5G. Another area is space. China landing on the Far Side of the Moon and Mars is not a flash in the pan.

China's economy continues to chalk up telling firsts: not just hard numbers but soft indicators. Tencent and ByteDance were the world's top-ranked companies by app revenue in the first half of 2022, Sensor Tower estimated. Byte Dance (owner of Tik Tok and Douyin) became the world's most downloaded non-gaming app in 2022: some 83% were outside China.

German publisher Springer gave the 2021 *Nature* Science Cities award to Beijing for contributing most to scientific advancement. In the last decade, China has jumped from 34th to 11th in the UN World Intellectual Property Organisation's (WIPO) Innovation Index. The list goes on. This is all leading to growing conflict. How could it be avoided?

A Grand Bargain to Reset US-China Relations

Although the chances of a Nixon–Mao rerun may seem remote amid current tension, distractions and hostility, another Marco Polo Mission looks like the only way to end peacefully the widening chasm of mistrust between the US and China. Exactly 50 years after Richard Nixon reached out to Mao Zedong, could Joe Biden do the same to Xi Jinping? Strike a Grand Bargain. Unthinkable? Consider this.

Time is running out fast. Soon the conflict could explode, literally. The Nixon–Mao detente worked well for both countries. Not without ups and downs but time enough to manage a potentially very difficult period. A similar three decades would be invaluable. Could Biden and Xi show similar leadership, to tell the truth about the future and grasp the opportunity? Could they be a clear-eyed American eagle and a long-life Chinese crane?

After Nancy Pelosi's visit to Taiwan, China stopped talking officially to the US. This was reversed ahead of the G-20 Bali summit but for how long is the question. How much damage will be done by stop-starts that sour relations? Not only US–China rivalry threatens the world's very existence.

Even more, it is their absence from leading on global issues where the US and China together are central to solutions. The US should work with China and its growing weight, not against it. Even when China's economy was a small fraction of the US's, Nixon wrote in *Foreign Affairs*, before winning the presidency in 1968, "there…is no place on this small planet for a billion of its potentially most able people to live in angry isolation".

Consider another dimension. After announcing in 1971 he had secretly sent Kissinger to Beijing to prepare for his own visit, Nixon stated, "They're not a military power now but 25 years from now they will be decisive. For us not to do now what we can do to end this total isolation would leave things very dangerous".

Ultimately the key to US–China relations is military. Those leaders with long-term vision could see the implications of China's growing economy. Half a century on, that is even truer because the power equation has altered radically. The economic gap has narrowed enormously, global demographics changed and Western competence is increasingly questioned.

Anticipate the future and ease its birth. Failure to do so, "would leave things very dangerous", especially when nuclear war is no longer unthinkable, tactical nuclear weapons exist and some US hawks contemplate "limited" nuclear strikes.

Accidents, non-nuclear and nuclear, do happen. In 2021, a US nuclear-powered submarine hit an underwater ridge in the South China Sea.

Details were scanty but damage was said to be severe: three top officers were fired, almost immediately. Luckily there was no nuclear meltdown. Nine nuclear submarines though have sunk or been scuttled in history: five from the Soviet Union, two from the US and two from Russia. Accidents do happen.

Incidents may not only be human or mechanical accidents. They can also result from policy. Pentagon official Daniel Ellsberg leaked secret papers in 1971 that revealed President Eisenhower received military advice in 1958 to launch a nuclear attack on parts of China during the Kinmen-Jinmen Islands crisis. He rejected it, for obvious reasons.

Forgotten, it should be remembered that US commanders in the field wanted to launch a nuclear attack on China. Unconnected to this, Chiang Kai-shek secretly began a nuclear programme in Taiwan, which the US closed. Nuclear proliferation always threatens.

Old China Hand Biden first visited China in 1979. He has known China longer and arguably better than anyone else now in US politics. He must also understand the current dangers, which explains why in his 2021 video call with Xi he stressed the importance of avoiding war and did the same with Russian President Putin. Biden knows the history.

Could Joe Biden reach out to Xi Jinping to strike a Grand Bargain for long-term stability, as Nixon did to Mao? What could it offer?

What doesn't it offer to solve the world's major problems? That should be the question. Without the US and China at the heart of discussions there will be no effective global solutions. For that they have to lead together; set the pace, harnessing themselves to the same plough. The US needs to recognise China's growing strength and work with, not against, it.

Vision is most needed: a practical vision not an ideological one. "Politics is the art of the possible, the attainable — the art of the next best", as Prussian Chancellor Otto von Bismarck observed. Economist and Ambassador J.K. Galbraith though was closer to the truth when he said,

"Politics is not the art of the possible. It consists in choosing between the disastrous and the unpalatable". What might the unpalatable look like?

Recognise what is off-limits to the other party. All countries have red lines not to be crossed, and special interests to be considered. Then find common beliefs: pure pragmatism and compromise. Both Biden and Xi believe in government's role, especially in difficult times: not Big Government but enabling government. Where to start?

A Manifesto for Cooperation

A manifesto would read like this. Define areas of common interest and cooperation. To some extent, this has been done but the US has demanded much more than China. That could be negotiating tactics.

Without providing mutual benefit they will fail. Zero sum advantage does not work. Both sides would lose and nuclear winter could descend. Binary thinking fails. Shades of grey and ambiguity work much better, for they limit objections to solutions.

Use supranational institutions as all existential problems are global. That is why the United Nations (UN) was founded. Some like the World Health Organisation (WHO) and World Trade Organisation (WTO) need reform to reflect 21st century realities but they do provide a venue and basis for global coordination. Others may need to be built, such as for chemical and biological weapons, like the International Atomic Energy Agency. Making the UN central to solutions will not come easily to many in the US.

Not to be ignored after all the gloom of COVID, is the one bright light that shone throughout: the extensive range, capability and *esprit de corps* of health experts. They cooperated across borders, often well beyond expectations. The same can happen from space to the environment, if permitted.

Grass roots communities and organisations contain a wealth of practical knowledge to incorporate into new thinking. Civil society has many ideas, often well ahead of governments. Include them more. They can leap over the heads of politicians and commentators, who are largely today's problem.

Enabling government, empowered by well-informed popular support, can face down vested interests, from healthcare to social media, security policy to arms proliferation. These are global and national emergencies. Things must be done. Thinking must be in decades, and that needs to start now. Three main areas — global security, domestic economies and the world economy — are obvious.

Global Security

It is hard to imagine the world surviving much longer without global cooperation. In Afghanistan, all five permanent members of the UN Security Council — the US, China, Russia, UK and France — are in complete agreement on handling terrorism: a rare event. Build on that.

In East Asia, China could provide defence guarantees to North Korea in return for denuclearisation of the Korean peninsula and military reductions in the rest of northeast Asia. Similarly, in Taiwan, China can give guarantees once the US has lived up fully to its commitments under the One China Principle and Three Communiques. Risks exist for all parties but the much greater risk is doing nothing.

Security is not just military. Cyber security online affects everyone: their communications, privacy and finances plus protection against identity theft and ransom demands. To most people, these are much more relevant than nebulous talk about insecurity thousands of miles away.

Plenty of opportunities exist to cooperate in science, technology, health and education. People can see the benefit of these to their lives. This will strengthen society and politics.

New standards can ensure technology does not interfere with security and privacy: quite the opposite. Technology can ensure compliance, as Britain's main surveillance institution GCHQ did with Huawei for years. Instead of banning competitors' products, often a costly burden to users and economies, technology can reap benefits for all, safely.

Domestic Economies

The most obvious is Joe Biden's aim to Build Back Better. Chinese firms could help rebuild ageing US infrastructure. They have done so before successfully, from New York's Alexander Hamilton Bridge to San Francisco's Oakland Bay Bridge, each time saving substantial costs.

Without a Biden–Xi accord, China could make financing harder by cutting its holdings of US Treasury bills, pushing up interest costs or/and requiring higher taxes. Even the threat of China boycotting T-Bill sales, let alone selling just some of its holdings, would hurt the US.

More US infrastructure spending would boost GDP growth and jobs. It could also extend the time beyond 2030 before China overtakes US real GDP. That should help smooth the way. People can gradually get used to the idea; and as benefits materialise see the threat disappear.

By the time China's GDP surpasses the US, the American public would know it is not the end of the world. The average American would still probably be much wealthier than the average Chinese. This would boost badly needed trust in government, especially among the disillusioned young, whose future it is. The economy would gain from better consumer confidence, triggering greater consumption and investment in a virtuous circle.

Politicians, by solving problems, should benefit at the polls. People value what companies or governments do, not what they say, opines communications consultant Richard Edelman. Higher US growth boosts the whole world, just as China's does.

World Economy

Swords into ploughshares: lessening distrust between the US and China would cut defence needs. Funds could instead be used elsewhere, dispelling uncertainty and boosting consumer spending.

Retrained soldiers could fight the world's greatest threats from natural disasters like floods, famine, earthquakes and volcanic eruptions. They could monitor compliance with global environmental standards and prevent or extinguish wildfires. Projects can address poverty and income inequality, as well as create sustainable economies: drain the swamp of instability. Only a little imagination is required.

A great symbol would be if the US cooperated with the Belt and Road Initiative and the Asian Infrastructure Investment Bank (AIIB). Both are powerful growth engines, not just economically, but also, if successful, for social stability. Similar, smaller projects can work in other trouble spots.

Germany has already proposed a private sector-led initiative to help industrialise North Africa. Creating jobs at home in unstable hotspots is much more logical than pushing the young into the arms of organised crime as refugees or migrants: not to mention humane. The same has been discussed regarding Central and South America.

Benefits for US and China

Clear benefits accrue to both sides. The US can avoid financial overreach, which often ends empires. Already spending twice as much as China on defence, as a percentage of real GDP, the US cannot afford more expense without reducing welfare elsewhere.

Defence and intelligence budgets are out of control. Farid Zakaria in 2021 wrote in the *Washington Post* that the F-35 fighter jet, whose most advanced version may never fly, is expected ultimately to cost $1.7

trillion to develop, whereas Zakaria said China has spent $1.6 trillion on the Belt and Road. Which is money better spent, he asked?

Apart from freeing up funds domestically, a security-enhancing agreement with China would improve US standing in Asia. Forcing nations to take sides in the US–China dispute does not work. Asians resent it. Give Asia something it wants such as more economic assistance, investment and trading opportunities. This would earn the US Asian diplomatic capital: soft power. Unless the US approaches Asia differently, it will lose influence in the most important economic and military theatre of all.

The almost 700 million people-strong Association of South East Asian Nations (ASEAN) has already established regional peace, finding security largely through greater economic integration. This is with both China and US allies in the rest of Asia. With transformative infrastructure, the US was once the great builder in places like Indonesia and Thailand. Now it is largely absent, relying on Japan and Taiwan to help out.

The benefits for China are equally clear. First would be a US pledge of non-interference in China's domestic affairs, just as the US demands from Russia. This would include reining in regime change groups, like the US government-funded National Endowment for Democracy. In his talks with Nixon, one of the demands Mao made was for the CIA to stop funding operations in Tibet: it did.

Securing its borders, not world domination, has been China's primary goal. Throughout history, China has not colonised distant lands (Chapter 10: *The New China-US Equation*). Traditional philosophy teaches such wisdom. If left in peace to reach its full potential, China can achieve its top priority: much higher standards of living and security. A peace dividend would extend to all neighbours, further strengthening China and the world through stability.

Then the US and China can *huo lu*, as former CIA Deputy National Intelligence Officer Douglas Paal says. Find a way to live together, give each other room to move: not to corner but to provide an exit out of an otherwise dead end.

Time, demography, history and geography are on China's side. The next move is the West's. It must think very carefully. Then a mutually beneficial accommodation to get through three very challenging decades ahead might be possible.

Of course, China competes with America and Europe. Yet fair economic competition is fine. It can bring out the best in people, driving efficiency and innovation, as Xi Jinping once observed in another context. Tilting though at a much larger adversary, as Don Quixote did at windmills, is most unwise. Recognise that healthy military competition is an oxymoron, a contradiction in terms; and very dangerous in a nuclear age.

Apart from a Nixon–Mao rerun, solutions, short of military conflict, are very few. There is one that will help. However, it cannot happen quickly. Nonetheless, a start should still be made. In 2019, there were only 11,000 US students in China, compared with well over 300,000 Chinese students in the US, a gross imbalance in knowledge.

Therefore, encourage Westerners to visit China. The young to study and travel: older people to see for themselves and share impressions at home. Link to China many more schools, institutions and other groups around the world.

Far more people, with knowledge of today's China, will then have the tools to discuss matters of common interest and concern. They can understand why others think differently: the beginning of any successful dialogue. However, it will be slow. That is why a Grand Bargain, à la Nixon and Mao, another Marco Polo Mission, is the best solution before great shocks get out of hand.

Chapter 3

Great Shocks

He who is last shall later be first.

2020, 2021 and 2022 pointed to what lies ahead. Great shocks lurk. Aftershocks will reverberate globally, touching all, from families and firms to militaries and science, nations to continents. Three will alarm the West most — economics, demographics and competence.

This should be no surprise but it will be. Denial is very human. Building steadily over four decades, China first, followed by India and others, will change world views. Facts on the ground will increasingly alter assumptions about future global economic and geopolitical power.

Nothing is inevitable. The great shocks might not happen. Wars, epidemics or insurrections could prevent them: much better though to be prepared. Do not bet against it. Having watched China from Asia for more than four decades, China's economic primacy looks ever more likely. China's return to global economic eminence and even pre-eminence, its rank for half the last two millennia, is very much on the cards.

Already among global brands, three of the most innovative and successful firms recently to break through to world recognition were founded by Chinese — Zoom, TikTok and Huawei. Energised private companies, competition, education and innovation combine with other factors to drive China's economy beyond the US this decade.

Global corporate leaders from China were once, to me at least, unthinkable. Asked in 2001 to name one Chinese global brand, I could think of none. Maybe Tsingtao Beer could hold its own against foreign competition, in China! In 2021, Shenzhen DJI had 77% of the US private drone market and Shein is the latest fast-fashion leader, while everyone seems to Zoom or Tik Tok: and Huawei has become one of the best-known global technology brands.

Economics

Taking the measure of GDP least favourable to China, the greatest future shock is that the US may no longer be the world's largest economy in GDP terms. By 2030, even earlier, China could well be. Shocking because economic size determines wealth, trade, capital flows and, most critically for some, security budgets to maintain military supremacy.

In rowing parlance, clear blue water should open up between the two economies in the 2030s, as China draws further ahead. Most Western politicians and electorates ignore the possibility. Psychologically unprepared, they plunge their heads deeper into the sand.

No one mentions it. Everyone, including China, talks about the US as the world's No. 1 Economy; and China as No. 2. Yet economies are dynamic; and, with China likely growing twice as fast as the US, rankings can change. As John Cleese, tip-toeing around Fawlty Towers, might have said, "Don't Mention the Economy" or as Bill Clinton did say, "It's the Economy, Stupid".

China and other large non-Western nations will soon punch more like their demographic weight: not just economically but politically and even militarily. Already Asia has overtaken the US and EU as the largest continental economy. This happened in 2011. Next may very well be China alone, and one day India.

COVID probably brought forward the changing of the economic guard by a few years. Major institutions in Japan (Nomura), Germany (Allianz) and the UK (CEBR) all sharpened their pencils, adjusted their forecasts and made this clear by 2021. Suddenly China as No. 1 was the headline: the expectation.

The forecast did not disappoint during COVID. Between 2020 and 2022 the IMF reported that China's real GDP growth averaged 4.5% annually, compared with the US of 1.3% and Western Europe's 0.8%. This fitted the expectation: competence, helped by cycles.

Full consequences have yet to register in most Western minds. Rearview driving dominates their vision. Some two centuries of Western economic and military supremacy fill the mirror.

Modern English's word for the lowest of the low, the poorest of the poor, is coolie. Originally an Indian word, it came to be associated with Chinese migrants who had nothing to sell but their labour. That is all changing. Now the last shall be first: the coolie the master. That drives fear among some in the West. In fact, the more likely multipolar world will have no master, only competitors and cooperators.

Logic dictates China's likely economic primacy for one incontestable reason. China's population is so much larger than the US. Not the same or even double but four times bigger — an unignorable fact.

Previously, this did not matter. Indeed, giants were enfeebled by size. Small was beautiful, flexible and dynamic: manageable. Small Singapore, Hong Kong, Taiwan, South Korea and Malaysia succeeded. China and India were vast, dirt poor and failed.

Large size now is no longer a hindrance. After lifting 850 million people out of acute poverty, according to the World Bank, and taking 400 million into the global middle class, China's size matters. It creates beneficial scale: big is a bonus and beautiful.

The equation has changed, radically. This is an increasingly Humpty Dumpty World. "He who is last shall later be first," as recorded from the Bible to Bob Dylan. This applies as much to continents as to countries.

Led by Chinese, Asians are increasingly the world's greatest consumers of everything from luxury goods to the most mundane items. China is already the largest market, from autos to travel, smartphones to social media: more than one billion are online. Images of Chinese consumers in Bond Street and Oriental tourists alongside I.M. Pei's pyramid at the Louvre are not new in the West but what exactly they say about the future has yet to be admitted, let alone digested.

Is China's economy likely to remain four times less efficient than the US? Hardly, given it possesses three powerful drivers — the world's largest population and hence often the largest markets that attract ever more investment; rapidly rising education levels that generate higher incomes, hence greater consumer purchasing power; and a proven ability to manage rapid change. So why wouldn't a four-times-more populous China replace the US atop the world's economic pole?

Demographics

This is a White Nationalist's worst nightmare. Not just about China but about the combined potential might of the non-Western world, the Rest. Yet, as demographer Clint Laurent states, the trends are set. The cake is already baked.

Barely 10% of the world's population will be Anglo-Saxon by 2025, the UN projects: less than three short years away. Alarm bells will start ringing ever louder. Only 4.2% will live in the US compared with 17.5% in China, while 27% of people in 2025 will live in Confucian-based economies: more than one-quarter of humanity. Most significantly for some, the world will be 90% non-Anglo-Saxon: very largely non-white.

The UN forecasts Nigerians will outnumber US citizens by 2050: Nigeria, yes. Who sees that today or that Pakistan, with 338 million, will have barely 40 million fewer than the US? The list of other non-Western economies and populations on the march is long. Next come Indonesia, Brazil, Ethiopia, the Democratic Republic of Congo and Bangladesh, followed by Egypt, Mexico, Philippines, Russia, Tanzania and Vietnam.

All will be more populous than the likely 17th largest in 2050, Japan, which may shrink by nearly 16%: just ahead of Iran, Turkiye and Kenya. Germany and Britain, respectively 6th and 9th in 1950, will only rank 22nd and 26th, respectively in 2050 (Table 8: *Top 20 Populations 2050*).

Stop for a moment. Go back. The US–China population gap is so telling: 4.2% versus 17.5% of the world in 2025. By a factor of more than four: China is four times bigger than the 334 million in the US, with another 100 million people on top. Even the EU's population is barely one-third of China's 1.4 billion, let alone India's projected 1.6 billion in 2050. This all translates into economic heft.

The significance of all this has not completely sunk into most Western thinking. Even readers with little interest in figures should re-read this Demographics section and look at the tables in the appendices. Then they can grasp not just the future but the existing reality.

Competence

As if economic and demographic shocks aren't enough to worry the West, there is a new one. Competence is now an issue in many things from politics and government to institutions and systems. The West always assumed competence was its advantage: and now?

Disastrous Western mismanagement of COVID has cast doubt on the wisdom of automatically assuming such competence. Increasing numbers doubt even democracy itself. The 2021 Harvard Poll of 19–29-year-olds found that 52% of young Americans believed US democracy is either "in trouble", or "failing" and only 7% believed it to have a "healthy democracy".

Hallowed institutions like Johns Hopkins have erred. It predicted, only three months before COVID was first reported, that the two best-prepared nations for a pandemic were the US and UK, while China ranked 51st. Reread that... slowly.

How on Earth did Johns Hopkins, with research by the *Economist* Intelligence Unit, get it so wrong? How was the pandemic risk assessed? We know how in 2020 Western governments managed COVID: most did terribly. What does this imply for the future? What other unseen disasters lie ahead?

Bluntly, what does it say about Western expertise and competence? How could such esteemed institutions be so wrong, so quickly? What else of importance could others get badly wrong? That is very frightening. How good are they at gauging risk?

There have been Triple A and F Grade countries. After 30 months of COVID, the top grade country by far was China with 3.6 deaths per million people. F Grade countries include the US (3,255), Italy (2,950) and the UK (2,800) deaths per million.

F Graders spectacularly failed a fundamental test of competence. The biggest test of government competence since 1945, as Martin Jacques called it. Don't though just blame government. Venerable academic institutions did no better, starting with health, as mentioned.

Best prepared systems to handle a pandemic? Remember the Johns Hopkins study in October 2019 made the US and UK Nos. 1 and 2: tell that to the Marines. Also mention China's GDP grew by 2.2% in 2020, while the US and UK economies shrank 3.4% and 9.9%, respectively. What did Johns Hopkins not understand? What did it think was unimportant?

Supposedly world leading health systems, political structures and social cohesion in the West are now questioned: in need of reform, new thinking. A growing sense has crept in that the US is no longer the world's undisputed leader, and may not remain the world's largest economy forever. Nerves jangle. Nightmares recur, and not only in the US.

Questioning comes not just from radicals but also from the old establishment. The British conservative *Daily Telegraph's* former editor and historian Sir Max Hastings wrote in 2019 that two leading contemporary historians, Sir Michael Howard and Sir Richard Evans, "have recently suggested — independently of each other — that Britain has entered a "Weimar period". Not in the sense of being threatened by a Hitler but instead by suffering the failure not merely of a government, but of governance."

Sir Richard, the former *regius* professor of history at Cambridge, highlighted,

> "the menace posed by politicians and tabloid newspapers that attack the judiciary as "enemies of the people" — a charge now being made about parliament itself. We should not delude ourselves that what is taking place represents any sort of normality, or acceptable political process.
>
> Our society has lapsed into a period of madness which we should recognise as such — as do most foreign commentators viewing our affairs — wherein dangerous forces are in play. We shall be fortunate if we prove able to escape from it with only the implosion of one traditional political party, rather than with a collapse of confidence in our entire system of democracy."

China's Economy as No. 1?

For decades, US scholars and advisers like Henry Kissinger, Samuel Huntington and Graham Allison have considered the question of "China's rise". Strictly speaking of course it is China's re-emergence.

All three scholars concluded that the US loss of largest economy status is almost inevitable.

China's population is four times plus larger. No big deal: just adjust to the new reality. Get over it. Move on. Don't be King Canute, haplessly ordering the tide to stop. It won't. That would be futile; and counterproductive.

However, the three professors' scholarly opinions are increasingly a minority. Even if President Biden listens, successors may not. All three have been part of an East Coast, largely Harvard, elite. This though is losing influence, out of step with its heartland, Republican and Democrat alike. Increasingly, US opinion is epitomised not just by Trump's MAGA to Make America Great Again, but by broad media, academic and bipartisan Congressional support to "Do Something About China".

Whatever it takes: US pre-eminence must be maintained at all costs, especially in economics, security and space. This is not an academic quibble, it is existential it is said. It is also a vote winner. Such emotional thinking makes this a dangerous decade, with plenty of room for grave misunderstanding and miscalculation.

Befriend China before it is too late. Agree on a safe path forward, as Nixon and Mao did half a century ago. If not, the unequal struggle will not cease.

Following in China's footsteps will be a string of other non-Western nations. These are large old elephants with long memories of past glory and weighty cultures, from India to Indonesia, Nigeria to Egypt and Iran: in shorthand Asia and Africa. They do not intend to remain in the shadows forever. Not all will become giants or even middle-ranking economies necessarily but don't expect all to fail.

Expect the unexpected. Few in 1978 rated China's economic chances, nor in the 1950s those of divided South Korea or Taiwan to rise above civil war and poverty. Singapore, once just another impoverished small, tropical Third World island, now nearly equals First World America in per capita GDP at $67,000. Seemingly against all odds, it succeeded.

Turn, turn, turn: the wheel of history turns. The unavoidable conclusion is that the West will decline *relatively*, though not absolutely, while some of the rest will rise. Rarely is the future spelt out so starkly but that is what it is. One day in the 22nd century, the US could even be an upper middleweight economy, no longer even a heavyweight. This was the fate of its predecessor, the British Empire.

Talk of Western relative decline will be resisted in the West; and downplayed even in the East, for fear of triggering concern or even conflict. Unsettling conclusions abound. Potentially, much turmoil and uncertainty lie ahead. Rules about global governance will increasingly reflect the voices, cultures and growth of the non-Western Rest.

Entrenched groups rarely take kindly to challengers. Nor do they usually foresee a changing of the guard, until too late. Friction is inevitable. Countries go to war over who gets to be Top Dog; and, crucially, who stays there. Britain and Germany clashed in 1914, just as Athens and Sparta did over two millennia ago: in between nearly a score of such wars occurred.

The spoils are rich, in material and psychological terms. Not just a seat at the top table, with a pleasing sense of self-importance and rich pickings, but the ability to impose one's will on lesser powers: to have one's way. That is the unpalatable truth, especially dangerous in a nuclear age.

As change accelerates, globally and locally, disputes will rumble ever louder, more frequently exploding into rage and conflict. US–China rivalry is just the largest and most immediate example. The same could happen as easily one day within Europe or Asia, among regions and overlapping cultures: even between metropolitan elites and laggard communities or simply young versus old, without even considering the ever-present great dividers of race, religion and class. Potential fractured fault lines abound.

Again though, stop for a moment. We are only talking about total size. US GDP per person will still be double or more. China surpassing America in economic size need not be the end of the world for Western individuals.

Indeed it presents a new beginning with many opportunities if approached rationally; and if the Age of Reason endures, with a sense of fairness. Democracy is about much more than holding regular elections. In a globalised world, it starts between nations and peoples. Everything from health to wealth, food to education is involved: greater uncertainty but also opportunity.

Many new questions will arise. What will it mean that half the world's Millennials in 2050 are African? How will mature economies cope with one-third of their citizens aged over 60? Critically, how will the West react to its relative decline and how will Asia take on new responsibilities?

Without a radical, honest rethink about how these three great shocks will reshape economic reality, geopolitical tensions will only rise. To the point where the ultimate price of human folly could be paid; and nuclear winter descends.

Hard power comes mostly from being the strongest economy. Dominance in military, security, technology, cyber and space flow from that. Everything potentially is in flux; and up for grabs, which is why next we have to consider Power and the Decline of Empires to understand where things stand.

Power transitions are always difficult. The past teaches the perils of ignoring this truth, both in recent and ancient history. To avoid unending conflict and even war, the declining power has to:

- be realistic about the likely future: a multipolar world lies ahead, with varying degrees of power

- have a sense of proportion: Americans will still be richer than Chinese for many decades to come.
- find common ground: from climate to health
- avoid hypocrisy and double standards
- avoid caricatures: most of all racial, ideological or religious ones
- recognise one's own failings or limitations
- provide a way out for the other party, *huo lu*: not a zero-sum fight to the death

This amounts to a process, adaptable to circumstances. Of course, both sides need to understand each other, not just listen without changing. Invest time and money to get to know each other. The rising power needs to be sensitive to all this but primary responsibility for a peaceful transition lies with the incumbent. That is why we must first understand The Power Equation and Decline of Empires.

Chapter 4

The Power Equation and Decline of Empires

The duration of different empires at varied epochs show a remarkable similarity.
[All]…occurring around us has happened again and again before.

Fate of Empires Sir John Glubb 1976

Before we examine the causes and consequences of China or India overtaking the US economy, there is a question to answer. What are the roots of power, especially of dominant power, imperial power?

Dominant power is a giant Rubik's Cube: often making only minor, imperceptible changes. Suddenly a crunching wrench occurs. Everything is turned inside out, upside down. This is where we are today, especially after 2020–2022.

Power

Key power factors for most of the last two millennia have been population and land area: mass. Innovation in government, commerce and warfare strengthen the two main factors but alone are not enough to maintain dominance. For over two millennia, only when parts of the Indian sub-continent or China combine all factors did either achieve pre-eminence. Then their wealth seeded unrivalled bureaucracies and armies to support power.

India and China though could only dominate their immediate worlds not the whole world: whether for reasons of limitation or philosophical choice is immaterial here. Only by the 18th century were they seriously challenged by Europe. However, Europe was divided.

No European country accumulated sufficient economic might to dominate the Asian giants; and hence the entire world until the early 1800s. That was when Britain harnessed the Industrial Revolution's intellectual energy to create the first truly global empire.

Technology, civil and military, was at its core. Taking advantage of other European states being at war with each other or within themselves, Britain forged ahead at home. It avoided treasury-depleting European wars for 100 years: unlike France, Austria, Spain and Germany, along with their neighbours.

Expansion in new continents changed the equation. Population growth and land mass reinforced Britain's innovation-driven technological advantage. The small islands off northwestern Europe amassed extensive colonies, bases and wealth on which the sun never set. One-quarter of the world map was painted Imperial Red, like Britain's post boxes and telephone kiosks. Red was a magnificent, confident colour.

The basic rules of power though could not be defied forever. Sheer continental-scale land mass and resources led to the red, white and blue eclipse by Britain's offshoot. Steadily the US caught up with its parent before leaving it far behind, not just in population but in wealth and military might. Reluctant to call itself an empire, an affront to its democratic self-perception, the US has far exceeded the UK, the first global empire, in scope and raw power.

In 2020, the Rubik's Cube of world power ground once more. After four decades of China's economic, social and governance change, as well as peace, China is a challenger. Only late in the day did the US even grasp what was happening. What was dressed up as a trade war increasingly became a technology war for what some US strategists see as a 21st century battle *royale* for global mastery.

Equation

We are talking about the rise and fall of great powers and empires. With apologies to professional economists, who would be right to point out some double counting and factors without comparable measurements, I shall use a very simple equation in words: Dominant Power = Mass (Population + Area) + Wealth (Income + Resources) + Education + Technology + Innovation + Governance + Peace. Numbers matter: both in absolute and relative terms, starting with size, both area and population.

Population numbers are pretty much determined decades in advance: irreversible, unless war or another Great Plague returns to stalk the earth. Not only are almost all of the world's 2025 population already born but so are the parents of 2050s teenagers and Millennials or soon will be.

The cake is already baked, three decades in advance. Remember these are among the most reliable forecasts that can be made, with a long, detailed history to help guide them: not to be dismissed by wishful thinking.

What cannot be predicted with as much accuracy are future economic weights (wealth). History though provides a guide here too. Population or land size alone is not enough, as India and China proved for most of the last 200 years. Wealth (income and resources), Gross Domestic Product (GDP), is even more important but the equation elsewhere could change.

China's mass, of area and population, could combine with wealth to make it by far the world's largest economy in the second half of the 21st century. Long before then it will be stronger than the US. India could be challenging China in the first half of the 22nd century and even overtake it.

This is not set in stone but after constantly underestimating China, the West would be well advised not to bet heavily against it. By 2030, China is likely to have added economic muscle faster than the US, enough to gain the No. 1 spot even by the popular but less meaningful GDP by market exchange rates. Face facts now before it is too late to adapt; and reset relations amicably.

Theory and Practice

Where to start this calculation? Is there a general theory about dominant power? Media commentators toss around the words of Samuel Huntington's *Clash of Civilizations* and Graham Allison's *Thucydides Trap* to constitute a debate about the future. These are far from sufficient.

Indeed, interpreters often ignore what Huntington and Allison have written, quoting very selectively. Especially misrepresenting conflict as inevitable, which neither intended. With the right steps, conflict can be avoided but not by doing nothing.

A better place to begin is the late 20th century predictions of Paul Kennedy and Sir John Glubb. Kennedy's *The Rise and Fall of the Great Powers: Economic Change and Military Conflict from 1500 to 2000* (1987) has a very contemporary feel. Over three decades ago, the Yale British professor spoke to today's world of increasing US confrontation with China.

Kennedy foresaw in the late 1980s the danger to the US of "imperial overstretch". In the popular narrative this became a prediction of "US Decline". In fact, Kennedy stated it would be a *relative* decline. However, the word relative was usually overlooked or unknown, in the best tradition of lazy journalism not to let facts get in the way of a good story or opinion.

Unquestioned belief in its invincibility or even right to intervene has indeed led the US to over stretch, to over play its hand, as Kennedy predicted. After the US defeat in Vietnam, who would have believed the US would ever again, and certainly not so quickly, become involved in "attachments and foreign entanglements", as George Washington called them? The new millennium's US armed invasions of Afghanistan and Iraq, interventions in Syria, Libya and Venezuela, would make the Greek gods and Norse fates frown with rank disapproval.

This was not just Trump overstretch but of several predecessors. Endless fighting, half a world away, has not won security enhancing victories. Instead, they weakened the alliances that hold together the US Empire. Coalitions of the willing for these expeditions became increasingly harder to assemble. Some nations, like Germany, often declined to join, just as Britain refused during the Vietnam War.

Setbacks for the US were not just military but diplomatic too. Obama's officials exploded in fury at traditional European allies Britain and Germany joining the China-backed Asian Infrastructure Investment Bank in 2015. This childish behaviour was soon papered over but never forgotten.

Crucially for the central argument of *America as No. 3*, Kennedy shows that hard power, military strength, "is inextricably intertwined with economic power and technological progress". That is why what was first dressed up as a trade conflict was rebranded a trade war before rapidly revealing itself as a technology war. Banning ZTE and Huawei were the first salvos to decouple China technologically, then economically, from the US and its allies: to hobble China's "rise".

Any new economic Top Dog can convert greater wealth into a world-dominant military budget to impose its will globally on others. At least that is the US view and fear, based on its own behaviour for over a century. The US presumes China will do the same: act just like the West. The question, to be answered later (Chapter 10: *The New China-US Equation*), is whether this is how China sees its best interests advanced?

Decline of Empires

Sir John Glubb's *Fate of Empires* (1976) has a very classical and ancient feel to it. Explaining the long sweep of world history for the last four millennia, Glubb analysed 11 empires he knew well. He admitted to not knowing China, India and the rest of Asia, Africa or Latin America but the 11 alone have a big enough conclusion. Arresting is the only word to describe Glubb's findings.

The average empire, Glubb found, lasts on average some 250 years or 10 generations. None lasted 300 years nor less than 200: 250 would seem to be a very dangerous age.

In 2026, the US will celebrate its 250th birthday. That does not mean it will collapse immediately but it would defy the history of empires if it lasts more than another 50 years; and the last decades will be rocky, as rulers from the Tang to the British knew. Who will break away first, Texas, California, Florida or New England?

This may seem fanciful but 37% of US respondents showed a "willingness to secede" in a 2021 Bright Line Watch-YouGov poll. This was most marked in the 13 Southern states, where 50% of Independents and 66% of Republicans supported secession of their home state. The highest number of Democrats showing willingness to secede was in the five Pacific states (principally California) where 47% did.

Glubb's findings are not iron laws of history, though similar patterns constantly repeated may be more than mere coincidence. No matter the widely differing conditions of climate, culture and religion or different levels of technology, education and governance, each empire has followed the same six stages of rise and fall.

Glubb called the six stages respectively The Age of Pioneers, The Age of Conquests, The Age of Commerce, The Age of Affluence, The Age of Intellect and finally The Age of Decadence (of institutions). All very recognisable in Asia where cycles, from Indian reincarnation to China's *Yi Jing* theory of change, underpin much modern Asian thinking. The US is seen as being in the final stage, the Age of Decadence: decaying institutions.

The 11 empires Glubb (Glubb Pasha as he was known in the Arab world) studied during his life as a soldier, then scholar, largely in the Middle East and Mediterranean, were:

Assyria 859–612BC *247 years*, Persia 538–330BC *208* (Cyrus and descendants), Greece 331–100BC *231* (Alexander and successors), Roman Republic 260–27BC *233*, Roman Empire 27BC–AD180 *207*, Arab Empire AD 634–880 *246*, Mamluk Empire 1250–1517 *267*, Ottoman Empire 1320–1570 *250*, Spain 1500–1750 *250*, Romanov Russia 1682–1916 *234* and Britain 1700–1950 *250 years*.

Historians may quibble about the exact length, start and end of each empire. These rarely fit into neat boxes, though interestingly similar durations are found in the major Chinese dynasties. The Big Four — Han, Tang, Song and Qing — also lasted around two to three centuries before starting to crumble or actually collapse: more confirmation or mere coincidence?

Time and technology are two other dimensions to consider. Contrary to common assumptions, Glubb concluded that the "duration of empires does not depend on the speed of travel or the nature of weapons. The Assyrians marched on foot and fought with spears and bow and arrows. The British used artillery, railways and ocean-going ships. Yet the two empires lasted for approximately the same periods. The duration of different empires at varied epochs show a remarkable similarity". Technology may differ enormously but imperial duration does not. The Assyrian and British Empires, two millennia apart, lasted roughly the same length.

All empires decline, so it should be no surprise that the US faces this future both abroad and at home. Signs already exist that the US (and West more generally) have entered the final stage: the Age of Decadence, the decline of public institutions.

There has only been one outwardly smooth global transition in modern times when the US overtook the UK. This though was more a change in personnel at the top. It was not a deep change in the dominant power's culture. This time will be more profound because the new power's culture will differ, sometimes significantly.

The existing dominant power is likely to be in denial, as Britain was until the 1956 Suez debacle. This did not matter so much. For the Second World War had made perfectly clear the changing of the guard, economically and militarily. The current US–China transition will be more gradual, leaving plenty of time for denial to feed conflict.

The implications of this should be sobering for the West. How can it maintain a global position when it cannot provide for social harmony, broad prosperity and public health at home? Could Western dominance and the US Empire be coming to its end? What do the radically different outcomes of COVID tell us about China and the West?

Roots of the growing conflict lie in economics. China's stronger economy rattles nerves in parts of the West — though, most interestingly, not much in the business community that largely only sees opportunity. The threat that business fears most comes not from China but from their own politicians and electorates.

Will the future be a Clash of Civilisations, Battle of Economies or a New Beginning for the whole world? We have now arrived at the heart of *America as No. 3*. It is time to focus on the all-important Economic Contest. This begins with what many underestimate about China before examining its ignored strengths, which reflect a very different reality from that in the standard Western narrative.

Economic Contest

Chapter 5

Underestimating China and Ignored Reality

100 million Chinese ranked among the world's richest 10%: the US has 99 million.

Credit Suisse Bank 2019 Survey

Never underestimate China, my colleague Anna Kieryk would always remind me if I expressed surprise at something new or achieved. It can be fatal. What has the West underestimated or ignored most about China?

Apart from ignoring China's reality, Western assumptions about China are based on its own thinking, practices and experience. Many therefore miss what drives China. Western opinions are accepted as fact, and their errors create myths.

Outdated caricatures blind many to China's reality. Filthy air, polluted water, low wages and mass poverty are not a good starting point. Increasingly they are out-of-date images, though glitzy cities are not the whole story either.

Take key indicators to form a more accurate picture — quality of life, wealth, market size, managing change, long-term thinking and creativity. By some absolute figures, China is already ahead. These give a completely different picture.

Quality of Life

Life expectancy, air quality and healthcare tell a tale of improvement. Still a work in progress, indicators point to the worst being well behind a China that is catching up with the West.

In 2021, China's life expectancy overtook that of the US. Reduced by COVID, US expectancy fell to 76.1 years while China's rose to 77.1, according to the US CDC. China has more than doubled its life expectancy from 36 years in 1949.

Newborn Chinese are projected to have more healthy years ahead of them than newborn Americans, who will have 10 years of poor health at the end of their lives. A Beijing baby has a life expectancy of 82 against 78 years for a newborn in Washington DC.

Chinese deaths from air pollution peaked in 2013. Drawing confidence from conquering its notorious sand storms, by 2019 China had driven down air pollution to 1990 numbers. In the 1950s Beijing had 56 sand storms a year: in 2018 only four. In 2021 and 2023 a major Beijing sandstorm made news around the world because it is now so unusual.

Healthcare access and quality have also improved steadily. For that, *The Lancet* ranked China 110th in 1995, 60th in 2015 and 48th in 2016: the same level as the UK in 1990. With the continued rise in healthcare spending since 2016 China has probably risen even higher. Some 95% of Chinese are reimbursed 70–80% of their hospital expenses.

Wealth

Rich Asians are no longer just a film title or a joke at their expense. Rich Chinese outnumber rich Americans for the first time in living memory. Credit Suisse Bank in 2019 recorded that 100 million Chinese ranked among the world's richest 10%: the US had 99 million. At the same time the US middle class is shrinking, China's expanding: a tale of two futures.

In 2003, hardly surprisingly, China had no billionaires. By 2021, China's billionaire count was the first to reach four figures: 1,058. The extra 259 in 2021 constituted over half the world's new billionaires, according to Chinese wealth expert *Hurun*. Bottled water magnate Zhong Shanshan, with a $85 billion fortune became the first Chinese to enter the world's 10 wealthiest group, rubbing shoulders with the likes of Bezos, Zuckenberg, Gates and Musk.

Yet, US average GDP per capita is 5.5 times higher than China's. Why get excited at all about China?

Four hundred million in the middle class is one answer. That exceeds the total US population of 334 million. Many are well-educated Millennials, the world's most sought-after consumers, according to consultant China Skinny.

On top of that there are still 1.1 billion people, outside the middle class, on lower incomes but with very similar ambitions. That is why many foreign companies have made China their prime foreign direct investment target. China's potential has arrived and should continue for the next three decades or more. No longer about tomorrow, it is happening today.

Some comparisons between China and the US can be startling. By the important measure of net worth, in one of those jaw-dropping statistics that can jump out of China from nowhere, urban China's median households are almost twice as rich as their US equivalent. That sounds incredible. A quick explanation is due.

Net worth is the value of assets (home, car, savings and investments largely) minus debt. The median number is the mid-point in the group, the 50th percentile, the "typical" Joe or Flo. Often this is much more meaningful than the plain average, which is a very crude number distorted by the top 20–30%.

Urban Chinese households' median net worth was Rmb1.4 million ($198,330), according to a 2018 central bank survey. US urban net worth, adjusted for inflation, was calculated by the US Federal Reserve to be $104,000 in 2016, barely half. However, because of the very rich, the US average was 80% higher than China, again because the wealth of the top 20–30% pulls up the overall average. What accounts for urban China's higher average net worth? Again, China startles: it is *private* property ownership.

Some 96% of China's households own their homes, compared with 64% in the US. When China privatised urban residential property in the late 1990s (homes in rural China were already privately owned) prices were very cheap. Many people acquired the often run-down state-owned property in which they had lived most of their working lives, at a fraction of the value, let alone of today's price. They did not need mortgages. In fact mortgages did not exist. If buyers found informal funding, it has been repaid.

That means only 57% of China's households have any debt. This compares with 77% in the US: almost twice as many Chinese are debt free. Furthermore, maybe up to 30% of Chinese urban households own a second property; and by one estimate 11% own three. That means Chinese household balance sheets are much stronger than many assume.

Three things create a virtuous circle. Less overall debt per household means Chinese can borrow more. Lower or no debt frees up more income to spend on everything from food to entertainment, travel and leisure: real disposable income. Lower household debt also means less risk for lenders, as Chinese borrowers find it easier to repay than those more heavily indebted.

Rising incomes, less pressure from debt repayment and the world's largest population all add to consumer demand. This may last for several decades at least: room for more household debt and more GDP growth. The UK's Centre for Economics and Business Research sees China's 2020 consumption almost trebling by 2035.

Such growth, scale and consumer power are what make China so attractive. The economic fundamentals of consumption-led growth are in place. This means China does not have to invest as heavily to maintain GDP growth. It comes increasingly from rising incomes, driven by education and productivity. This translates into market size.

Market Size

For the first time in more than a century, the US retail market is not the world's largest. This had been anticipated, given China's population, but COVID brought it forward by a few years. In 2020, China's retail market was estimated at $5.07 trillion to the US's $4.84 trillion: advantage China. The key point though about China's market is not sheer size.

Character defines it. Chinese consumers love the new, maybe because for many decades new was not on the menu. Whatever the reason, this makes Chinese adventurous, willing to try anything new, exactly what all consumer companies and consumption-dependent economies crave.

Electric vehicles, EVs? Count us in. A 2021 survey found that 86% of Chinese car buyers could imagine buying an EV. In Germany, it was 35%, in France 28%, not even one-third as many. Maybe it was the high price? That put off 55% of Germans, 46% of French but only 20% of Chinese. Most will either first save a little longer or use their stronger balance sheets to borrow. This makes Chinese steady, attractive customers for brands that meet their expectations.

Detailed books can be written about the Chinese Consumer: analysis and articles proliferate. There is no need to add to the pile. Four eye-grabbing facts tell the consumer story far better than any voluminous account, presenting a powerful snapshot of future spending.

Vehicles: China is the world's largest auto market. Already it makes and owns half the world's electric vehicles. By 2022, China had 315 million motor vehicles, slightly more than the 295 million of the US yet still less than one quarter the vehicles per thousand people. Nearly 435 million Chinese have driver's licenses, under half the potential number. Plenty of room is left in auto sales growth, maybe a doubling, not to mention rising profits from upgraded models with higher sticker prices.

Tourism: China is already No. 1 in global tourism. Chinese made 150 million overseas trips in 2019, according to the UN World Tourism Organisation. Now the biggest individual tourist spenders, Chinese have replaced Americans and Japanese.

Luxury: Chinese account for 50% of world luxury spending, according to consultants McKinsey. Louis Vuitton's French parent LVMH in 2021 had 160 outlets in Shanghai alone: 160 in one city. Driven by luxury tax cuts, more Chinese are buying in China, especially during COVID overseas travel restrictions.

In the land of tea, consumers are also sipping more coffee: a small luxury given its price. Shanghai in 2021 had 6,913 stand-alone coffee shops, almost twice as many as Tokyo, three times London and six times New York City.

Millennials: The world's most sought-after consumers are China's 400 million Millennials (not to be confused with a middle class of the same size). Consultants say Millennials lead some global trends, rapidly adapting to change, especially in technology and formats. Think Byte Dance (Tik Tok), Xiaomi and Shein. This new name overtook H&M and Zara in 2021 to become the largest brand in US fast fashion. Its app was downloaded more than Amazon's.

Opportunity Abounds: Healthcare

One large industry will illustrate: healthcare. COVID simply heightened interest and concern in the sector. Revenues are projected to treble by 2030. That is why foreign firms are so keen on China.

No other market can compare for immediate potential size or growth. China answers the question all companies ask. Where will they find strong profit growth? It is very unlikely to be in mature Western economies

China's growth is already fast, and higher incomes lead to rising expectations. Health, therefore, becomes a political issue. Government has to respond, especially after SARS and wide income inequality. COVID merely reinforced the pressure. In 2021, Xi Jinping called for better public health systems.

Looking one decade ahead to 2028, *Global Demographics* wrote that, "The combination of an ageing population (which has a higher incidence of health conditions), improved diagnostics as a result of a steadily improving and increasingly accessible health service combined with significant lifestyle changes (such as diet and exercise) means that the number of conditions needing treatment in China over the next decade increases dramatically": much more demand.

If China follows other older Asian countries such as Japan, China, instead of spending 5.3% of GDP on health as it did in 2018, would spend 7–10%. *Global Demographics* sees a $1.67 trillion healthcare market by 2028. That is a 9.3% per annum growth rate, a trebling.

What other underestimated economic strengths does China have? Eight ignored sources of dynamism should keep China's economy on its present trajectory. There are two main pillars and six essential buttresses.

Chapter 6

Sources of Dynamism

A furious sea of private sector sharks, enormous state sector whales and pursuing piranhas.... Harvard Business School has no words to describe the intensity *of competition.*

Michael Enright, Hong Kong University

China is already the Workshop of the World: manufacturing in all 360 of the UN's industrial categories, unlike either the US or Europe. This is a good start but no guarantee of China becoming the dominant economy, let alone power.

The last chapter outlined China's current reality by using some big numbers. What though will make it continue on this path towards becoming a fully mature economy? What are the wellsprings of China's dynamism?

If two facts about China's economy are remembered after reading *America as No. 3* they should be these: the private sector and competition. Critical ingredients of success, they tell how much longer China can continue to grow faster than the West.

Private Sector

For *America as No. 3* to convince people, it must blow out of the water some strongly held Western ideas. The biggest myth is that China's

57

economy is state dominated. This implies it lacks entrepreneurship and financial discipline, thus doomed to fail. This simply is not true. Indeed, nothing could be further from the truth.

Today's China is neither the Soviet Union nor the China of 1949–1978. This is a modern, mixed-ownership 21st century economy. The private sector pays 50% of taxes, produces over 60% of GDP, employs 80% of workers and creates 90% of jobs, according to Vice Premier Liu He, Xi Jinping's top economic adviser. The vibrant, vigorous and generally more efficient private sector is China's primary engine of prosperity.

In the memorable phrase of Michael Enright, China's economy is, "a furious sea of private sector sharks, enormous state sector whales and pursuing piranhas". The only thing that has changed in the decade since Michael spoke is that some private-sector sharks have become enormous whales while more piranhas have become sharks.

Constantly at battle, full of great energy and ideas, firms regroup after setbacks to review, learn and change course. In China, this is standard operating procedure. Companies reinvent themselves before rich veins of profit near exhaustion. Permanent renewal, *weixin*, comes as second nature from millennia of experience.

Firms know that no bullet-proof business models exist. There is no alternative to working hard, fast and taking risk. Today's entrepreneurs have known this since childhood. It does not scare or discourage them. This is normal. They get on with it and get things done.

Ironically, China's harshest foreign economic critics miss the private sector's leading role. Free enterprise ideologues obviously don't visit China or, if they do, clearly don't get out much. They should go to Zhejiang province and try to find all the state-owned enterprises (SOEs) of their imaginations. A few banks and old industries exist but the rest is a forest of relatively new private firms, many encouraged by government. As one Zhejiang entrepreneur remarked, "of course the government supports us, who else is going to pay tax and create development."

Nor do ideologues appreciate or even seem to know the importance in China of two major ideas — the primacy of markets and the rule of law. Neither is remarkable in the West but in post-1949 China they appear revolutionary. The fifth generation of leaders, headed by Xi Jinping, approved these two ideas in 2013 and 2014. They have reinforced them ever since with more detailed regulations and active implementation.

Markets and the rule of law are the fifth generation's most important economic ideas. Both support the private sector. Yet they are ignored or doubted in a West that cannot believe a communist state would value let alone promote them. Maybe Western name tags mislead, clouding judgment. Furthermore, China's time-frame is different. No one expects overnight change but give it a couple of decades and things could be very different: as with the environment.

What matters is that the process has begun. The principles have been enshrined in the Party's ideological canon for safekeeping: to become permanent, implemented and usually successful. It is not like switching on a light. This all takes time for pieces, awareness and refinement to fall into place: to be built (Chapter 8: *China's X-Factor*).

Top leaders' walks-about are carefully chosen to reinforce major messages. Prime time is just before the Spring Festival (Chinese New Year) holiday when families reunite with much feasting, catching up, including to discuss the economy and personal prospects. In 2021, Xi Jinping chose to visit a privately owned supermarket in the distant, southern province of Guizhou. There he sang the store's praises.

The private sector, Xi said, should provide the skills and enterprise, while the government regulates in the public interest. One brief video clip and a few words captured where China is heading, for those with the ear to hear — namely 1.4 billion Chinese.

The evolution of China's private sector has been very rapid. After the late 1950s, any firm with more than seven employees was illegal: until about 2000. Private enterprise came of age after the 2008 Western financial crisis. Until then, most private firms were very small, largely lacking sophistication. All that mattered was to produce, produce and produce. Get goods out of the factory gate as fast as possible. Production growth and speed, nothing else mattered.

Grab whatever was available. Use what worked. Everything was short-term. Otherwise, firms would not survive. There was neither time nor point in detailed long-term planning, only for ambitious goals. This was a golden era for nimble Chinese entrepreneurs, whose containers of cheap goods filled the shelves of Walmart, Target and Costco.

There was though one hitch. The go-go years of 2002–2008 bred some really bad habits. The Western Financial Crisis, none of China's doing, cruelly exposed them. Many, many small firms went to the wall.

The skills to found and steer an early Chinese private firm were not those most needed after 2008. Character, determination and perseverance were all very well for the first private companies. However, in the new turbulent times, when two decades of global boom turned to bust, professional management was required everywhere to navigate through the new depths, raging storms and hidden rocks. China was no exception. Knowledge of business basics was required, not the bull-in-a-china-shop never-say-die mentality of most 1980s and 1990s company founders.

Founders had much to learn, and some did. If not, they had to bring in professional, non-family executives or face extinction. The list of new skills required was long.

Learning just one skill would have been a challenge. Now there was a whole palette of basic business problems. How to manage customers? How to manage suppliers? Why build a brand? Build, buy or acquire? How to price to maximum advantage? What is premium pricing? How to improve wafer-thin profit margins?

Profit-and-loss questions required immediate, solid answers. Everything was needed, from putting distance between themselves and competitors to building strong distribution channels. How to create a steady flow of new products? How best to manage rising costs, especially of labour? Should they relocate work to cheaper areas or was there a better, more effective strategy?

Last but not least, they had to focus on competition, local and foreign. Literally often a life-and-death battle: though for survivors it was not all bad. Valuable lessons were learned not just through everyday struggle but directly from foreign multinational companies.

These global giants increasingly outsourced work to Chinese firms. They demanded three things: ever-higher manufacturing quality, good governance and global best practices. The firms learned new standards under the world's sternest taskmasters, setting Chinese entrepreneurs on their way for many years to come; and for some to inherit the earth.

The post-2008 era was so different from earlier break-neck expansion. Then annual sales could grow 30%, year after year, for seven biblical, unrelenting years. In retrospect this was absolute madness. No time was left for anything else: certainly not for sustainable best practices. This was no preparation for a world of new challenges, dangers and opportunities.

Competition

The next myth is that China is full of either zombie companies, the financially walking dead, or very fat, lazy, corrupt and uncompetitive state companies, verging on collapse: the next Soviet Union, Cuba or Eastern Europe. This could not be more wrong.

Stumped by a question about competition in China, Michael Enright told a Research-Works investment workshop that Harvard Business School had no words to describe "the *intensity* of competition". The word *intensity* rang around the room. His 2004 insights into manufacturing in Guangdong, (then with a resident population of

100 million) opened investors' eyes to the advance guard of China's industrial future — and future competition for the West.

Firms from Huawei to ZTE, BYD to Tencent, cities like Shenzhen, Guangzhou and Dongguan: these names were barely known then, even to intrepid emerging market investors like this group. Only foreign competitors and collaborators like Cisco knew, half a decade or more ahead of the 2004 visitors.

Peppered by questions, Michael, a former Harvard professor, plumbed the depths of his on-the-ground knowledge. Surprising himself, he discovered something he had never before realised. Parts of China's economy, and the high growth parts at that, are the most competitive in the whole world. Competition was building the Workshop of the World.

The first spur came when China removed internal trade barriers between its more than 30 provinces, municipalities and autonomous regions. Local protection had shackled China's full potential by denying the best outsiders entry to exploit China's greatest advantage, its scale.

When China's leading brewer Tsingtao listed on the stock market in the late 1990s its share of China's beer market was only 1.6%. I proofread the prospectus and flagged it as a typographical error, assuming it must be 16%. No it was 1.6% came back the reply promptly: miniscule, with minimal presence outside its home province or even city.

Only a few ministry-led firms could operate throughout China. National state companies alone could benefit from China's great scale, yet many were not interested. They were largely unmotivated monopolies. Anyway, there was no Ministry of Beer, only thousands of small, local breweries excluded from exploiting the benefit of China's scale.

Local vested interests wanted competition even less than the monopolies. Indeed, they were increasingly a drag on the economy, as well as a drain on national finances. By the early 1990s it became obvious all this was financial madness; and unsustainable. So, Beijing opened inter-provincial trade and investment to companies throughout China: a boost to economic activity, efficiency and competition, just as the EU did by creating its Common Market.

External barriers were addressed in 2001 by China joining the World Trade Organisation (WTO). This increased competition further. Steadily China opened up. Competition was injected slowly, not in a US-style Big Bang for which most Chinese companies were completely unprepared; and would have been crushed. Two decades later, far more Chinese firms can now face and withstand foreign competition. With enough now ready, there is renewed emphasis on opening up to help drive efficiency through competition.

New industries were the third spur. In the 1980s, this was light industry. SOEs, mainly in Soviet-style heavy industry, were not very interested in such simple things. Most were happy sticking to their heavy engineering, with well-defined protection; and reasonably risk-free employment.

Requiring much less capital, light industry suited new private firms perfectly. For most entrepreneurs had very little money or even access to bank credit. They did though have a healthy appetite for risk and hard work. Just like their forerunners in 19th and early 20th century Europe and North America.

In the 2000s, a new set of industries in information technology (IT), social media and e-commerce emerged: becoming China's hottest sectors in the millennium's second decade. SOEs largely spurned these too. Private entrepreneurs though were much quicker to seize the opportunities.

As in geographic exploration, new areas usually offer new wealth — even if only for the few survivors. In each sector they learned from experience, theirs and that of failed firms, to build strong innovative companies. Aided by China's great scale and appetite for the new, almost all were private firms, forged by the white heat of competition.

Not just among themselves but from the even more ruthless smaller, private piranhas in hot pursuit: *intense* competition.

Foreign firms were not spared this competition. When I moved to China in 2002, Motorola and Nokia shared 60% of China's mobile phone market. Where are they in phones today? Not the global giants they once were. Now Chinese firms have 60% of the China market through intense competition, which has driven innovation in manufacturing technology, function and marketing.

Mind you, China's once largest phone maker fared no better than Motorola or Nokia. In 2002, Ningbo Bird, with almost 20% market share, had the first enormous flickering neon advertisement on Pudong's waterfront. Very much a bold statement: Bird had arrived, and was taking on top global competition in an industry of the future.

Dominating Shanghai's night skyline, across the river from the historic Bund, Bird's neon-lit logo scrolled up and down, up and down, endlessly from top to bottom of a riverside skyscraper. No more: the last I read, Ningbo Bird ranked No. 100 among Chinese phone makers — but it has survived. He who is first can later be last: foreign and local alike.

With much greater corporate size has come China's first substantial regulation to boost competition. Not to protect state ownership, as many foreign commentators report, but attempts to curb monopolistic and oligopolistic practices, so as to promote the competition essential to healthy economies. Anyone knowing US history after the 1929 Crash and Great Depression would know this awaited China's *wunderkind*. Their Wall Street advisers seemed absent among the knowing.

Notice was first served in 2008 by China's US style anti-trust laws: a small step but it put an anti-trust policy on the agenda. Then in 2010–2011, deep official concern arose about the rapidly deteriorating Gini-Coefficient, which measures income inequality. Not normally a subject of dinner conversation or even the nighttime news, China had rapidly become one of the world's most unequal societies.

Finally, in 2020, worldwide clamour against Big Tech spread to China. This included the misuse of personal data, abuse of market power and profits of gigantic new economy firms. Increasingly the terms "people-centred policy" and "common prosperity" crept into Party language.

After three decades of maximising their own interests, heady from enormous success, some entrepreneurs paid no heed. They acted as if they were the golden geese that laid China's economic eggs: an essential, protected species. Hubris had hit.

Several had achieved greatness, overtaking and even vanquishing global leaders. Who wouldn't have let this go to their heads? However, it was only a question of time before pro-competition regulation and data privacy legislation brought them down to earth. Official media was already hinting at it 18 months beforehand but many ignored the signals.

This though is not the death knell for China's private sector as some foreign observers maintain, based only on their experience in the West. There is no killing of its "animal spirits", as Keynes called entrepreneurship. Chinese companies will adapt, they always have. Young entrepreneurs aren't put off: piranhas neither. Indeed both will be incentivised by more economic space opening.

Private sector sharks welcome the opportunity to compete fairly with their former brethren, who have since become giant whales. Some of whom have become like the original state-owned whales, believing they are beyond reproach. As a species they have now lost their protection.

Leading China-Watcher of his generation David Bonavia wrote in 1980 of the Chinese, "Their civilisation is based on the most forthrightly materialistic value in the history of mankind... The trick is to find how things work, and manipulate them for a better life for oneself, family and or social group". Nothing has changed. Accept the new rules of the game and adapt.

The private sector and competition, twin central pillars of China's dynamism, need half-a-dozen solid buttresses. Education, innovation, technology, new growth areas, urbanisation and inclusion are essential to help transform China into the world's No. 1 economy.

Chapter 7

Strong Buttresses

China has become an innovation hot house.

Former World Bank China director Bert Hofman, 2021

By 2030 some 37% of the world's scientists will be Chinese.

DW TV, 2020

Private sector enterprise and competition are the two central pillars of China's continuing dynamism. Yet, collectively, even more important are six buttresses. Not all strictly economic in nature they are indispensible.

Education, innovation and technology are needed for growth. These then fit in with new growth areas: different geographic regions, industries and processes. Beyond that urbanisation and social inclusion provide new kickers to economic growth. All are connected.

Education

Already, some 200 million people in China have university or professional qualifications. The number exceeds the entire US work force of 160 million. Not all may be exactly comparable with countries overseas but the data indicate China's existing strength and future potential. Imagine every American worker with a tertiary qualification. Let's start though at the beginning of learning.

Time in the classroom is a key economic development indicator. Primary school alone is not enough to move anyone far up the development ladder. A full 12-year education is needed for that: to be able to handle much higher value added work. With greater skills people earn higher incomes. That makes them much more valuable consumers: many rungs higher up the ladder.

Human capital though is not just created by formal education. Time in the workplace counts for much too: experience, on the-job-learning. Secondary school or university graduates are much more productive after 10–20 years of work than right after graduation. The full pay-back on the rapid expansion of tertiary education since 2000 is only now being felt economically: the proverbial gift that keeps on giving, as it will for the next two or three decades.

Much has changed since 1990. Then 37% of China's workers only had primary school education, while another 17% were illiterate. In other words, half were still low productivity, poorly paid workers with little spending power: though better off than in 1964 when 33.6% were illiterate.

Many have since moved from farms to factories to offices, shops and platforms, from low productivity agriculture to higher value added manufacturing and services. By 2018 barely 3% were illiterate; and many of those will soon retire. Brains have replaced brawn and muscle to power the economy.

Government spending on education almost doubled to 4.4% of GDP in 2017 from 2.3% in 1995. With the modern economy requiring more secondary and tertiary educated students, in one of China's characteristic leaps, university intake trebled from two to six million around 2000. Now it totals some 11 million, including half a million from overseas.

Enrolment has quintupled to about half of the university age group, from under 10% in the late 1990s. In addition, China had an estimated 370,000 students in the US in 2018, while 770,000 students worldwide returned to China in 2020 and more than one million in 2021. The Ministry of Education estimates that since 2012, some 80% of students abroad have returned.

What frightens the US most is that some 40% of China's graduates are in science, technology, engineering and maths (STEM) subjects, more than double the US share. The World Economic Forum estimated in 2017 that China had 4.7 million STEM students and India 2.6 million. The US in 2016 had only 568,000: more than eight times fewer than China. Furthermore 70% of US STEM PhD candidates were from overseas, mainly from China and India.

One fact establishes the quality of Chinese education. While Chinese comprise about 33% of overseas students in the US, in the top 100 US universities it is 53%. Now they accept China's famous two-day marathon university entrance exam, the *Gaokao,* as suitable qualification.

Sheer quantity is seen from a German global TV channel forecast that by 2030 some 37% of the world's scientists would be Chinese. True or not it makes the point. A substantial foundation has been laid over the last two decades. Germany, today's world leading high-end manufacturer, would only provide 1.4%.

DW bemoaned that Chinese scientists and geeks have rock star status, with appropriate celebrity treatment. In Germany, the media does not cover significantly, let alone celebrate, German AI successes, science competitions or game contests: a cultural disadvantage today.

China sees science and technology in very positive terms. Thomas Edison and Albert Einstein are known by every Chinese schoolchild. The political elite has this perception too: a cultural advantage.

Innovation and Intellectual Property

US attacks on Huawei drew attention to China's manufacturing advance; and US weakness. China now has 30% of cutting-edge 5G patents for the key manufacturing industries of tomorrow. Europe and South Korea have more than 20% each but the US lags far behind: no more a leader.

Whereas Chinese firms and Europeans, like Nokia and Ericsson, use the mainstream sub-6G spectrum, it is not available to companies in the US. There the military and government use it, unlikely to give up much: a sign of where the nation's priorities and power lie.

Innovation is not all about the relentless Long March of R&D spending, year after year. One example of innovation, which says so much, is the role not of scientists or engineers but of China's consumers: the most demanding in the world, as mentioned.

Nestlé, pushed by demanding consumers, has shrunk its average China new product cycle from 18 months to six-to-eight. This introduces more new products, more often; and refreshes old ones. In the process much innovation is discovered, needs met and economic activity generated.

China has become an "innovation hot house", in the words of the World Bank's former China director Bert Hofman. R&D spending as a share of GDP has risen from 0.6% in 1995 to 2.56% in 2022. In 2020 it was 2.4%, compared with 3.5% for the US and 3.1% for Germany.

Overall, measured by patent applications in the West, China ranks second to the US, ahead of Japan. Helped not just by government incentives and tax breaks common in most countries, Chinese firms benefit from long-term government thinking outlined in regular five-year programmes. These identify new long-term trends, adapting policy and support to them. This reduces risk, giving investors more confidence to develop new areas.

The emotive topic of intellectual property (IP) cannot be considered without a long-term global perspective. Throughout time, all nations have copied others. The Greeks, the fount of Western civilisation, took the alphabet from the Phoenicians, medicine and sculpture from Egypt, maths from Babylon and literature from Sumeria.

Was porcelain invented in 1759 by the Wedgwoods in England's Potteries or in Germany's Meissen? No, it was reaching its heights in Jingdezhen, China more than eight centuries earlier. From there its knowledge spread slowly to Europe, with no royalties for IP paid.

America's modern US textile industry was not born in New England. It was carried across the Atlantic in the head of Francis Cabot Lowell, after spying on a leading UK cotton mill. Industrial espionage, IP theft, was much lauded in the US. Indeed, US manufacturers openly advertised for it; and US Treasury Secretary Alexander Hamilton called for it to be rewarded.

Britain was very serious about keeping its IP for itself. Death by hanging was the penalty for exporting industrial drawings let alone machinery. Not surprisingly, for the risk he took and for what he later achieved, Lowell is called the Father of America's Industrial Revolution. For many decades other American entrepreneurs followed Lowell's example, hiring skilled workers from abroad or smuggling machinery to build US industry.

In its early modern days of industrialisation, why would China differ from the US or Europe? Both had taken IP from Asia, especially China two centuries ago. That is how the world has always worked.

China being a world market leader is so common today it is hard to be surprised. However many will be shocked to learn that China is home to the majority of the world's IP litigation cases: more than the rest of the world combined, according to veteran IP consultant Luke Minford. "Chinese entities have become extremely litigious and actively use their court system to challenge and protect IP claims", he told the 2022 Papula-Nevinpat IP Summit in Helsinki. Many Chinese now have "skin in the game", in the form of IP investments they and the government strongly wish to protect.

China's courts now have 300,000 IP cases a year. As for backlog, Minford, whose firm Rouse has 300 people in China alone, says "it only takes about six to eight months for a foreign plaintiff to get to trial, which is quite fast. The judges are more sophisticated than you would think, and will often consider similar cases from outside the country. The courts are also adopting technology to speed up and improve different aspects of civil procedure, particularly in evidence preservation".

China now has 400 specialist IP courts. "Huge developments have happened since 1980", Minford relates. "China has gone from nothing to an internationally competitive system". That is China Speed. The old quip, that China did not do R&D but R&C (Research and Copying), is no longer reality.

"There is a perception that IP cannot be protected in China. I would say there are aspects to this narrative that are true, but that there are also certain parts of China where it's not true at all", Minford said. The chances of winning are high, especially for foreigners. Out of more than 1,000 IP cases, Minford continued, he could "count on one hand the number Rouse has lost in the last two decades".

Some 99% of cases are between domestic Chinese entities. Non-Chinese plaintiffs win 82% of their cases, whereas domestic plaintiffs win 69%. Foreigners are likely to receive more compensation than domestic plaintiffs and are more likely to secure an injunction.

All is very professional. Cases are held online, site visits are made to understand the claims. The three main courts of Beijing, Shanghai and Guangzhou are very good, said Joerg Wuttke, head of the EU Chamber of Commerce in 2020. They are less good outside the main centres, where implementation can be a problem because local jobs are often at stake — always the top concern of local officials. That may well change over time.

Like much in China, this is a work in progress but progress has already been very real. The American Chamber of Commerce in China, Amcham, in its 2021 survey found IP protection or theft not ranking among its members' top 10 China concerns: not in line with Western media and politicians' tropes. Consistent with reality, the fear is steadily receding.

More than four out of five respondents had no fear of doing R&D in China. Only 17% were put off by the prospect of IP theft, down from 26% in 2019. The Amcham survey found that only 3% of member companies had been "pressured informally" to transfer technology or IP by "business authorities".

The US China Business Council found in 2020 that 61% of US firms believed IP protection had improved in China. Four years before it had only been 37%. Evidently neither Washington politicians nor media received the memos or chose to ignore them — ID, intellectual dishonesty, self-deception: not helpful in facing up to the China challenge.

Technology

As with Chinese consumers, who deserve entire books in their own right, I shall limit this section on Chinese technology to four cases. Two are very well known so need only the briefest mention. Namely, the world's fastest high-speed trains, cruising up to 450 km (281 miles) per hour on a network that comprises half the world's high-speed track; and China's space craft landing on Mars and the Far Side of the Moon.

Two are less well known, so merit more description. One seems prosaic, illustrating China's advances in automation, innovation and managing large scale, mind boggling nonetheless. The other reads like something out of science fiction.

China is adapting one of the world's oldest forms of infrastructure, with a very 21st century twist. The Maritime Silk Road will spread these new systems around the globe. China was once known for Ghost Cities, a totally erroneous label incidentally, but now it does have Ghost Ports.

In Ghost Ports, containers move around day and night, without a single human touch. Lasers scan and position each container, before guiding them into driverless trucks. The original was built in Qingdao by 2017 and expanded in 2019. The first took three years to build, compared with a decade previously. The second terminal took only 18 months, five times faster than normal: China Speed.

Artificial intelligence (AI) cut labour costs by 70%, while productivity rises 30% as the port can work at night 24/7. Previously it took 60 workers to unload a ship, now just nine. Going one big step further, Guangzhou is building the world's first automated unmanned parallel container quay — with no workers at all: truly ghostly.

The final example sounds like pure science fiction. Neither Alexander Graham Bell nor Jules Verne could have imagined it nor understood the science. Quantum physics was unknown: "uncrackable emails" unfathomable. Vast quantities of information can be sent almost instantly through a space network to people or machines 3,000 miles away: *incroyable*, incredible. Yet this is what is now declared to be scientifically and technologically possible.

First a Chinese team under Pan Jianwei at the University of Science and Technology of China (USTC) showed how powerful Quantum computing could be. In a 2020 *Science* paper, he and colleagues wrote of, "beams of laser light to perform a computation which had been mathematically proven to be practically impossible on normal computers". *Nature* magazine reported, "The team achieved within a few minutes what would take half the age of Earth on the best existing supercomputers".

To be more precise, they can, "perform certain computations nearly 100 trillion times faster than the world's most advanced supercomputer", *Bloomberg* wrote. *Xinhua* reported that the USTC researchers claim their new prototype can process 10 billion times faster than Google's prototype, which in 2019 could compute in 200 seconds what would take the fastest supercomputers about 10,000 years. "This is certainly a *tour de force* experiment, and an important milestone", said physicist Ian Walmsley at Imperial College, London.

After two-years of testing and study, the USTC scientists, with others from Shanghai and Jinan, published in the British science journal *Nature* a paper confirming, "the feasibility of space-ground station quantum communication work that ... lays the scientific and technological foundation for achieving a quantum communication network that covers the world".

Implications are tremendous. Real secrecy, no hacking: no wonder governments want to know much more. So do we all: no snoopers, no junk mail, no unwanted fake news — a whole New World?

Ironically, according to Harvard's Graham Allison, the spur to China's quantum communications research came from Edward Snowden's 2013 revelations of how much the US spied on China. Quantum knowledge is also critical to any military, including how to jam radar and stop stealth technology. China now ranks top not just for the number of publications on quantum sensing but for citations of new scientific papers in the last five years.

New Growth Areas

There are other new growth engines. Not just new industries but different regions are altering China's economic growth map. Geographically and within industries: it is not just hard technology but soft processes that drive productivity and innovation.

Think of China as a continent, as opposed to simply a country. Each of more than 30 administrative units is like a European state, only on average larger. Then it is easier to grasp what is happening to China's economy: the benefits of scale and diversity.

Successive waves of change wash over the continent, spreading what worked before in China or elsewhere. They distribute knowledge, systems and models. Each generates its own momentum and network effects. These have driven China ever since Reform and Opening Up began in 1978.

From China's three main gateways of Guangzhou, Shanghai and Beijing, the first wave of high economic growth rippled along China's 1,200 mile-long coastal belt in the 1980s and 1990s: then inwards in the 2000s. This was transformational but only 39% of China's population lives there.

The other 61% saw little progress until central China's economy started to spurt around 2005. Initially it happened around the provincial capitals, with budgetary injections from Beijing and the first inland property booms, which then spread internally. West and northeast China still largely missed out, except for their capitals and principal cities.

These laggards are today's third wave of growth leaders. They are at the forefront in the 2020s. Many are helped by cross-border trade and investment with China's 14 land neighbours. Inland China only housed 13% of China's middle class in 2015. By 2022 it would treble to 40%, consultants McKinsey predicted.

This is all part of a process: not a one-off wonder. Successive, though slightly smaller, waves always follow the first big wave, bringing the next stage of economic development. Each subsequent wave is faster because the coastal economy has lit the way. Each time, mistakes are fewer as people learn from earlier lessons, often from coastal pioneers relocating to less costly inland areas. This is nothing new. The US has been doing it for a couple of centuries.

Global best practices are adopted, new systems introduced and devised. Not all powered by AI but many are. Traditional manufacturing's contribution is maturing while new industries and services have only just begun to drive the economy. The lagging service sector, not manufacturing, is the biggest example of higher productivity. Surveys show that government is learning too, as its response to COVID confirms. This is particularly true at the local level, where officials' education levels — and hence effectiveness — have risen significantly.

Growth in old industries like textiles, shoes, steel and cement is replaced by newer industries in IT, e-commerce, tourism, entertainment, logistics, transport, health and education. These are the new growth generators. They have a long way to go before maturing across the whole of China.

Urbanisation

Urbanisation has been China's biggest economic story in the last quarter of a century: even more important than exports. Like China's growth itself, the nature of urbanisation is changing.

China's urbanisation growth still points to very large absolute numbers and change, though slower in percentage terms than in previous decades. The National Academy of Economic Strategy estimates that more than 70% of China's population will be urbanised by 2035, (maybe more) compared with 58% in 2018 and 64% in 2021.

This will mean at least an extra 160 million more people live in towns larger than 20,000 by 2035: earning much higher incomes. That is two Germanys or four Californias.

China's new factor is that urbanisation is not principally about the number of new buildings, requiring so much steel, granite and cement. It is about what people do with their existing homes, whose mortgages by now have usually been reduced and often repaid, leaving much more money for other things.

Among China's near one billion urban dwellers, the top priority has been to buy their own home, with the maximum space they could afford. This is as much a long-term investment as about buying a home. Don't worry much about furnishings. They can come later, ditto white goods. First, get on the housing ladder; and only then think about the interior.

Today, people increasingly spend to upgrade their homes: renovate. Owners remodel extensively their homes (very common in China), buying more expensive white goods and plusher furnishings. This trend began more than a decade ago in coastal China but is only now appearing inland.

The life cycle pattern repeats itself. The first decade builds the space, the next two decades fill and upgrade it. On top of that, now come "smart cities". Using resources more efficiently, often through employing AI, they will boost future growth.

Inclusion

Inclusion is very much in vogue. China has long used the concept since 1949, recognising gender equality and minorities' needs. Acknowledging the reality and complexity of managing change on such unprecedented scale, inclusion has been gradual. Now, after other basic priorities have been met, it has more central government focus.

Going in two generations from the land of bound feet to having the highest percentage of women working outside the home is quite an achievement. That is the story of China's women, within living memory, not ancient history. Tse Oy's grandmother hobbled along, with painfully shortened, disfigured feet all her adult life. So unbearable was the tight binding, her mother succumbed to her daughter's pleas to remove the bandages: too late though to stop the permanent damage that crushed her young bones in the interest of "beauty" and marital prospects.

Women Hold Up Half the Sky was the slogan. China has made good on the promise to emancipate women. Apart from six million getting divorces from often tyrannical and loveless marriages within the first year after 1949, women have gone on to comprise more than 52% of tertiary students, almost double the percentage of 1978. Their rising numbers in higher-echelons of government are increasingly visible. Some 60% of the world's new female billionaires are Chinese.

Women in China are considered adventurous. They found 55% of internet startups and make 66% of cross-border online transactions. Some 58% of independent overseas travellers are women: men prefer group tours. Women buy half of all luxury cars, from Porsches to Maseratis and BMWs. Women's inclusion has had a major impact on China's economy, in ways unimaginable seven decades ago.

A similar story can be told about the inclusion of other previously marginalised groups. Social attitudes have begun to help those excluded by disability to join the mainstream. Apart from women and the disabled, the other major beneficiaries from greater inclusion are China's 130 million from ethnic minorities.

Inland China, especially along its borders, is where most of China's 55 ethnic minorities live. As these areas grow, minorities benefit from cross-border trade and investment. Not to mention China's ever-growing development funds, designed to end not just extreme poverty but poverty itself.

China's economy probably has another three decades before becoming fully mature. That means 30 more years of growth above the Western average. China should average 4% real annual GDP growth over the next three decades, 40–50% faster than the 2.8% the US achieved in the last two decades, which seems to be its average mature rate. Each time China's absolute GDP growth outstrips that of the US, the more it closes the economic size gap.

The sources of China's dynamism, along with its strong buttresses, highlighted in the last two chapters, give China the muscle to compete in the global geopolitical contest. What else drives China? Managing change is China's X-Factor.

Chapter 8

China's X-Factor

The Yi Jing, the Book of Change *is transformation ... the principles of fortune and calamity, the process of waxing and waning, the Dao of progress and retreat, of survival and extinction.*

Cheng Yi, Song Dynasty (11th Century)

Managing change has been overlooked as China's X-Factor. China has no "special sauce", as some claim. Indeed China's success shows great similarities to 20 signposts along the Western route to economic development in the 19th and 20th centuries.

In *China's Change*, I wrote, "Managing change can be described in barely 70 words. For China, the main goals are harmony, stability and moderation: in other societies goals will differ. They can though be crystallized using the same long-term thinking and vision, along with a good grasp of cycles and priorities. Implementation then follows with research and field work, pilot schemes and correct sequencing. Pragmatism, flexibility, gradualism, restraint and constant renewal are central to success. Educating people for politics and administration is essential". How this worked during COVID is explored in Chapter 14: *How China Works*.

All 20 ideas are needed for a 360-degree view of any problem. If forced to choose four of the greatest importance in China, I would select a very clear sense of priorities, long-term thinking, gradualism and pragmatism. "Black cat, white cat, it doesn't matter as long as the cat catches the mice", as China's paramount leader Deng Xiaoping said — very unideological. China had had more than enough ideology by the 1970s.

Long-Term Thinking

Asia's post-war Economic Miracles were built around outline planning: long-term economic thinking. These were not Soviet-style five-year plans but painting the next big picture. Japan, South Korea and Singapore still keep a close watch on long-term trends, adjusting policy when needed. Both macro and micro thinking are led by long-term thinking. China has taken long-term thought to another level altogether.

When I first moved to Shanghai in 2002, I was surprised to learn that by 2020 the city would have 20 crossing points across the Huangpu River that divides the city, west from east, old from new. There are now seven bridges and 15 tunnels: 22. How did Shanghai know? How could it be so sure?

Shanghai then had just two bridges, one road tunnel and an under-river pedestrian walkway, closed to the public. Such expansion of infrastructure, involving all that lay behind it in terms of administration, road systems, property construction and funding, was unimaginable in the West: yet it happened. The same occurred in macro-economic policy.

Resetting China's government's economic default position happens every decade or two. This gives the whole country a sense of long-term economic direction. Companies can better see opportunities. Meeting consumers' needs by improving capacities, standards and efficiency is made much easier. A focus on specific areas helps firms handle relentless competition, at home and abroad.

Government involvement in the economy was not uncommon in Europe or the US for three decades after World War II. Eisenhower built the National Inter-State Highway System, Kennedy set steel prices, while Britain fashioned a mixed economy and the welfare state. Then the West, mired increasingly in economic problems, turned to the Reagan/Thatcher revolution for their panacea of cutting the state through privatisation and deregulation.

When that ran its course, the UK, France, Germany and the EU became more enamored of state-assistance, something COVID reinforced. Joe Biden is certainly not shy about using the state to Build Back Better or to help private firms compete with China.

China has reassessed its long-term economic thinking three times in the last four decades. First, in 1978 through Reform and Opening Up; then rebooting this major reform, after Deng Xiaoping's 1992 Southern Tour; and thirdly under the fifth generation of leaders, headed by Xi Jinping. This latest phase originated in 2011, when China began thinking about the next two decades.

A long report, *China 2030*, published in 2013, resulted from a close collaboration between three institutions: the State Council's think tank the Development and Reform Commission (DRC), then headed by Xi Jinping's Harvard-trained economic adviser Liu He, China's Finance Ministry and the World Bank. The aim was to "build a modern, harmonious and creative high income society". To raise skills and incomes, a major systemic overhaul was the goal.

Prime focus is to upgrade the two main economic laggards of finance and other services. This enormous task would stretch over three five-year programmes, as plans are now called. What had already worked on China's coast would be spread inland. The whole country would learn more from Western best practices, systems and cutting edge technology.

On top of services, China set three decades of targets for Chinese manufacturing: all the way to 2045. By then, China aims to be the world's dominant manufacturer. Not an unreasonable target given its population size but how to do it?

The first stage is Made in China 2025. Big data, real time information and sensors speed up decentralised decision making: incorporating inclusive, holistic and all-round 360 degree thinking. This depends heavily on the private sector to upgrade existing systems.

China's Next Big Thing should raise workers' skills, productivity and incomes, not to mention corporate profits. The Internet of Things (IOT), cloud computing, 5G and all the other components of artificial intelligence (AI), already provide services to forecast and diagnose mechanical failures.

Washington met this with horror. As with the Belt and Road, the US was slow to appreciate the significance. Its roots of thinking about economic decoupling began to grow. Europe's initial reaction was different.

Much of China's core industrial strategic thinking today is based on Germany's Industry 4.0, the Fourth Industrial Revolution. Germany has partnered with China on this, each for its own good reasons to secure their futures (Chapter 9: *The New New World.*) The EU followed more tentatively, finally signing the outline of a Bilateral Investment Agreement at the end of 2020 but then put it on ice.

Industry 4.0 showed the path. China had placed innovation at the heart of *China 2030* but lacked a detailed structure of analysis, let alone implementation strategy. Innovation, not more physical inputs of steel, concrete and workers, was to drive China's transformation: especially through private sector growth. The state, *China 2030* wrote, would have to reduce its role in production, distribution and resources but change could not stop there.

China 2030 was not organised around statist language or thinking. Indeed, it acknowledged government does not have all the answers: admitting the state might even retard growth.

More individual rights and space, *China 2030* said, would have to be "granted to encourage broad participation" in this enormous enterprise.

The middle class and the private sector gained recognition in ways unthinkable three decades earlier. Only time will tell what this means precisely but it signaled that more than economic reform lay ahead.

Creativity

China 2030 can talk of a modern, harmonious and even high income society within 15 years but creative? Surely everyone knows Chinese are not creative? One 2015 Harvard study pointed to China's reliance on rote learning, while British media cited that China won no Oscars, suggesting only endless lines of worker ants, who could only follow instructions not create. Only free thinkers in free societies could innovate, not those in "authoritarian regimes" shut out from the latest global knowledge by the Great Firewall of China: right?

Before answering if China lacks creativity, think about whether your definition is derived principally from the West. If it is, this may be too narrow a way to capture other arts or strengths outside the Western experience.

Jump into a cab in London or New York City and pop music may well be on the radio. In Beijing it would often be cross talk, a great love of local taxi drivers and passengers alike. Combining clowning humour with witty word play, pace and great timing, cross talk has survived and adapted to the modern era. However it is unknown overseas. Cross talk certainly counts as part of China's cultural heritage; and is very creative. No Chinese would say that London or New York are not creative because they do not have cross talk on taxi radios.

It is easy to stereotype Chinese education as simply rote learning or having too much emphasis on a few subjects, cramming and enormous amounts of out-of-school tuition. That was once partly true but had been changing steadily until a major overhaul.

A new school curriculum was introduced in 2021. This places much more emphasis on the arts, humanities and sport, less on maths, science and a crippling homework load. Correcting this is all part of Xi Jinping's China Dream. To develop creativity and critical thinking is the new imperative. Singapore faced the same problem a few decades ago, just as Britain did in the 19th and 20th centuries. The answer was to broaden the curriculum and boost extra-curricular activities, as well as to free up more time out of school.

True, traditional arts like Chinese opera and music have declined. Once every rich business man had his opera troupe, complete with dancers, musicians, singers, acrobats, technicians and props: no more. Without financial support, very few performers since 1949 could study for 10 or more years to learn their craft. The state had higher priorities. Initially these were to provide the very basics of calories and security: understandable. That has changed and when it did China had significant cultural assets to develop.

First came technical skills, including traditional props. When Ang Lee's *Crouching Tiger, Hidden Dragon* wowed Western cinema audiences in 2000, China's viewers rated it as average for a Chinese martial arts TV series: nothing special. Traditional techniques using hidden springs and wires were not new. They came right out of traditional theatre and opera. On stage they are even more real, dramatic and breathtaking than in film.

China has a rich history, providing plenty of content for its arts. Other traditional skills are well advanced. China's most famous living film director Zhang Yimou draws on China's traditional capacity to organise large numbers and space, be it coordinating crowds, colour, lighting or music. Stunning blocks of colour were Zhang's original *motif*. His scripts though were not up to much.

Far richer can be Red Dramas: films or TV series with revolutionary themes. Weaving complex webs, which would make modern Western spy or thriller writers proud. Many are based on true events in history, ancient and modern.

Modern Chinese writers like Nobel Literature Laureate Mo Yan draw on their personal experience from the turbulent 1950s to the 1970s or like Yu Hwa from observation posts on the new economic margins of the last four decades. They have lived far more complex lives than most Western writers, many of whom base work on their own lives, which are often remarkably unexceptional by comparison.

Tik Tok may not be high art but it is certainly creative. The world's most demanding consumers, China's Millennials, love novelty; and have the numbers (400 million) to get their way. The technicians come from the millions of young Chinese who want to found the next Byte Dance or at the very least land a job.

Markets quickly spot market gaps, new needs. Lack of time is one of the most pressing: hence Tik Tok's super short videos, some only 15 seconds long. There is one brand that is even shorter, another niche. As Chinese social media discuss more about national and international affairs, Byte Dance (Tik Tok's owner), originally founded to provide educational content, has added a new format. Going in the opposite direction, it now has longer videos, some up to four minutes: all responding to market demand.

Not only are Chinese consumers driving this but energetic entrepreneurs, with creative business models, make it possible. So do rapidly evolving financial markets to provide funding, as in the US, though often faster. China's private equity fund raising far exceeds Europe's and has overtaken the US. The NVCA 2021 Yearbook estimates China raised $134 billion of new money for venture funds in 2020, the US $75 billion and Europe about $20 billion.

China has become the world's leader in electric vehicles (EVs) not just because it has the largest auto market but because it is the leading electronics manufacturer. All very logical, prompting many of the world's leading auto makers to invest heavily in Chinese EV operations to open up new frontiers in China.

Gao Feng consultants Edward Tse and Bill Russo note that EVs are, "the next big thing in the era of the IOT, so intelligent connectivity is becoming standard in today's vehicles... past success won't be a guarantee for future success. The winning companies will be the ones that can learn, adapt and strengthen along the way". Be creative.

Similarly in the arts, technical innovation in cinematography, lighting, video, computer graphics and music support creativity. It doesn't all have to be hi-tech. Imagination also works. What could be more creative than live camels and roaring, splashing waterfalls in a stage production I saw in Xinjiang? Everything went without a hitch. Local knowledge, in this case of camel husbandry and water management, came in really handy.

Merely to survive, Chinese in their everyday lives have to be creative. Some rubs off onto artistic creativity: much more into business or work, the top priority in life for most Chinese. Living in such a large, complex society, they must be nimble and innovative to face competition, bureaucracy and change. When state-owned enterprise reform began in earnest in the 1990s, tens of millions of workers were laid off. Their iron rice bowls of guaranteed lifetime employment smashed.

Many decided to *xia hai*, jump into the sea, the Chinese expression to become a private entrepreneur. That was not easy, pitfalls or deadly riptides were everywhere but they released untold energy.

Problem solving, the essence of creativity, became second nature. From it rose the world's most entrepreneurial generation since the Silicon Valley founders of the 1970s and 1980s. That is how China learned speed, low cost and responsiveness to demanding consumers.

China becoming the world's undisputed largest economy has so many dimensions. Geopolitical consequences are legion. A New New World is evolving. We have reached the heart of *America as No. 3*: the Geopolitical Contest.

Geopolitical Contest

Chapter 9

The New New World

By 2030 RCEP will add $500 billion to members' exports; and $186 billion to income.

Peterson Institute for International Economics, 2021

The New World for more than two centuries has been America. Great celebrations will mark the US's 250th birthday in 2026. Remember though Sir John Glubb's discovery that empires on average last just 250 years (Chapter 4: *The Power Equation and Decline of Empires*).

Should the West worry? Is the US already in its final innings? What would the New New World look like?

For two centuries the Atlantic Ocean has been at the heart of the world economy. Two world standards remind us. Greenwich Mean Time and zero degrees longitude are based on maritime London's Greenwich, the centre of all globes. Europe, then the US, dominated commercial geography: north to south. Now a new phenomenon the Belt and Road could reset the main axis of world trade through Eurasia: east to west.

For more than a century, the US has been by far the largest economy and military. In 1950 it accounted for half the world's manufacturing and wealth. Yet today the US faces a competitor and quandary unlike any other. US GDP no longer towers over China nor is 8.5 times larger, as in 2000. That advantage has shrunk to just 36% by GDP at market exchange rates and is 27% smaller by the OECD's real GDP on a PPP basis.

All Change

The US is no more the New World. Nor is Europe necessarily the Old World. Neither are ancient civilisations and former regional power centres. From India, Nigeria and Indonesia to Brazil, Egypt and Iran, all seek to re-emerge like China.

The New New World connects all these former powers, offering new opportunities for economic growth; and alternatives. That challenges US global dominance. Many may become part of the BRICS, the Shanghai Cooperation Organisation (SCO) or both. Not militarily but for development, investment and trade among its 30 members*: though the SCO does cooperate to combat terrorism, separatism, extremism and cross-border crime that is its primary security concern.

Nothing symbolises the New New World like the Belt and Road. This could literally redraw the world's economic map. With the majority of the world's population living between Europe and China, the vast stretch of land between the Atlantic and Pacific Oceans could be the proverbial global game changer. Three basic economic instruments — markets, investment and communications — redirect trade, create jobs and boost consumption in places few can locate on the map. This is all very different.

---

*There are eight full members — China, India, Kazakhstan, Kyrgyzstan, Pakistan, Russia, Tajikistan and Uzbekistan, with Belarus and Iran approved for membership, leaving two observers — Afghanistan and Mongolia; and nine dialogue partners — Armenia, Azerbaijan, Cambodia, Egypt, Nepal, Qatar, Saudi Arabia, Sri Lanka and Turkey, with another five approved for dialogue partnership in 2022 — Bahrain, Kuwait, Maldives, Myanmar and UAE. Four guest attendees are ASEAN, CIS, Turkmenistan and the UN.

Regional Comprehensive Economic Partnership (RCEP): Regional Economic Integration

Even with its mind-boggling scale and imagination, the Belt and Road is not even the most important economic factor the US has to consider. Hidden in clear sight is Asia's growing economic integration, with China its engine and beating heart. Easternisation, as Gideon Rachman of the *Financial Times* calls it.

Western focus has been principally on China, not the continent as a whole. That has been a strategic error. Asia's economy is already a very large fact on the ground, indeed the largest. Combined, Asian economies overtook the US and EU in size one decade ago.

Growing steadily larger, China contributes ever more, through developing communication networks by land, air and sea. At first internally, then with neighbours, China helps knit together Asia's previously disparate economies and societies.

Asian economic integration is accelerating through the world's largest free trade project. The Regional Comprehensive Economic Partnership (RCEP) began in 2022; and from a much larger economic base than the Belt and Road.

By 2030, RCEP will add US$500 billion annually to world exports, each year generating US$186 billion extra income for its members, according to the Washington-based Peterson Institute for International Economics. China's trade with the rest of RCEP comprised almost one-third of its foreign trade in RCEP's first six months, growing 20% faster than with other trading partners.

All 15 RCEP economies* need a permanent boost. Realistically, only China's growth can provide that. The mature US and EU markets

---

*There are 15 signatories: the 10 members of ASEAN plus Australia, China, Japan, New Zealand and South Korea.

have little new access or capital they wish to offer. Increasingly they cannot even guarantee what exists, as firms like ZTE and Huawei have learned.

Birth of the world's largest trade agreement went almost unnoticed in the West. Few have heard of it, let alone grasp its future significance. Covering 30% of world GDP and almost one-third of the world's population, RCEP is bigger than NAFTA/USMCA or the EU's common market.

Notable absentee is the US, which withdrew from RCEP negotiations as it failed to contain China. This opened the door for China to join US allies Japan, South Korea, Australia and New Zealand, with the 10 Association of Southeast Asian Nations (ASEAN), the original promoters.

Just one example shows what could happen to boost intra-Asian trade. ASEAN has 20 "smart" cities, with more to follow. These can work with China, Japan and South Korea whose companies specialise in this new technology. Geography and proximity talk, facts cannot be undone or wished away by ideology or others' self-interest.

Belt and Road with 21st Century Marco Polos

To the north, an enormous land bridge connects the Pacific with the Atlantic: almost 6,000 miles as the crow flies, along the old Silk Roads. To the south the Maritime Silk Road links China with Southeast Asia through the South China Sea, before connecting, via the Indian Ocean with West Asia, the Middle East and Africa, to Europe.

In less than a decade, the Belt and Road has evolved substantially. Since its announcement in 2013, it began largely with developing economies, often poor trouble spots like Pakistan, Afghanistan, Myanmar and the Stans.

Now the Belt and Road is taken much more seriously in Europe and, even in its opposition to it, by the US. The first G7 country has joined,

Italy. Two-thirds of EU members and 33 international organisations are involved. Currently 149 countries have joined the Belt and Road by signing a Memorandum of Understanding.*

A complex web of rails, roads, ports, airports and pipelines grow constantly as trade expands in all directions. Not along a single artery but through nine existing rail routes, nine road connections, ever-denser air networks and numerous sea links.

In concrete terms, China and the Pacific are linked to the Rhine that opens onto the Baltic; and to Porto on the Atlantic, which faces the Americas. Adding power to the idea is that these economies are more complementary than those that drove previous Atlantic or even Pacific trade.

There is more diversity. Not the old formula of rich consumers at one end and largely poor raw material producers or low-end assemblers at the other. Belt and Road connectivity brings into play countries like Italy, Greece and Bulgaria: even Argentina and Brazil. All need infrastructure, so that is the first priority. Firms from rich countries like Switzerland and middle-income China work together along the route: mostly in high-end manufacturing and services.

This is not promoter (China) takes all. Projects are often very large because distance magnifies scale, complexity and cost. Pooling resources to reduce risk makes sense. Collaboration works better, including in management and sourcing. China National Building Materials Group buys half its Belt and Road machinery from foreign companies. Beneficiaries include Siemens, Caterpillar and Komatsu: German, American and Japanese, respectively.

---

* Regional membership, as defined by the World Bank, comprises: 43 from Sub-Saharan Africa, 35 Europe and Central Asia (18 EU), 25 East Asia and Pacific, 20 Latin America and Caribbean, 18 Middle East and North Africa and six in South Asia: seven others had not confirmed membership by March, 2022.

The Belt and Road creates new markets, which did not exist for economies constrained by 19th and 20th century fractured communications. Old trade routes are reopened, new ones forged. Initially from the Chinese end, though not exclusively by Chinese: far from it. Participants come from around the globe.

I was surprised to see so many consultants, accountants and financial advisers from leading global firms when in 2017 I attended *Euromoney's* Green Investment conference in one of China's poorest provinces. In the north-west corner of China, they were following their clients' business. Five years before that a conference in Xining, capital of Qinghai province, would have only had Chinese companies; and I would have been one of the very few Western individuals.

A caravan of global advisers and companies was now on the move, looking west into the seemingly endless heart of land-locked Eurasia. That is what I saw, driving deep into Eurasia's little known, let alone understood, mosaic of peoples, states and histories.

The unlikely travellers were the latest foreign group to find opportunity along the Silk Road. Marco Polo in the 13th century wore loose fitting garments not a well-tailored suit but he is the pioneer many now emulate. Their clients comprise the world's largest companies, often led by those from the West.

Through here Asia-based firms have a new opening to the West, while European business has new access to the East. Nothing captured this more than the 2020 overland rail trans-shipment of COVID personal protection equipment from China to Europe: two to four weeks faster than shipping, not to mention cheaper.

This is a work in progress. It combines classic Chinese long-term thinking, vision, *weixin* (constant renewal), regrouping after setbacks, flexibility, sequencing, gradualism and inclusion. It is collaborative, not a top-down rigid Soviet-style plan of some Western imaginations. With markets as its guide, it is a pragmatic 21st century economic attempt to see what works, for the mutual benefit of many people and countries: ask the companies themselves.

In a world struggling for economic growth, firms need little encouragement to find profit. Asian firms too, working along the Belt and Road with neighbours, often for the first time. With it comes a new sense of identity.

Surely Asia is as old as the hills, with millennia of culture, history and proximity binding the region's economies and nations together? Well, no, not much, so far.

Asia is not an Asian idea. It is European. Europe defining the other: what is un-European. There is no single Asian identity, only many, overlapping cultures in a host of 20th century post-colonial nation states. Previously there were no countries, with today's borders, called India, Indonesia, Pakistan, Bangladesh, Myanmar, Malaysia, the Philippines or Singapore.

Like China, Asia is not one vast monolith. Asia is multilayered, linked to other cultures by different languages, philosophies, religions and history. Some similar government cultures and practices exist but not as much as in Europe. The 21st century is when Asia will be knit together, principally by geography, communications and economics.

Asian identity, as opposed to much smaller local identities, is emerging: principally through economics. This is new. First the Northeast Asian power houses of Japan and South Korea restored commercial links with China. Now Southeast Asian countries of ASEAN have overtaken both and it has replaced the US and EU as China's largest trading partner. Princeton's Wilson Center wrote in 2023 that "the days of America's trade dominance have passed". In 2022, the US was already No. 3. The Belt and Road is turbo-charging this change; and not just for Asia.

China's Growing Importance to the West

In exaggerated fashion, China's importance to the West was illustrated during COVID-hit 2020. Then China was the only major economy to grow; and so give the rest of the world any economic boost at all. Its markets are often the largest or second largest in the world. For some 130 countries, China is their top trading partner.

Take the world's largest manufacturing industry, autos. China has been the world's largest market for half a dozen years. Not only in internal combustion engine vehicles but in new energy vehicles and autonomous driving. China will be the future, simply because the largest market attracts the most global investment to develop new vehicles and technologies.

This though is not only about the future. In practical terms and in 2020 hard money, China meant Daimler made an overall profit of $4.8 billion, despite global sales falling 11% when European and US operations dived into the red. China more than offset this. Not for the first time did China aid foreign auto makers. The China market helped bail out General Motors in 2009, arguably more than did the US government. It certainly cost the US nothing: the ignored benefits of international trade.

China's greatest attraction to US companies is that it offers higher profit margins than any other country. How can this be if there is so much competition in China? Most Western firms occupy the market's high-end, not the intensely competitive low-end crowded by Chinese manufacturers. Chinese consumers pay a premium for perceived quality and status. Foreign has cache: *yangqi*, foreign air, as local sales staff constantly stress.

In autos, first time buyers may well buy local but aspire to a Mercedes: an Audi is equally fine and BMW has its fans, especially among younger, rich women. As incomes rise, buyers move up the quality curve, through the South Koreans, Japanese, US and assorted Europeans, to where the top German makers have long awaited China's consumers. In VW's case the People's Car has been Made in China for almost four decades, upmarket BMWs since 2003.

When profits worldwide collapsed, often into losses, many Western firms earned rare first-half 2020 profits in China; and not just auto makers. Greatest of all was in the European-dominated luxury sector. With COVID travel bans, Chinese domestic sales soared for the likes of Louis Vuitton Moet Hennessy (LVMH) and Kering (Gucci, Yves Saint Laurent and Bottega Veneta). Not only does China matter as an auto or luxury consumer market.

China is a major contributor to world development and welfare: take renewable energy. In 2019, Nick Butler of King's College, London, pointed to the, "significant gains for the world as a whole. Without its [China's] development of wind and solar power over the past decade, the growth in production from renewables would not have taken place and the transition to a low-carbon economy would hardly have begun".

World leader China helped make solar and wind power competitive with fossil fuels. Wind and solar power costs fell 69% and 88%, respectively, in the last decade, mainly because of heavy investment and innovation in Chinese turbines and panels. Imagine what China will do in renewable energy and environmental technology in the next two decades. The global energy transition needs China not just in these fields but also in advanced grid technology, lithium ion batteries, civilian nuclear power and nuclear waste disposal.

The New New World is now emerging, not just in Asia but in the West. Nowhere is it more critical than for Europe. Once the Old World, Europe has plentiful new economic opportunities but acute immediate dilemmas. Notably how to co-exist with Asia and America, while maintaining the benefits of both: not easy, even before Russia invaded Ukraine.

Changing Role For New World Europe

The Anglo-Saxon world built the West on either side of the Atlantic. The main nations of Old Europe, all imperial powers to varying degrees — Britain, France, Spain, Portugal, Netherlands, Germany, Belgium and Italy — looked west to associate with the then New World of the Americas for five centuries. They had much in common, from ethnicity, religion and philosophy to skin colour.

Creating a common identity named the West seemed natural. Especially in juxtaposition to Eastern Europe, Russia, Turkey, the Middle East, Africa, the Pacific Islands and Asia. To the West, Asia was the Orient, literally the East.

Several generations since their imperial heydays, Europe wants to move on but is not sure how. Indeed the whole world is moving on: needing new arrangements, "global architecture" in the jargon, between countries and regions, including within the West. Interests evolve, challenging centuries-old relationships. A new Europe is being born, less Anglo and more Saxon. At least that is how it looked before Russia invaded Ukraine. Whatever transpires there, Europe's role is changing.

Much has changed since the invasion of Ukraine but, beforehand, German Chancellor Angela Merkel put it succinctly, "Europe needs to reposition itself in a changed world. The old certainties of the post-war order no longer apply". She added that China, Russia and the US, "are forcing us, time and again, to find common positions. That is often difficult given our different interests".

Have these different interests changed permanently or only temporarily? They certainly have been rearranged. Will German and EU words be the same in 2025, let alone 2030, as they were in early 2022 when every US statement emphasised the word unity; and Europe kept repeating it. Energy and defence security are understood but overlooked are other critical consequences. Europe has much to lose and ponder.

New Europe has to face the fact the US is no more the New World but the New Old World. Yet, even before Ukraine, Europe was unsure if it wanted to embrace China fully in a New New World. A new generation in the EU and individual states is in power. It talks about values more than economics, without admitting that means voters' jobs, incomes and welfare. That contradiction has yet to be resolved.

Nowhere is this more evident than in Germany. Merkel's generation's world view, based on two World Wars, a Cold War and decades-long struggle with the Soviet Union in a divided Germany, is giving way to a generation that only recalls, with great emotion, the Stasi secret police; and therefore prioritises individual human rights, universally. This has very unpredictable implications for future foreign policy, particularly towards China. Just allowing the Chinese shipping line COSCO to invest 24.9% in a single terminal at the Hamburg port divided the ruling coalition.

Therefore, a bumpy, much less predictable road lies ahead, just as the globe turns once more, again pivoting westwards. This time though it takes a head-spinning long journey from the Pacific through Eurasia to Europe, the Atlantic and Baltic, if left to economic forces.

Go West young man. No one ever thought the northern leg would start in Xining on the roof of the world, the Qinghai–Tibetan Plateau. Let alone end in Germany on the Rhine in the world's largest inland port of Duisberg or Hamburg, adjacent to the North and Baltic Seas.

Prompted by Germany, the EU stole a march on its business rival the US through the EU–China Investment Agreement. Whether it is ever signed is unclear. However it indicates the economic geography that some in Europe see as a New New World.

The calculus between the US, EU and China, is complex. Each has to consider the other two in a triangular 3D brain-teaser. This is better solved by mastery of Chinese *weiqi* (*go*) than linear chess, let alone rush-and-grab poker.

Weiqi is all about patience and long-term vision, building positions to command space until the encircled opponent cannot move; and yields. It is a very Daoist continuum, a flow, a marathon: not a deal, play, take or fold finish, then reset to begin all over again, with the last hand forgotten.

Poker-playing Americans seem to find the calculus harder to grasp than chess-playing Europeans. Incoming US Secretary of State Antony Blinken blundered in late 2020 when he publicly told — not suggested politely or privately — the EU not to sign the investment agreement outline with China before the EU had talked with the incoming administration.

This was literally after more than seven years of negotiation and only days before signing. Significantly this was just as Merkel, the driving spirit behind the EU–China agreement, completed her term as EU President: the result?

The EU ignored Blinken, went ahead and signed the outline: quite a slap in the face for US power, demonstrating its new limits. Of course the old EU generation did. Some 450 million people, their interests and independent collective pride counted for much more than a troubled 334 million, no matter how many nuclear warheads or aircraft carriers it has.

"America Is Back", sounds a little different in German, French and other European tongues than in Peoria, Illinois. It sounds like the Old America giving orders, telling allies what to do. After Trump that can never happen again, Europe likes to believe: partly because it thinks the US does not hold all the cards anymore.

The US is less dominant economically by the year. Often it is no longer even most countries' top trading partner, let alone best future economic growth prospect. Allies see they have to protect their own interests: current and future. A possible Trumpian return to power makes this all the more urgent.

The EU does not want to be a mere pawn in a US contest with China. It has all the credentials to be a full player, with different interests, thinking, history and size: a 35% larger population than the US, with similar economic weight to it and China. Yet, the changing EU has to show it can be a third major power. Otherwise it will be a minor actor, even in its own neighbourhood, as the Ukraine war in 2022 illustrated.

Biden's pitch to the G-7 and NATO in 2021 was all about US interests, cloaked in common benefits and values. Biden brought hope, so was excused publicly for his America-centric ideas. He promised action on Europe's top concern, climate change; and everyone was so relieved after Trump's erratic and often crude behavior.

Not all though were in lock step with Biden over China. Phones and the internet had to be switched off to maintain the G-7 discussions' secrecy. Much is uncertain as the US pushes Europe to support it against China. As noted in the Prologue, Germany has rejected decoupling. Either there will be a major row or Washington may have to accept meekly Germany's stance, as it did when Quad ally India bought Russian oil and refused to join US sanctions: making the US look weaker.

Bad News for Biden

Bad news from friends is often the worst. Imagine Joe Biden's feeling when he heard that 60% of Europeans believed China will be more powerful than the US, within a decade. Ukraine may have changed all that for now, although by the end of the decade the view could still be the same as in 2021, especially if China's economy outstrips that of the US.

After a century as Top Dog, having slain its ideological foe the Soviet Union to become the only superpower at The End of History, the US light is fading. The dusk of American dominance suddenly looms in the eyes of its friends: China No. 1, US No. 2 in power.

The rarely spoken issue was re-opened by a European Council on Foreign Relations survey, conducted in late 2020, among 15,000 people in 11 European countries. This was even before the damaging invasion of the US Capitol.

Not only did 60% believe China would be more powerful than the US by 2030, more than half wanted the EU to be neutral in any US–China conflict. Furthermore, 67% would not trust the US to help defend Europe. Friends? Allies? Time will tell.

The final piece of bad news to greet Joe Biden on arrival in the White House was that in 2020 China became the world's favourite investment destination. Foreign Direct Investment (FDI) is not a popularity contest but a serious commitment. It is hard dollars and cents invested: money on the table and subject to foreign laws.

How do the US and China view the arrival of this New New World? How do they see relations with others? Different perceptions will shape how they approach this conundrum. It is not without hope for those wishing for peace and global economic recovery but it will require hard work, especially after the invasion of Ukraine.

Chapter 10

The New China—US Equation

Wu ji bi fan *(when you go too far, you rebound): overreach, overstretch.*

Traditional Chinese saying

Appropriately on May 1, 2021, I read the latest thoughts and fears of America's leading strategic thinker for half a century Henry Kissinger. With loud echoes of May Day, May Day, the international distress signal for emergency, Kissinger said in his slow, gravelly voice that, "US–China tensions threaten to engulf the entire world and could lead to an Armageddon-like clash between the two military and technology giants".

Certainly Joe Biden in his first 100 Days report to Congress beat the drum, "We're in a competition with China and other countries to win the 21st century". Not exactly peace, love and understanding but excusable for a politician with a very difficult job to do at home where the majority do not share his previous views on China.

Then Biden said he had told Xi Jinping, "we will maintain a strong military presence in the Indo-Pacific just as we do with NATO in Europe, not to start conflict, but to prevent conflict". After NATO's eastwards expansion, despite US assurances to the contrary, this would not have reassured Xi. Especially a little later when NATO, the North *Atlantic* Treaty Organisation, decided that China and the South *China*

Sea, 6,000 miles away, were an area of great concern and legitimate interest.

Biden's rallying cry may have been largely for domestic political consumption. However, it would be wrong to ignore it altogether, coming right after the Senate Foreign Relations Committee voted 21-1 for the 281-page Strategic Competition Act.

Designed to stop China's rise, the act said China's growth is, "contrary to the interests and values of the US". This must be prevented by all means, including military: military no less. Domestic politics are one thing, a flotilla in the South China Sea, conducting war games across 17 time zones is quite another. Sabre rattling possibly but not for China to ignore.

Foreign Relations and Colonialism: China

The first mistake many in the West make about China's future intentions and behaviour is that it sees or should see things in the same way as the recently successful West. Sometimes it does, sometimes it doesn't. For China's much more extensive history and resulting Confucian philosophy may teach very different lessons.

Traditional Chinese philosophy did not have the concept of global power. That was only possible after the Industrial Revolution enabled Britain to harness new technology to project power globally: through greatly advanced transport, communications and arms. The US took this to a new level. Everything was a zero sum game and a fight to the finish. Traditional China did not think in such terms. Modern China does not either.

China's traditional view of foreign relations begins with neighbours. Historically they have always been the major threat, whether nomadic raiders from the Eurasian Steppes or Japanese pirates and military from across the sea. To secure its borders, China seeks to bind neighbours into mutually beneficial arrangements. That is its top goal. Simply because the US chose global domination, backed by force, does not mean all other countries will do the same.

China knows that power and influence decline as distance increases: for practical reasons of geography, cultural understanding and supply lines. China knows that overstretch, financial, geographic or both, often sounds the death knell of empires.

If expansion goes too far *wu ji bi fan* (when you go too far, you rebound). Technology does not alter this, only the details, as Sir John Glubb noted. It cannot replace proximity or cultural affinity in importance. The neighbourhood is key.

Therefore why seek World Domination? Only during a few years in the 1960s did China's radical ideologues want to export its system. Ever since, securing the homeland has been the primary goal of foreign policy: easier and ultimately much safer. China's leaders, starting with Mao Zedong and Zhou Enlai, agreed on that with the 1972 Mao-Nixon accord.

Stability of major powers is China's global goal, the immediate neighbourhood its primary concern. That should never be forgotten. On the map that means peace with northeast and southeast Asia plus along its Eurasian border. For this the US is important. A friendly West Asia and even the rest of the world would also be nice for China to have, though not as important as peace with its 15 bordering neighbours and one superpower.

Get the priorities right. With secure borders, China can pursue prosperity. Economic development has been China's primary goal since the early 1970s, pushing the military to a subsidiary role. Radical ideology exited the picture altogether, including abroad, replaced by pragmatism and *realpolitik*. Leaving the broader questions of Chinese philosophy to Chapter 11: *Challenges* and Chapter 19: *What Can the West Learn From Itself and China?*, it is worth here considering whether China will be just another colonial power, as the Western narrative asserts, without any evidence; and taking advantage of widespread Western ignorance of Chinese history.

History records that China has never had colonies. They would be greatly out of character with its traditional philosophy or practice as demonstrated over two millennia of contact abroad: much longer than the US has existed. Those who claim China will colonise should consider Melaka.

The Malay Muslim Sultanate, founded in 1402, made Melaka (Malacca) into a major port by linking traders from the Indian sub-continent and Middle East with those of Southeast and Northeast Asia, especially China. This was long before Singapore, Penang or Jakarta became regional trading centres.

China recognised Melaka as a state when mariner-cum-diplomat Admiral Zheng He visited in 1405. In return for tribute, China offered defence (notionally) but had no role in government, let alone sovereignty. One of China's princesses later married the Sultan, bringing 500 attendants, who settled with her in Melaka. Enhanced trade and peace ensued.

What happened in the following five centuries was in marked contrast. The Portuguese invaded in 1511. In the words of historian Daniel Headrick, they "spared the Hindu, Chinese and Burmese inhabitants but had the Muslim inhabitants massacred or sold into slavery." Through incompetence, the Portuguese then destroyed the delicate mechanisms of trade that had built Melaka's wealth, allowing other ports to grow at its expense; and other European powers to rule Melaka. This pattern of violent colonialism continued until its ejection after World War II.

In contrast, China's trade and travel first began with India more than 2,000 years ago. Between the two large countries, Chinese traded and invested extensively in maritime Southeast Asia without colonising any territory. Gold mines, gambier plantations and Chinatowns are testimony to this along with settlers and their descendants, who made it their home but never under the Chinese flag, let alone guns.

An example of non-interfernce in modern times comes from Africa, where China funded and built the Great Uhuru (Freedom) Railway during the early 1970s. This connected Tanzania on the Indian Ocean with landlocked Zambia in the heart of central Africa. Located on the frontline against White–ruled and US-supported *apartheid* Southern Africa, the railway was negotiated during the radical Cultural Revolution. Yet China sought no military bases, as it possibly could have done, had it wished. It was not in Chinese thinking to colonise, very aware of the danger of overstretch.

As well as wrong, colonisation would be foolish in Chinese eyes. Empires don't last forever, as Sir John Glubb recorded. Exceptionalism is a lethal delusion, bringing about its own downfall, often a case of *wu ji bi fan*: imperial overreach and eventual collapse of the dynasty. China knows all about the fall of dynasties, they study them hard.

China is Ready

With economic size moving towards the cross-over point of the two GDPs, who, overall, is better prepared? Why is this so?

Long-term thinking is the big difference between the two. China thinks long-term on every issue, policy and problem, including war. Meanwhile, US politics are trapped in endless short-term politics and the 24-hour news cycle that cloud or block out the long-term.

China has been preparing for its economic comeback for decades. Even after Deng said China should hide its light and not alarm the US, Chinese TV in 2006 made a special 12-part series reflecting much of Paul Kennedy's analysis in *The Rise and Fall of the Great Powers*. This would have been years after China's leaders and strategists first considered it. Demography is on China's side. No need to rush. Just be ready for when the economy is strong enough to make its next moves.

Many in the West assume China welcomes chaos and erosion of the Western-led post-1945 global institutions. That is certainly not what has happened in finance and economics nor in health, as COVID has shown. This is an inter-connected world. Even if it wished to gain advantage, China knows it loses from a crippled world economy. Demographic advantage alone should ensure China finds the security and prosperity it seeks, as long as it has peace and gets along with everyone.

The global economy is important to China's domestic economy, a top Beijing priority. Strengthening its own and all other economies, China has had very good relations with the International Monetary Fund (IMF), which were cemented first during the 1997 Asian Financial Crisis.

Cooperation not confrontation: the record speaks for itself. For quarter of a century, China has aided global financial and economic stability, especially after the 1997 and 2008 financial crises. China did not seek competitive advantage by devaluing its currency after the Asian Financial Crisis, as many in the West said it would. After 2008, China was actively involved in the world's economic recovery through domestic stimulus and policy coordination: again it did not take advantage through devaluation.

Instead, China added about one-third of all world growth — almost double its population share — in the decade to 2019. This was more than the three giant economies of the US, EU and Japan combined.

Imagine a world, without China. It would have to rely on the old, slow growth economies that once dominated the 19th and 20th centuries. No wonder German industry is so keen on good relations with China; and US business keeps very quiet during government tension with China.

Even though China has twice as many bank assets as the US and is already the second largest economy by all measurements, China has accepted the US's significantly greater IMF equity holding, along with the unwritten rule of having a European managing director. Relations were once so good that the early Obama administration proposed a bigger say for China, until European *armour-propre* and possibly US pre-Pivot-to-Asia strategic reassessment nixed that.

To avoid being seen as a challenger, the China-initiated Asian Infrastructure Investment Bank (AIIB) has gone out of its way to work on projects with the US-headed World Bank and the Japan-led Asian Development Bank: not go head-to-head as competitors. Both have expertise and funds, so it makes sense for AIIB to work with them. The lack of infrastructure in Asia is enormous: the deficit cavernous. There is plenty of work for all.

China's view is that what benefits its neighbours benefits China. This differs fundamentally from much Western, especially US, zero-sum thinking that assumes one side wins, the other loses in every transaction or encounter. As the larger economy, China can usually manage relations with neighbours so both sides benefit.

China assumes that if its population advantage and economic size are allowed to develop unhindered, then China will achieve its goals. Namely, securing its borders and prosperity, something it lost almost two centuries ago to foreign powers and internal weakness. Skirmishes may occur beyond the current high tension if provoked along the way to achieving its primary goal of securing its borders. This came to a head in 2010, brought not by an "assertive" China but by a fundamental change in US military strategy.

Is the US Ready?

The US as a country is not ready — psychologically, politically or economically. Geopolitically, its thinking and understanding faces in the wrong direction, still largely focused across the Atlantic on familiar Europe, Russia and the Middle East as opposed to over the Pacific to Asia, no matter what the Pivot implies. This is just like British guns facing the wrong way and underestimating its enemy when the British Empire lost to Japan the critical Far Eastern base of Singapore in 1942.

The British Empire never recovered. Despite helping defeat Germany and Japan in the war, within two years the empire was in decline: a victim of financial overstretch. Within two decades, the sun had set on most of the British Empire. Could the changing of the world's economic guard see a repeat? Could this be a case of fighting the last economic war?

Economically, Biden's US is focusing domestically, mainly on things China has already largely done, such as infrastructure and new industries. China meanwhile is much freer to focus both at home and on new priorities abroad in trade, investment and security. Militarily, the US employs a Cold War strategy of containment, which may prove to be out-dated. Again an empire undermined by hubris and incompetence.

Looking backwards rather than forwards, the US acts in the new millennium with last century thinking. Republicans recycle Ronald Reagan's Cold War rhetoric while Democrats replay the riffs of Bill Clinton's ideas about rules (with exceptions and exemptions unmentioned): some do both. Neither is appropriate to the real world of the new millennium's New New World where the US is no longer the lone superpower.

Three major differences from the former American Century shape the New New World. America's main rival will have a growing economic advantage, from which it could gain the military upper hand; US allies increasingly pursue their own national or regional interests; and old, often populous, civilisations aim to do what China has done, come back to create a multipolar world.

Regional powers may re-emerge economically: think Indonesia and Nigeria. By 2050, Indonesia is expected to be the world's fourth largest economy, while Nigeria will have the world's third largest population, bigger than the US. A very different world from the unipolar one assumed by most in Washington or by the American public.

The US does not consider how China sees the world. Blind to likely Chinese strategy, misunderstanding the difference could be fatal. Importantly, China sees economics having the final say in a military conflict — if avoided until China is strong enough. Increasingly China is confident population size will tip the balance. First, economically, then technologically and eventually it will be decisive militarily.

Military Invincibility or Financial Vulnerability?

Today it may look as if militarily there is no contest. Everybody says so. US military expenditure is roughly three times that of China. The US has 11 nuclear powered aircraft carriers, China two. No one comes close. As for overseas military bases, China is barely on the map.

The next nine countries combined spend only the same as the US. Estimates vary slightly but, from the world's two leading institutes on military spending, recent annual numbers are just over $730 billion for the US and $193–261 billion for China: $178 billion in 2020, according to CGTN. US intelligence spending is estimated at another $80 billion. Not a small amount nor to be ignored in the power equation.

The US in 2013 admitted to "around" 600 bases overseas, others count 800 or more. China is said to have three, though only one fully operating: in Djibouti to combat piracy in the Indian Ocean, next to a US base that is four times bigger. The US military is still supreme: its technology superior, no doubt, today. This is the conventional view but ignores two very important factors.

Economics and focus threaten this seemingly eternal US military invincibility. Economic threats to the US come not so much from China's GDP but from financial vulnerability. The Stockholm Peace Research Institute calculates the US in 2020 spent 3.8% of GDP on the military, while China spent 1.9%, only half that of the US.

How much higher might the US have to go, if pushed further by China Threat perceptions? Some 5–6% or even 10%: to double or more? That question should cause concern when the US has so many pressing domestic issues to fund; cash is not unlimited while foreign opposition to US dollar-printing monetary policy grows.

One day the US may well have to choose between guns and butter. That day may be closer than many realise. Cuts were made in 2012. That is a recent precedent. Biden's first military budget had no increase in real terms, i.e. it merely kept pace with inflation. This pleased neither hawks nor doves in striking a note of realism.

The other concern, apparent to anyone in business who knows China, is that some Chinese new equipment manufacturing costs can be half those in the West: 30% less is common. Not just because of lower wages or subsidies but mainly because of accumulated decades of Chinese learning, innovation and competition.

An example is wind turbines. China already leads technologically in onshore and offshore wind power generation. *Bloomberg* reported in 2021 that top-end wind equipment prices were 40% lower in China than in Italy, where China made its first European sale. There seems no reason why Chinese arms should not be much cheaper to develop than the West's.

Spurring China's arms industry has been the West's arms embargo. From 1949 to 1972 and after 1989, this forced China to make its own military equipment. Evidently China is quite good at it, as in other areas of manufacturing.

China, literally, now gets more bang for its buck — even before considering legendary US armament cost overruns. China gets more for its *yuan* than the US gets for its dollar. This should be factored into calculations about what budgets can buy. Only development time or war can slow China's weaponry from closing the gap with the US.

Anyway, does China need so many aircraft carriers? China's only theatre of major concern is the West Pacific, where China has the advantage of geography. That provides all the bases it needs for its missiles and aircraft: much better than building carriers that are last century's strategic technology and, in truth, sitting ducks thousands of miles from home especially in an era of submarines with hypersonic missiles and laser weapons.

The Soviet Trap and a Ring of Fire

The great irony would be if the US increases military spending to counter China and falls into the same trap, as some argue, did the Soviet Union. This forced Moscow to spend more than it could afford. Using up scarce resources, overburdening the economy with debt, while failing to address domestic concerns, some US Cold Warriors believe this deadly formula brought down the Soviet Union. That should be a warning to the US.

The US would have to double or treble its military budget to approach a similar impact on China. If, instead, the US limits spending but tries to persuade allies to increase theirs, which seems to be the plan, it may eat into precious diplomatic capital, slow allies' economies or speed up independent security plans: whichever way the US loses.

Other troubling factors come into play. Printing dollars may not always be a risk-free option. China is a large creditor of the US: creditors have individual and country limits. The US bond market has long worried about what would happen if China sat out the US Treasury bill auctions, let alone sold heavily. That is not unthinkable.

All bets are off if China's core interests are threatened, notably Taiwan, Hong Kong, Xinjiang, Tibet and the South China Sea, let alone red lines crossed. Note that China's US Treasury holdings, as a percentage of GDP, have been falling steadily while China's GDP rises.

How much of the Belt and Road is funded by these often US dollar investments? Good question. Asset diversification is a sensible investment strategy, especially if it strengthens vulnerable neighbours and their stability. The US confiscation of Afghan and Russian assets will have made China think very hard about their reserves' safety.

China has announced its intention to transform its military into "a world class force" by 2049. To keep up with this, the US will face tough budgetary and tax choices, if it is to avoid paying the penalty for overreach. Matching China's military modernisation could require a large politically unaffordable rise in the military's share of the US budget — and or higher taxes.

Bases in the Middle East, Europe, Latin America or the Caribbean are of no interest or cost to China. Therefore, recalculate military budgets. China does not need a global military budget the size of the US's.

The West Pacific is what matters to China. China has increasingly funded this for a decade now, ever since the US in 2010 began to change its military operational strategy. This is China's Cuba and Caribbean. In it lie Taiwan and the South China Sea: these are what matter.

Not to mention a ring of 400 US military bases from South Korea to the Indian Ocean, armed to the teeth with missiles, all pointing at China. The US base in Okinawa, Japan, is barely 500 miles from Shanghai; and little more from provincial capitals Hangzhou and Fuzhou. Then there are the islands of Hawaii and Guam, both on US soil, yes US soil: 2,479 and 6,098 miles from Los Angeles; and just over 3,000 and 5,000 miles, respectively, from Shanghai.

China is nearing parity of forces in this critical theatre of the West Pacific. That is the 2021 assertion of Chinese strategic specialist Senior Colonel Zhou Bo of Tsinghua University. All the more alarming because China has home team advantage, with geography, culture and economics on its side. Bo's comment though should not have come as much of a surprise.

The leading US strategic think tank, the RAND Corporation, had already said that the US often loses in simulated war games, should China try to take back Taiwan by force; and even when the US retaliates it could still lose. There is no guarantee of success. That could be end of empire.

Change in US Military Thinking

US–China relations were good for most of the new millennium's first decade. President George W. Bush, informed closely by his ambassador in Beijing, his old China-knowledgeable Yale fraternity friend Sandy Randt, made it clear to Taiwan's leaders to back off independence and provocation. The One China Policy held firm.

US–China trade was booming and welcomed. It dampened US inflation, helping offset stagnating real incomes for half the population. A majority of Americans in Pew Surveys thought well of China: US student numbers in China rose. The Beijing Olympic Games in 2008 were applauded, not boycotted by the West as were the 1980 Moscow Olympics or downgraded by some Western governments like the Beijing 2022 Winter Olympics. In retrospect, the summer of 2008 was the high point in US–China relations.

Matters began to reverse in 2009 after the US military reconsidered its strategy towards China. Not surprisingly China pushed back: in US language China became more "assertive". Which country wouldn't react if the world's largest power moved from peaceful long-term friendship to preparing for the possibility of war? Then followed a policy of containment, which some believed brought down its rival superpower the Soviet Union: regime change.

The line of new US military thinking was unmistakable. Apparently, without consulting the new president — Obama in his first year was focused on the post-2008 Financial Crisis domestic and global recoveries he inherited — the US military discussed what to do about China. In

2009, a classified memo circulated to consider possible military confrontation with China, according to John Ford of the US Army JAG Corps.

Ford wrote that Secretary of Defense Robert Gates openly discussed the need to counter China's growing military capabilities. The first public sign of a fundamental change in thinking came in mid-2010 when Secretary of State Hillary Clinton declared the South China Sea to be a "security interest" of the US.

This was the first anyone had heard of it. Just like the East China Sea, the name South China Sea had been around for rather a long time. Back in the 19th century the British simply called it the China Sea, all the way down to the east coast of Peninsula Malaya. British publishers such as John Murray in 1883 had maps with that name and delineation: no one questioned it and no one in the US considered it a "security interest". It is like the Indian Ocean, which in some areas is much closer to parts of Indonesia, Malaysia, Thailand and Myanmar than India but logic does not matter, it remains the Indian Ocean.

A tussle over China policy, if not outright battle, soon gripped Obama's White House. From late 2009, "there was a different strand of thinking in the State Department, supported by some in the Pentagon that sought a tougher stance toward China", observed Bill Clinton's former Special Assistant for National Security Affairs and Senior Director for Asia on the National Security Council Kenneth Lieberthal.

Obama's first two China-related appointments were for Deputy Secretary of State and senior director for East Asia on the National Security Council. They worked closely together on China policy until their views lost out. Both left government in the spring of 2011. Other opinions were in the ascendancy, more to Hillary Clinton's assertive liking.

Called the Air-Sea Battle Strategy, the new thinking became US operational doctrine in 2010. In 2011, it morphed into the much catchier

Pivot to Asia, the new centre piece of US global policy. The Air-Sea Battle strategy was renamed in 2015 to the wonderfully innocuous-sounding Joint Concept for Access and Maneuver in the Global Commons (JAM-GC), which sank without trace, as presumably intended.

That is the new China–US equation. Increasingly a military one with business and trade caught in the cross-hairs. Though nothing is as simple as that, we next have to consider the tricky challenges of Philosophy, Values and Psychology.

Chapter 11

Challenges of Philosophy, Values and Psychology

What the world needs is Cultural Literacy. What is needed between civilisations is respect not tolerance.

Irina Bokova, UNESCO Secretary General (2009–2017)

The New New World, an emerging multipolar kaleidoscopic world, throws up many challenges. Fundamental to meeting them is to understand each other's cultures, starting with philosophy, a combination of history and the thorny question of values. Then there is psychology, a dimension too often ignored.

Understanding

Understanding Asia is crucial. Misconceptions must be corrected. However, some in the West have simply not moved on from empire. Hubris and ignorance remain. A comment in the *Financial Times*, epitomised this in 2019, saying, "a new [British] prime minister should learn lessons from the Swiss in democracy, Germans and Swedes in economy and society, Australians in work force planning and ourselves in stoicism".

Were no non-Caucasian examples considered? Japan's Just In Time manufacturing, China's record-breaking growth, India's IT prowess or

ASEAN's record of peace and prosperity? Apparently not: the reader's world was still totally Caucasian.

In the last two centuries, much of Asia has not been so much anti-Western or anti-modern as anti-imperialist. Indeed many Asian revolutionaries were modernisers. Their main 19th century philosophers were German — Marx and Engels. The principal demands have been for equality of treatment, freedom to make their own decisions and to be safe from foreign invasion, domination or rule: sovereignty.

Asia is looking increasingly to Asia for identity. Professor Wang Hui of Tsinghua, Beijing's Oxford, told a conference about Asian Culture in 2019 that China has principally defined itself in relation to the West: one-sided. Now Wang says China needs to develop much more understanding of Asian cultures and regions. Then China can define itself better, from a second side: the East.

The loudest applause came when Xi Jinping said Asia should translate its classics into each others' language so as to deepen knowledge and promote tourism within Asia. All this is strengthening, for the first time, the basis for a common pan-Asian identity, interests and economic development.

Philosophy

All civilisations should be treated equally, each has value. That was Xi Jinping's central point in an ignored 2014 landmark speech to UNESCO in Paris. This addressed directly the US State Department policy head's view that the problem the US faces is a rising power that is not Caucasian.

Goodness: nearly 90% of the world isn't. Quite a thought stopper in the 21st century, especially from a country built on migration of many ethnicities, including non-Caucasian. Its only merit was its honesty.

Xi maintained in Paris that the whole world could benefit from all civilisations, if understood. Each civilisation has its own personality, with contributions to make to solving problems and disagreements.

In foreign relations, look for areas of mutual agreement and cooperation: Biden and Xi agree on that, to get started, to build trust. Large countries are complex. Therefore understand the need to respect diversity and dialogue. Diversity enriches experience. Change is rapid in the 21st century, often where least expected.

Be prepared for anything but don't interfere. Change is strongest when it has cultural roots that thrive in local soil, a fact the US often misses when it sides with one group against another. US support can be the kiss of death for local allies, accused of selling out to a foreign power: counter-productive.

Asia talks of true globalisation and the need for civilisations to live together. None are superior. All have a common future. No country permanently benefits from a Clash of Civilisations.

Whatever the differences, people can agree to disagree: the ASEAN Way. That principle underlies the success of the 10-country Association of South East Asian Nations (ASEAN). The regional group was formed in 1967 as Southeast Asian dominoes seemed to be falling to communism. The Western prescription was for the US to beef up SEATO (the Southeast Asian equivalent of NATO) with Caucasian allies – UK, Australia, New Zealand and France – along with three Asian nations.

Instead five and eventually 10 Southeast Asian neighbours took matters into their own hands. More than two-thirds of a billion people strong, ASEAN has largely enjoyed peace and growing prosperity since its foundation in 1967: non-communist and communist alike, Muslim, Buddhist, Catholic, Protestant, Confucian and secular — with results so unlike the foci of US activity in the Middle East and Europe.

Traditional East Asian philosophy taught the value of consensus, flexibility and patience. Ambiguity is an art, especially in Southeast Asia. Difference does not prevent communication. Indeed difference should be a starting point for communication to resolve problems or open new opportunities. That said, there are similarities to be found between Asia and the West.

Confucius, half a millennium before Christ, said do to others what you would want them to do to you, just as the Christian Bible says. Asian values of family, community and respect for elders are held by many non-Asians. Much of importance is shared.

Most great religions originated in Asia. All preach of humanity as one; and the great virtue of peace. Yet the Eurocentric view of history is full of religious wars; and the seeming inevitability of them, the Clash of Civilisations. Even if not pursuing outright holy wars, religions like Christianity and Islam can be evangelical. Some want to spread their faith, to "enlighten" others. Such thinking spills over into politics, with some, especially in the West, hailing democracy as the new perfect faith, even after centuries of democracy-denying Western colonialism and forever war.

In Chinese philosophy, there is no desire to proselytise, let alone colonise. "China's history is the record of an expanding culture, more than of a conquering empire", is how the great British–Australian Sinologist C.P. Fitzgerald described it in 1935. Assuming that when China has power it will act just like the West ignores this very obvious point: it won't.

Daoism and Confucianism are the foundations of Chinese traditional thought. They are philosophies, principally ways of looking at the world and behaviour, providing a moral code that can say much of relevance.

A leading Confucian scholar, Tu Weiming, sees the scale of today's global problems. Tremendous challenges abound from climate change to redefining humanity in relation to technology, science and communications.

Listen to Tu's expert voice. He has impeccable credentials. Professor Emeritus at Harvard and Director of Peking University's Advanced Institute for Humanistic Studies, Tu was born in Kunming, China, grew up in Taiwan, lives in the US and has worked extensively in China. He sees many resources in Chinese philosophy to address current problems.

Confucianist Tu advises the individual to start with self-cultivation and self-reflection. How can I be a reasonable human being, good to others, public spirited, respecting others? He then continues with society-at-large.

Acknowledge that many politicians have lost their way, some their humanity. The political animal therefore must start with the individual. A person is not an island but part of a group: able to think of others and their aspirations, to respect their dignity and reciprocate consideration. Life is not a zero sum game. There has to be dialogue, rules of the game and etiquette. Otherwise society, let alone the world, cannot survive.

How does equality of treatment among nations and individuals work, in Tu's view? Five points: Concern for others, with sympathy and compassion; a sense of Justice not just law; Civility; Trust; and Humility. These five elements can develop a critical but open spirit, without social media anger: not showing off but contributing.

That is what Confucianism offers. How to learn the best from the rest of the world for peace and prosperity? That requires confidence, without arrogance. Who can argue with all of the above, unless they wish continual conflict or worse?

Process vs. Results

Many assume unbridgeable differences between Chinese and Western philosophy. Even before the 1949 communist revolution there was a strong collectivist streak in Chinese thinking. Yet as Tu Weiming says, Confucianism starts with the individual. So what divides West and East so much, starting with governance?

Current Western political philosophy is more interested in process: China with results. The West highly values electoral democracy, regardless of the quality of governance. It argues that problems can always be remedied at subsequent elections. This is true up to a point but as democratic Europe proved, plunging into totalitarianism in the

1920s and 1930s, that is not guaranteed. Today it is an open, unanswered question.

The big divide comes in human rights; and their perception. In the West these are defined principally by individual political rights and civil liberties. In China and to varying degrees the rest of Asia, they are defined more by economic and social rights.

For instance, China values greatly the fact that none of its 1.4 billion people live any longer in extreme poverty, whereas 80% did as recently as 1980. Compared with Indian women in 2020, Chinese women live 10% longer, six times fewer die in child birth and 95% are literate compared with 54% in India.

Singapore, classified as only partly free by Freedom House and not invited to Biden's democracy summit, values highly its three-decade rise "from Third World to First World", in the words of founding Prime Minister Lee Kuan Yew. This has raised Singapore's GDP to $67,000 per person in 2021, only $2,000 below the US. Each has different priorities.

Over time these may change or be reformed. Differences today are often because each society has its own starting points for process; and for desired outcomes. Asia may later establish more of the rights valued in the West but not all. The West may focus more on basic economic rights like employment, income, housing and health, much as it did in Europe for more than three decades after 1945: the pendulum continues to swing.

COVID has already forced a limit to the absolutism of some individual rights and freedoms in Europe and Australasia. For both China and the West it is a work in progress. In the meantime, some in the West are going in a different direction, sanctifying their own values and wanting to impose them on others just like some earlier evangelists.

Values: Here Be Dragons

Values may seem to be beyond reproach. Beware: this is dangerous territory, especially if the intention is to impose them on others. When earlier map makers' knowledge ran out, some would warn Here Be Dragons: danger.

A two-edged sword, values can be uplifting but they must be lived not mouthed: confirmed by actions not words. Otherwise they breed distrust, resentment and conflict. When people fail to live up to self-proclaimed values they are called hypocrites: despicable in both East and West. Apply them rigorously, first at home.

The West can claim Christian core values but must live up to them. Otherwise the charge of hypocrisy will undermine good intentions. The Christian Bible is very clear about three things — compassion, judgmentalism and hypocrisy.

Compassion: Take in refugees: aid even your enemy in distress. The parable of the Good Samaritan says so in Luke 10:25-37.

"Love thy neighbour as thyself", the Book of Leviticus instructed in the Old Testament and the third book of the Torah. How many Syrian refugees did the US or UK take in and shelter from war? Only the Lutheran pastor's daughter Angela Merkel and Germany lived up to that.

Judgmentalism: "Why beholdest thou the mote (speck) that is in thy brother's eye, but considerest not the beam (plank) in thine own" as Matthew 7:3 says. Correct one's own faults first: do not judge others.

Hypocrisy: "He that is without sin among you cast the first stone", John 8: 1-11. Otherwise keep quiet; and again correct your own faults. The last two strictures apply equally to improving domestic human rights and correcting colonial legacies.

Hypocrisy is particularly dangerous and offensive. It loses the moral high ground by following the self-serving dictum to "do as I say, not as I do": a.k.a. double standards.

Double standards stick in the throat. They play very badly outside the West. Propping up "power privilege", often acquired by superior arms and invasion, is not a good 21st century look. Not that it looked good previously but those impacted were too weak to resist.

Psychology

Hearts and minds matter during power transitions, not just economics, philosophy and values. The challenged and subsequently displaced Top Dog has feelings too, often incoherent or expressed very crudely. The rising power has to consider these, for its own good. This has happened before, when the US replaced Britain as the dominant power.

People overlook how long Britain resented the US replacing the British Empire. Burning down the White House and Capitol in 1814 was not a Guy Fawkes accident. It was angry retaliation after its former colonies burned and looted the British capital in Upper Canada at York (Toronto).

Three decades later, before the US had even overtaken Britain economically, Charles Dickens would not return to the US. Dickens feared for his safety, after writing *Martin Chuzzlewit* in 1842. Simon Callow called the book a, "wild satire tinged with personal animosity: the sense of grievances being settled is palpable. His personal loathing of the pomposity, bragging, lying and spitting he found [in the US] are not counter-balanced by any intimation of merit whatever".

One hundred years later still, little had changed. When the US was well established as top economy and world power, the London quip, reflecting British grievance at its displacement, was that, "the problem with Americans is that they are overpaid, oversexed and over here". Expressing no gratitude for their contribution in the war against Nazi Germany, this was grudging acceptance of changed times.

Stereotypes lingered in Britain for several decades more: a felt need to release resentment for declining fortunes in economic leadership, relative wealth, status and loss of Empire. Similar feelings now underlie many US attitudes towards China. Resentment is a very powerful sentiment. Modern US anti-China sentiment has been rising, seemingly since 2008. Why only then?

Previously US surveys found the majority were positive about China. American consumers appreciated cheaper products, especially when real wages stagnated or even fell. China helped people keep their heads above water. For business and government, it helped bring stability to financial markets by not devaluing its currency in the 2008 Western-created Financial Crisis, as many had feared. China made positive contributions.

That was not enough after 2008. Resentment rose, bursting out with great consequence through Donald Trump in 2016. Establishment elites, especially in defence and intelligence, had begun to turn actively against China even earlier. This began with their ideas in 2009 for an Air-Sea Battle Doctrine (Chapter 10: *The New China–US Equation*) that evolved formally into the 2011 Pivot to Asia. Politicians fell in line fairly quickly. Dedicated followers of fashion and funding, some in academe and many in the media followed suit. Why then only after 2008?

Up until 2008, Americans saw their own prospects improving. From the collapse of the Berlin Wall and the 1990s peace dividend, through the dot com boom, the new economy and the rise of the Dow, these were good years. There was no reason to blame anyone for anything.

After 2008 it was a very different story. Not just the economic crash and the prolonged Great Recession but the disappearance of many manufacturing jobs. The fact that many jobs in the US and Europe were lost to automation not to China (one US study estimated 80%) was irrelevant.

Politically, there was a need to blame someone for stagnant real wages, lost jobs and a worsening outlook. Blame the "other", in this case China. The pump of blame was well primed when COVID hit the US and Europe. Psychologically, it was the easiest immediate response.

China in turn believes its development is unfairly blocked by US containment. Therefore its back has stiffened. It feels unappreciated by the West, even insulted, after what it has done for global welfare. From the World Bank's estimate of lifting 850 million people out of extreme poverty to technological breakthroughs and record economic growth that boosted world trade and incomes, China feels it has already contributed its fair share, without recognition.

When the Philippines foreign minister in 2016 told the US that his country could, "not forever be the little brown brother of the US" and that it "wanted mutual respect", many Asians smiled. Someone had finally spoken truth to power. The wheel of history turns. Another cliché comes to mind: the genie cannot be put back in the bottle.

The UN named 2001 the Year of Dialogue Among Civilisations, an idea which Iranian President Mohammad Khatami put forward. What came of that? Two decades have been wasted but there is still time for the older and younger civilisations to secure their common future by understanding each other much better. This is not some goody two shoes or milquetoast remedy.

Dire necessity demands it. COVID revealed the inability of many in the West to learn from other cultures. Millions died unnecessarily. This only exposed its incompetence. The next two sections look at why this happened in public health, society and especially the media. All are examples of what Glubb called the Age of Decadence, institutional decay at the end of empire.

By mid-2022 a new interpretation of handling COVID emerged in the West. China did well in the first part of COVID but the open societies of the West did better in handling the exit: a breath-taking air-brushing of history.

Since Omicron began in October 2021, world COVID deaths rose 25%: more than 1.3 million people. This included some 300,000 in the US, hardly a successful exit, especially considering new variants continue to emerge the longer the virus is left alive. Only 58,220 Americans died in the Vietnam War: five times fewer.

Competence: COVID

Chapter 12

This Didn't Have to Happen

What China has demonstrated is, you have to do this. If you do it, you can save lives and prevent thousands of cases of this very difficult disease.

Dr Bruce Aylward, head of WHO–China Mission, February 24, 2020

"This is not an Italian 'Wuhan'," insisted Ivana Jelenic. Jelenic, President of the Italian Tourism and Travel Agents' Federation, added that, "Avoiding all travel ... would just be alarmist", according to the Associated Press (AP) on February 23, 2020. Complacency? Folly? Hubris or was it something much more complex?

A health crisis or one prolonged by a failure of Western governance and society? Was it rank incompetence or all of the above? COVID was a real life test of competence that the West failed.

A Question of Competence

By the next year, not just Italian travel agents but all Italians must have rued the tourism president's rash words. They must have regretted their own inadequate responses: government, society and individuals alike.

If only Italy had been a Wuhan or even the whole of China it would have suffered barely 5,000 deaths or 3.6 per million by late 2022. Instead, 182,000 died in Italy of COVID: some 3,000 per million. The US was even worse with 3,300 deaths per million people: 1.1 million died. Collectively the world has had 655 million cases: deaths reached almost seven million.* That is the true measure of incompetence given the early warning and clear advice.

Of all places in Europe, Italy has the least excuse. Europe's largest concentration of Chinese is in Prato, just outside Florence. Apart from boasting a fine medieval cathedral, with Filippo Lippi frescos and an outdoor corner pulpit by Donatello looking into its downward sloping square, Prato prospered six centuries later during Italy's post-War textile boom, before giving way to bust in the 1980s.

Bust gave thousands of Chinese the opportunity to migrate to Prato for work and business. Many came from China's most entrepreneurial city of Wenzhou. They now manufacture some 95% of Prato's textile exports, having revived a dying industry.

When Wuhan's lockdown sounded the alarm on January 23, 2020, Prato's Chinese immediately began to isolate. Fully grasping what could be happening in China, they knew what might well lie ahead. History had taught them that. This was weeks before Italy registered its first COVID case; and exactly one month before Jelenic said Italy was not Wuhan.

Not a single Prato resident of Chinese origin, some 10% of its 200,000 inhabitants, tested positive for the virus, officials told *Politico Europe* at the end of April 2020. "Many Prato Chinese in late January went into self-isolation, closed businesses and kept children at home. Social pressure from the community ensured a scrupulous adherence to the rules and a fastidious attention to hygiene", Hannah Roberts reported. Scrupulous adherence to the rules and a fastidious attention to hygiene: words to remember.

---

*The source Worldometers uses data from each government. Some is disputed, including China's, though the devil is often in the definitions. When 2022 excess deaths data are calculated a more accurate picture may emerge but the relative magnitudes are unlikely to be changed significantly.

The Prato Chinese influenced their fellow citizens. Prato suffered fewer COVID cases than any other area in Tuscany. Mayor Matteo Biffoni remarked that indigenous locals, "said to themselves, if Chinese, who normally work all hours of the day, are not working, it must be serious.… we all got into line". Evidently this information did not reach Italy's Tourism Federation or was dismissed as inconvenient. The whole country could have learned so much from its Chinese community — but did not. Italy was not alone.

Error compounded error. One day after Ivana Jelenic's assertion, an even worse error was made throughout the West. Most Western governments and people ignored the World Health Organisation's (WHO) stark warning. This came on February 24th at the Beijing press conference to announce the WHO's key findings from its 10-day experts' joint mission to China.

The WHO communicated more than enough for the world to know what to do to avoid another Wuhan. Few in the West listened or even heard it. Many thought the virus couldn't touch them. They were strong: immune, their systems and societies robust, even, to some, superior. They had no reason to fear. I quote extensively *verbatim* from the press conference to prove this common assertion wrong.

This Didn't Have to Happen. The West's struggle against incompetence and the world's nearly 7 million deaths could well have been avoided.

WHO Warning and Blue Print

The virus is "very cunning and tricky … our knowledge is not sufficient" warned the Chinese team leader Dr Liang Wannian. "Very cunning", "tricky" and "knowledge not sufficient", the words leapt off the screen as I read the 45-page account of the press conference the day after it was given. That was February 25, 2020.

Beside the pool in Bali, Indonesia, China seemed a world away but the message was crystal clear. Don't be complacent. There is still much to learn. Dr Liang had my attention.

Bruce Aylward, head of the WHO-China Joint Mission, repeated Dr Liang's warning. Then he laid out China's approach to reduce the number of new cases. China's "traditional classic method really works", Aylward said, "Let us do the same". He kept repeating this, "Let us do the same". This blue print "really works".

The report was unequivocal, "The world needs the experience and materials of China to be successful in battling this coronavirus disease. China has the most experience in the world with this disease and is *the only country to have turned around serious large scale outbreaks*". Engage with China, learn from it.

The 25-person enquiry comprised experts in epidemiology, virology, clinical management and public health. There were 12 international experts and 12 from China. Canadian Dr Bruce Aylward, former assistant director general at the WHO, headed the team, while Dr Liang Wannian led the Chinese side.

The WHO-China Joint Mission began work on February 16, 2020. After visiting Beijing in the north, the mission went south to Guangdong, west to Sichuan and then southeast to Wuhan. Wuhan, whose name will never be forgotten.

Capital of Hubei province, epicentre of the first China-reported COVID outbreak, Wuhan is a major industrial and communications centre. The world's third longest river, the mighty Yangzi, swings passed on its near-4,000 mile journey to disgorge its waters more than 400 miles downstream into the South China Sea at Shanghai.

The COVID mission had four main objectives. To find:

- **Characteristics:** Infection source, transmission routes and susceptible populations.
- **Severity:** Breakdown between mild, moderate and severe cases.
- **Measures:** Prevention, control, overall and in different provinces. Effectiveness.

- **Recommendations:** For the Chinese government and the world, especially on cooperation and research priorities.

The Mission made five main findings:

- **Knowledge:** There was no obvious variation in the 104 strains found in China: no major mutations.
- **Epidemic characteristics:** The average age of confirmed cases is 51 years old. Nearly 80% are 30–69 years old. 78% of cases are in Hubei province. Some 80% of cases were mild, 13% moderate and 6% severe. Case fatality was 3–4% nationwide, though only 0.7% outside Wuhan. Some patients are asymptomatic. It is unclear if they can spread the disease.
- **Hosts:** Bats and pangolins could be the source but more work has to be done.
- **Transmission:** Most common routes are through respiratory droplets and contact with surfaces infected by the virus. Stools and aerosol transmission are possible in small, enclosed areas but again more work is needed.
- **Susceptibility:** Against a new pathogen people have no immunity. Most cases in other provinces came from Hubei. Special places and conditions like hospitals were more susceptible: over 3,000 medical workers were infected nationwide, the vast majority in Wuhan before the need for PPE and protection was known.

China's Approach

The first major problem in late December 2019 was that China did not know what this new illness was: no small matter. Only that it was a pulmonary condition of "unknown origin". First thoughts were of SARS or flu. Such speculation quickly hit a dead end when the disease was found to be a new pathogen (an organism that can cause a disease). It was much deadlier than either SARS or flu. How to treat a new virus? What approaches might work with a previously unknown disease?

Basic pillars of Western medicine were absent. The virus being new, no vaccine existed. Nor did the COVID genome sequence. What was it exactly? Effective treatments had yet to be found: all very alarming.

Large gaps in knowledge have to be filled during the first few days and weeks of any disease's discovery. Normally all this is very time consuming. Yet China did it at surprising speed, as WHO spokeswoman Dr Margaret Harris remarked with evident admiration. That carried over into treatment. Within seven weeks China had its sixth edition of its clinical guidance: done at China Speed. Few in the West thought it could succeed.

"China did not approach the new disease with an old strategy. It developed its own approach and *extraordinarily* has turned around the disease with strategies that most of the world did not think would work", WHO Mission leader Aylward declared. Furthermore, to make them more effective, strategies must always be adapted to local conditions, necessary in a country of 1.4 billion people in more than 30 provinces, municipalities and autonomous regions.

China simply had to make do. Work with what it had. COVID could last for months, possibly years. A start had to be made: first find the genome sequence, observe the disease's nature and characteristics. Then determine treatments until vaccines proved effective and safe.

What did China have? There was traditional knowledge like case finding, contact tracing, isolation, quarantine, medical observation, hand washing, mask wearing, social distancing and temperature monitoring. This was not exactly high tech or even modern science. These were ancient measures developed literally over millennia.

As Aylward pointed out, these are not even control measures that many, "people know how to do any more. They don't do case finding or contact tracing, except for Ebola in West Africa or in DR Congo. This is old fashioned stuff using tools like these to try; and that is what China did".

For once, knowledge of traditional methods was an advantage. They helped get China started.

Very quickly new methods and treatments emerged. The one-size-fits-all approach evolved with flexibility into a science and risk-based one. This took note of different containment measures, depending increasingly on the context, capacity and nature of the virus. Strategy was constantly refined, learning from new discoveries and experience.

"This was probably the most ambitious, agile and aggressive disease containment effort in history". Aylward told reporters. Within a month after Wuhan's lock down, China had taken, "an old approach, then turbo-charged it with modern science in ways unimaginable even a few years before": most ambitious effort in history ... old approach, turbo-charged with modern science ... unimaginable.

Public health systems were adapted. Hospitals were cleared to make way for COVID cases. Near-instant giant hospitals materialised. Most famously, the 1,000-bed Huoshenshan hospital went up in 10 days; and the 1,500-bed Leishenshan hospital in 15. Other facilities were pressed into service. COVID patients were separated from people with other conditions, preventing further spread. Things happened; and largely in a logical sequence, avoiding chaos after the initial mayhem.

Much routine medical care went online, using cutting edge technology. Patients in remote parts of Sichuan were treated with the help of 5G communications, linking medics in the villages with experts in the main hospitals. This was all new.

Government systems were adapted. There was a, "tremendous collective commitment and will of the Chinese people from bottom to top": note from bottom to top. Aylward stressed the individual's importance. While government had to take large, difficult decisions like travel bans, stay-at-home orders and timing of measures, the compliance of individuals was essential, as the West later learned to its cost.

Everyone, to use the cliché, was in this together. Aylward called this an all-of-government and all-of-society approach, something "rare to see". Provincial governments followed national priorities. They all had local concerns but ensured that enough medical workers and PPE were sent to Wuhan and Hubei: the top national priority. Almost immediately, nearly 40,000 medical personnel arrived from other provinces. Party secretaries and governors worked together across provincial borders under a unified government system.

China's team leader Liang Wannian added that, "All work was carried out under unified leadership but follows the principles of scientific, localized, and tailored decision-making that enables the constant adjustment and optimization of strategies and measures". Far from being a monolithic one-size-fits-all policy, this was flexible, local and responsive.

"China's *bold approach* to the rapid spread of this new respiratory pathogen changed the course of this rapidly escalating deadly epidemic", Aylward asserted. When the WHO experts arrived in China, new daily cases were running at 2,478. Two weeks later they were just 416. This was not simply one government number. In the field, evidence supported it. For instance, patient visits to fever clinics fell sharply. Beds became available and wards emptied.

The most compelling evidence was that China's anti-viral trials could not find enough infected people to recruit. They had to be conducted overseas where there were far more infected people. Starting with Brazil, Turkey and the United Arab Emirates, they also provided a valuable range of ethnicities and conditions.

Traditional Chinese medicine was not overlooked. Liang Wannian said that, "Effective measures, such as the use of traditional Chinese medicine and comprehensive therapy, should be taken to prevent the large number of mild cases from progressing into severe cases".

Lessons From China

What were the main lessons others could learn to avoid what China had experienced? How to improve on what China had done?

Junk first thoughts: they were wrong. "Unless the world realises COVID is different from SARS or flu, it will not be able to respond with China's *agility of thinking* and approach required to beat the virus globally", Aylward told the media.

Late comers have an advantage. They could learn how to, "move faster, to act earlier on alerts, organize front line protection better, enhance collaboration, communicate frankly and share information better". All could be improved; and lives saved. The great tragedy is the advice was ignored, people did not learn.

"The single biggest lesson is speed.... What worries me most is has the rest of the world learned the lesson of speed?" Aylward asked. He evidently feared it had not; and was correct. If the rest of the world had followed Aylward's February 24th check list, things would have turned out very, very differently.

"Much of the global community is not yet ready, in mindset and materially, to implement the measures that have been employed to contain COVID in China", the Canadian epidemiologist continued, "These are the *only measures* that are currently *proven* to interrupt or minimise transmission chains in humans. Fundamental to these measures is extremely proactive surveillance to immediately detect cases, very rapid diagnosis and immediate case isolation, rigorous tracking and quarantine of close contacts". He added that, "an exceptionally high degree of population understanding and acceptance of these measures" was also necessary.

In the West in particular, Aylward saw, "ambivalence to using non-pharmaceutical measures when they don't have vaccines or therapeutics. People repeatedly throw up their hands. [Whereas] China says this is what we have. Get out the old ones [measures]. Adapt, innovate. Let's stop the virus and save lives. And that's what they have done". Not just in COVID but in life itself. Manage change, be creative (Chapter 8: *China's X-Factor.*)

The press conference finished with Bruce Aylward addressing three of the most frequently asked questions about handling COVID.

- **Lockdowns:** Full lockdowns are *not* necessary everywhere, *only where the virus is out of control*. The Wuhan method is a special approach due to the many clustered cases in one community. It was not applied nationwide in China. Indeed the number of people under full lockdown in China at COVID's peak was about 8%. Less intrusive stay-at-home orders went out to about half the population.
- **Data:** broad trends rather than individual data points are what Aylward, like any good analyst, sought. He found trends in China to be "incredibly clear and consistent" with the official data — as is usually the way in my experience.
- **China's Approach:** China's method is to "conduct *exhaustive* case identification and close contact tracing, quarantine, and basic hygiene measures, including constant emphasis on the importance of frequent hand washing".

For the first time in 30 years the WHO published a report, with recommendations. Aylward emphasised, "This was done for the general public. For without the collective will of the population this cannot work". Everyone in the world had to know.

Aylward concluded by saying, "I wanted to make sure that after a very intensive program of work here, we shared with the rest of the world just how extraordinary the effort was here. And this is not to praise China.

It is to open the door, and have the rest of the world realize *there is something that can be done as people despair over what we can do. What China has demonstrated is, you have to do this.* If you do it, *you can save lives and prevent thousands of cases of this very difficult disease*".

That was said on February 24, 2020. Many darkly prophetic words were spoken that day, while shining a light for the world on how to avert unnecessary death.

Rereading them three years later is achingly painful. History unfortunately proved Aylward both right and wrong. The West could have nipped the virus in the bud. This Didn't Have to Happen but it did. Later chapters (15–17) examine Western Failings, especially the failure of the media. First though, how did China bring COVID under control so rapidly?

Chapter 13

First Antidotes

Zizhi Tongjian: Aiding Governance: A Comprehensive Historical Mirror (403 BC–959 AD).

Sima Guang 1084

When I heard Wuhan was locked down I had two instant reactions. First, how could China possibly stop COVID overwhelming the whole country? China has 93 densely crowded cities with populations exceeding one million: 93. These include 10 megacities with more than 10 million: Wuhan is just one of them, with 11 million. Then there are the 360 cities that exceed 100,000 people.

The scale is truly scary, mind numbing, when expressed in such stark terms. Indeed almost impossible to imagine. Worse still, Wuhan, dubbed China's Chicago for more than a century, is a major national crossroads: north, south, east and west for air, rail, road and river transport. Potential rapid spread was enormous.

To make matters worse, the Spring Festival or New Year holidays were only two days away. This was China's Thanksgiving or Christmas. Nationwide, hundreds of millions of people had already returned home to celebrate with their families: an estimated five million from Wuhan alone. Wuhan has more university students than any city on earth. Most were heading home for traditional family reunions, all over China. These were not comforting thoughts. I had no immediate answer. My mind went blank.

My second reaction was that if any society and government could do it, I believed China could. On-the-ground observation for almost two decades gave me some confidence. I had seen so often how China's individuals, families, firms and different levels of government function and react, especially when seriously challenged: usually with surprising speed, sure-footedness, focus and competence.

This made me think China might survive the crisis. How precisely, I knew not but a general sense of "Can Do" permeates China today, from individuals and government. Furthermore, as noted in Prato, Italy, the Chinese in a health crisis have a, "scrupulous adherence to the rules and a fastidious attention to hygiene". Amid all the fear and uncertainty, my slight optimism surprised me.

China's governance is based on ideas that have stood the test of time. As Max Weber, the German sociologist and political economist, who incidentally died in 1920 from the Spanish Flu, said China has been a "precociously modern state" — for more than 2,000 years.

Modern state systems have existed that long in China. Making its bureaucracy a fine-tuned delivery machine, Pulitzer Prize Winner Ian Johnson declared the Wuhan lockdown, "emblematic of the bureaucratic *élan* that underlies much of China's rise over the past few decades": a very important observation.

One deeply ingrained idea in Chinese governance is the importance of history. From this well of experience are drawn solutions to new problems. In January 2020, this meant the epidemic would be taken with utmost seriousness, from top to bottom in society and government. Danger lurked; and must be respected. History had taught that lesson; and much else.

Plague History

"Everywhere, I saw people suffering from high fever, coughing blood and dying suddenly", a Chinese doctor recorded in his autobiography. Writing about the world's worst outbreak of pneumonic plague since the Black Death, which had wiped out nearly one third of Europe's population in the 14th century, he continued, "As far as the eye could see, the roads were covered with corpses.... The plague brought life in Manchuria to a standstill. Towns and villages barricaded themselves against strangers. People left home as little as possible; if they did, they walked down the deserted streets wearing facemasks".

Fatalities were said to be 99.99%. Some 63,000 people died in northern China's Manchuria, as well as in neighbouring Mongolia, over seven months in 1910 and 1911. Writing of this in 2020, Mark O'Neill described how,

"Those infected coughed sputum streaked with blood and their skin turned purple. Death followed within a few days. The first victims were trappers and fur traders in Manzhouli, on China's border with Russia.

The epidemic came from marmots, a rodent caught for its fur that when properly dyed could pass as sable. High prices for fur and sable persuaded 10,000 people to hunt for marmots in the forests of Manchuria. Many were inexperienced. Instead of killing healthy marmots that roam the field...they dug burrows and collected sick marmots — and it was these that carried the virus".

The Chinese doctor autobiographer who had written, "Everywhere, I saw people suffering ..." was Wu Lien Teh. Over his life, Wu collected a remarkable string of firsts. In 1896, Malaysian-born Wu was the first ethnic Chinese to study medicine at Cambridge. Before returning home to Penang in 1903, he had also studied at St Mary's Hospital, London, the Liverpool School of Tropical Medicine and the Pasteur Institute at Halle University in Germany.

Despite his qualifications, Wu knew that British colonial policy would bar him from reaching top positions in the land of his birth, Malaya. So he moved in 1907 to China, his father's homeland, where he worked until the 1937 Japanese war.

Today, Wu is remembered as the person who strangled the 1910–1911 Manchurian Plague. He innovated. Cutting up dead bodies was taboo but Wu defied this to conduct China's first autopsy. He introduced quarantine, told people to stay-at-home, disinfected buildings and, prior to rebuilding it, burned down the old plague hospital.

Cremation also was taboo in China: indeed illegal. With the ground too frozen to bury some 2,000 seriously infected corpses, Wu appealed to the emperor for permission to cremate them. Imperial consent came. Cremation was the turning point: the devastatingly deadly disease was eradicated within a few months. How?

Wu discovered that the plague spread through the air. To stop airborne infection he made masks, inspired by masks he had seen in Europe. Wu improved on them by adding extra layers of gauze and cotton to filter air. In 2020, these were considered the forerunners of N95 and KN95 masks.

Afterwards, Wu organised the disease's first international conference. He brought together scientists from Europe, the US, Mexico, Russia and China for a three-week conference cum workshop in April 1911. In August, he gave a paper to the International Congress of Medicine in London, which *The Lancet* published.

Wu became the first President of the Chinese Medical Association in 1916, the first director of China's quarantine service in 1930 and, in 1935, the first Chinese nominated for the Nobel Medicine Prize. A public health pioneer, he modernised China's medical services and education.

There is plenty of history here to inform solutions for Wuhan. No matter it is more than one century old. In many ways 2019–2020 mirrors the history of 1910–1911. It was not forgotten.

My experience of understanding the danger of epidemics is not unusual in China. I lived through one, day in day out, for months: the 2003 outbreak of Severe Acute Respiratory Syndrome (SARS). Context, perspective and history were the first things I learned: then innovation.

My Shanghai work required me to forecast China's economic and stock market recoveries for worldwide investors from Boston to Hong Kong, Edinburgh to Singapore and Sydney. The epidemic crashed share prices. Having to study SARS' dynamics, I turned to my wife's cousin Weibin who had been a medical student during Shanghai's last major epidemic in the 1970s. In 2003, as new mysterious cases and deaths mounted, he kept a cool head. He quietly advised me to do the same.

When I asked why he was so calm and detached, Weibin gently commented this was nothing like the 1970s when one Shanghai district hospital recorded more than 400 new cases in a single day. He knew precisely: his job was to chalk patients' names on a black board, until he ran out of space. That is why he was sure new cases exceeded 400: the remainder went unrecorded. There was not an empty inch on the black board, commandeered when note paper ran out. That is how rudimentary China's public health data systems had been.

Things were not as manic or desperate during SARS in 2003, Weibin explained. We simply must remain calm while hygiene and other measures did their work.

The main outbreaks were in Hong Kong and neighbouring Guangdong province, though Shanghai had a few fatalities; and deserted streets. Our research did the obvious. We tracked daily Hong Kong hospital admissions against the number of patients discharged. The time to turn positive on the stock market and economy would be when discharges outnumbered admissions. Market bulls would catch the scent.

This proved uncannily accurate. The market began a 20–30% rebound the very day of the trend's inflexion. Neither Harvard's Business School nor Medical School teaches such analysis: maybe after COVID they will. It is common sense.

Make do with what you have, however limited. Just as Bruce Aylward noted China did. Among families, SARS awoke tales of earlier epidemics and progress made since in China's public health, kindling some hope.

In 1922, two small children stood outside the curtained entrance to the main bedroom of the widower scholar's home. Their father motioned for them to enter, to come to him. The young boy brushed aside the cotton curtain and rushed in to hug his bedridden father. His elder sister, all of four years old did not move. An innate sense of danger possessed her. She froze, rooted to the floor.

Next day her father and brother were both dead, from the plague. Most of Woo Mingfeng's village in Jinjiang, a prosperous textile district in coastal Fujian, was wiped out. Only four years old, she must have sensed what was happening.

Her grandfather, a traditional doctor, taught her much about herbs and traditional treatments. Woo Mingfeng was my mother-in-law. She passed on much advice to her daughter, my wife, Yang Tse Oy. Decades later, immediately after Wuhan was locked down, Tse Oy phoned our son Matthew in London to warn him of the danger. Nothing was specific but everyone knew what to do.

Take precautions, stay home whenever possible and keep up with the news. The same was happening in Prato, Italy, where Chinese heard from relatives and friends in China. There was no vaccine to provide protection, only knowledge of conquering past plagues. To his credit and our relief Matthew listened to his mother, taking precautions and adjusting behaviour weeks before this was standard practice in London.

China has always given the highest respect to its leading doctors. Yang Sugong received the title *Taiyi Zhenren* after curing the Tang empress of breast tumours in the late 9th century. His name, along with those of all male heads of Yang households in Se Zhuang village ever since, is inscribed on tablets in Tse Oy's family memorial hall.

In a more recent reminder from history, Tse Oy received two photos that had been displayed in the Malaysian office of Eu Tong Sen. Apart from building up the traditional medicine firm Eu Yan Sang, which remains pre-eminent more than 140 years later, Eu became Southeast Asia's richest man in the early 20th century. A public health pioneer, he helped Ipoh rise from malarial swamps to become a prosperous, developed town within two decades. He was also a leader of the Malayan 1907 Anti-Opium Movement and the first Chinese member of the Legislative Council of the Federated States of Malaya.

His grandson Dickie Eu sent Tse Oy the photos as mementos for helping research into Eu Tong Sen. Found in a drawer in Dickie's grandfather's old Ipoh office, both had inscriptions in traditional Chinese characters. He wondered if Tse Oy could read them to identify the youngish, bespectacled man in the white suit. A large decoration was held together by a fine broad, silk sash, tied tightly, diagonally across his chest.

The man was Wu Lien Teh, China's Plague Fighter of 1910–1911, honoured by the government of his adopted home, possibly even by the last emperor himself. The photo was signed by Wu for Eu Tong Sen, his old friend from Penang, their birth place. In return, Eu showed typical high regard Chinese have for doctors and scholars by displaying Wu's photo in his office.

All the history of overcoming previous plagues and respect for doctors convinced me in January 2020 that Chinese had a real appreciation of the danger; and to whom to listen. Collectively, people knew immediately what to do. Take personal responsibility, like the little girl of Jinjiang in 1922.

History: The Raw Material for Governance

History is the raw material not only for action during plagues but for Chinese philosophy and strategy overall, the basis of Chinese governance.

Plenty exists: some 3,000 years written, another 2,000 years as oral history.

War, death, instability and disaster have been the greatest influences. How to avoid these afflictions has been the primary goal of Chinese governance. After 500 years of near-continuous fighting and death during the Spring and Autumn period (771–476 BC) and the Warring States period (476–221 BC), the search for peace and good governance occupied China's greatest minds.

This was the Golden Age of Chinese philosophy. It gave rise to many philosophies but Confucianism, short hand for many traditional philosophies, was the one that survived. Bizarrely for Westerners, Confucius was not even the first Confucian, only the most prominent. He did though have the best sound bites. Confucius also injected a moral dimension that most ignored.

Like history itself, the quality of governance ebbed and flowed. After Qin Shihuang completed China's unification in 221 BC he laid the basis for a strong economy and hence state. Standardising weights, measures, coins, cart axles and most of all the written language, he enabled China to have the scale that shapes it to this day. Managing scale and mobilising vast resources are among China's greatest strengths, as proven by its response to COVID in a country of 1.4 billion people.

What the Qin, father and son, failed to do was to provide stability or peace. Their dynasty lasted barely 16 years before being overthrown by the Han Dynasty (206 BC–220 AD). Three major periods of new thinking in politics, administration and economics followed.

The Han created a permanent foundation for government, strengthened by meritocratic competence. The Sui and Tang Dynasties (581–907) built on this Han foundation to strengthen and expand the bureaucracy to take China, in many Chinese eyes, to its highest peak. Finally the Song Dynasty (970–1269) completed the search for good governance and morality. It gave China its most comprehensive book on governance.

Sima Guang's *Zizhi Tongjian* covered almost 14 centuries of China's history from 403 BC to 959 AD: plenty enough raw material for governance. Doing it full justice took three million words and 294 chapters, written over 19 years.

Not only did the Song emperor praise his senior minister's work but, one millennium later, so did Mao Zedong. The emperor gave it a title; *Aiding Governance: A Comprehensive Historical Mirror.* Mao, the strategist, said he read it 17 times. He directed 21 scholars in 1956 to rewrite the *Zizhi Tongjian* into simplified characters so ordinary people could read it.

The rise and fall of dynasties in China were studied in great depth over a millennium ago, if not before: almost 800 years before Edward Gibbon's *The History of the Decline and Fall of the Roman Empire.* The *Zizhi Tongjian* praised good rulers, damned bad ones: doing the same for policies, structures and strategies.

These were the lessons of good governance: including how to maintain stability and sustain a grip on power. Even today, leaders frequently use historic examples. Xi Jinping is very fond of them. Words, phrases and allusions are scattered like Shakespearean or Dickensian quotations: for the educated elite James Joyce-like references.

In the West, they may draw a blank look or wry smile but considered obscure, obsolete or plain irrelevant. In China, they are reality, still informing and communicating today's thinking on governance. Five millennia or more of rich folk wisdom is also imparted at grandmothers' knees.

Trust in Governance: Reality From Surveys

The greatest surprise in this book for some will be that China's government is the most highly trusted in the world. This is hard to square with the relentless criticism Western governments and media make about China. Being among the worst governed, most distrusted and unpopular would seem much more likely.

Yet for the fifth year running, China's government was the world's most trusted government by its people. The November 2022 survey of US communication consultants Edelman recorded China's government having an 89% trust rating. China ranked first also in the other three categories of business, media and NGOs. Edelman was not one outlier. Other surveys have found similar results.

"From the impact of broad national policies to the conduct of local town officials, Chinese citizens rate the government as *more capable and effective than ever before*", Harvard's Ash Center reported. Since 2003, it has conducted face-to-face interviews with 31,000 urban and rural Chinese, the largest independent survey of its kind in China. This was Edward Cunningham, Tony Saich and Jessie Turiel of Harvard recording in 2020.

Satisfaction with China's central government rose to 93% in 2016 from 86% in 2003. Not in a straight line. It had fallen to 80% in 2005. The improvement, Ash said, was driven by Xi's focus on things like healthcare, education and other public services as well as anti-corruption and environmental protection.

Satisfaction with local township government — the lowest level in authority but where people most frequently encounter officials — was lower but still leapt to 70% in 2016 from 44% in 2003. Previously, over half of interviewees saw local officials as good at "talk only": useless and worse. By 2016, 55% saw local officials as practical problem solvers, with only 36% disagreeing. Officials' constantly rising education levels would have helped, along with better supervision, clearer policies and leadership.

The score for officials' "cleanliness" also improved markedly, rising to 65% from 35%, while approval of anti-corruption efforts doubled to 71% in 2016 from 35% in 2011, before Xi came to power. Alfred Wu, at the National University of Singapore, said the 2016 Ash findings were consistent with his own World Values Survey research from 1995 to 2018.

Deng Yuwen, former deputy editor of *Study Times,* the Central Party School's newspaper, and now an independent analyst in the US, said people's attitudes appeared to respond to "real changes in their material well-being". They might not be too concerned about democracy but would react if material lives were affected, Deng believed. It's The Economy Stupid.

Can surveys in China be trusted? The results of a 2019 survey of 51,606 people by the State Council's Development Research Centre (DRC) would suggest yes. The results sound credible.

Far from a characterisation of near-100% approval in a totalitarian state, the DRC found only, "49.6% of residents in urban and rural areas were "very satisfied" or "satisfied" with their overall quality of life, down from 52.8% in 2017 (probably explained by the increasingly discussed income gap between urban and rural China). Those "relatively dissatisfied" or "very dissatisfied" increased to 13.4%, up from 12% in 2017. Nonetheless, 68.9% were "confident" or "very confident" about the future, compared with 10.2% who were not. This seems reasonable given the economic performance; half satisfied but expecting more.

China ranked first in the 2020 Ipsos World Happiness Index, with 93% of people happy or very happy. Since 2011, China has risen an unequalled 15 points, with an 11 point gain in 2020 after COVID. In March 2023, China was again top. Another 2020 indicator, before vaccines were available, came from *Nature* magazine. Its worldwide survey of willingness to have a government-recommended vaccine found China was the most trusting country: acceptance was 88.6%, negative responses a mere 0.7%.

How representative are these surveys? The first thing to remember is that with the exception of the DRC's survey, which had by far the *lowest* percentages of satisfaction, the rest are all non-Chinese. Harvard, Ipsos, Edelman and *Nature* are all Western global leaders in their fields.

With knowledge of history that shaped governance, together with high trust in government and confidence in the future, China was well armed to tackle COVID in ways the West knew not — or chose not to know. So how did China make things work during COVID?

Chapter 14

How China Works

Be the first to worry and last to share joy,

Fan Zhongyan, *Memorial to Yueyang Tower*, 11th century

Some argue China's approach to eradicating COVID is irrelevant, it cannot work elsewhere because China is deemed to be authoritarian. Nonsense: former Harvard Medical School Professor of Public Health Policy William Haseltine said, rejecting this ideological notion. He told *CNN*, "Driving China's confirmed cases down from 60,000 to zero is not a totalitarian approach, *it is a public health approach*": relevant to all.

Successful methods are not ideological. As New York Mayor Fiorello La Guardia said in the 1930s, there are no good ideological approaches to cleaning streets, only those that work. "There is no Democratic or Republican way of street cleaning", only good systems or bad systems.

These are processes. Specific approaches are parceled up in strategy and philosophy to address the problem or opportunity. That has proved to be the competent way to administer. This chapter highlights competence before considering why the West could not emulate it.

China's Process

As mentioned (Chapter 8: *China's X-Factor*), I found while writing *China's Change* an insight that was most relevant to how China approached and overcame COVID. There were 20 main ideas to manage change: 18 the same as those the West used to dominate the world economy and hence power for two centuries. They were not only Chinese ideas but universally understood, derived from common experience. Two and two make four, whether in Wuhan, Prato, Sao Paulo or San Francisco.

Assembling these ideas, I grasped how China manages change and makes things work. First, the process separates all elements into three categories: goals, means and people. Looking at COVID, the divisions are clear. The goal, stated early from the very top by Xi Jinping, is to save peoples' lives and health: kill the virus. Nothing more, clear and concise: save life, make health the top priority, kill the virus.

Everything else follows from that goal. Means include mobilising vast resources, long-term thinking, extensive *yanjiu* (research) and communicating a clear vision to gain widespread support: buy in. Last but not least, as in the Manchurian Plague of 1910–1911 and SARS in 2003, people are critical to success.

China's 20th-century experience brought to traditional strategic thinking one particular idea: the importance of regrouping after setbacks. The communists learned this lesson the hard way during the two-decade long civil war with the nationalists.

Their very survival depended on it: no mere academic theory or bureaucratic exercise. They did the same during the 1937–1945 Japanese War. The Communist Party took this well-honed military practice into government in 1949. Regrouping after a setback, for a quick but deep analysis of what went wrong, proved invaluable in the fight against COVID. New strategies and personnel changes followed swiftly.

That is what happened in January 2020. COVID's precise origins and early days are clouded metaphorically in the Fog of War, as former US Secretary of Defence Robert McNamara described the beginning of the

Vietnam War. "There was too much complexity, too many variables to contemplate all at once", McNamara recalled. January 2020 was no different, yet a new course was quickly charted.

What is known though is that China recovered. It brought COVID under control, unexpectedly fast. On February 24th, one month after the January 23rd lock down of Wuhan and much of 60 million-strong Hubei province, the WHO-Joint China Mission delivered its findings (Chapter 12: *This Didn't Have to Happen*). The roots of China's successful process lay in traditional strategy and philosophy.

Strategy and Philosophy

Strategy looks simple: to achieve goals in the best, fastest, safest and most cost-effective way. Good luck: things are never that easy. Details are very complex subsets. Befitting a culture that invented the board game *weiqi* (*go* in Japan and the West), China has much to teach. Kissinger said all students of China must study *weiqi*. More complicated than chess, let alone poker, no wonder *weiqi* is taught at US military academies. There are plenty of other classical teaching aids.

Sun Tzu's *Art of War* is just one of many Chinese strategic manuals, full of insights into psychology and human behaviour. The *Art of War* has taught rulers and administrators ever since the sixth century BC. Disdaining brute force, except as a last resort, Sun emphasised mind over muscle.

In literature, *The Romance of the Three Kingdoms*, tells of how the Han Dynasty fell and China split into three kingdoms in the third century AD. As any Chinese student knows by heart, the 14th–15th centuries Ming Dynasty classic novel begins, "Under heaven the empire, long divided, must unite: long united must divide", providing crucial perspective and warning for rulers and empire watchers alike.

Daoism teaches other aspects including the Big Picture: to understand the whole, to get everything in perspective. To grasp a situation's true dynamics, to know that the small can be large, the large small, depending on the reference point. Everything is relative, everything is dynamic and everything changes.

How China manages change, with all its twists and turns, is analysed in the *Yi Jing*, the *Book of Change*. Based on ideas from the 11th century BC Zhou dynasty, it reflected history from the previous two millennia. That is how China comes to have 5,000 years of history, not an idle boast.

The *Yi Jing* is a How To Manual: How to Manage Life. Ideas like goals, clear priorities, pragmatism, flexibility, vision, 360-degree view, sequencing, detailed research and leadership wove China's response to COVID. These were not uniquely Chinese ideas. Indeed, as mentioned, they were part of a similar toolbox that enabled the West to become dominant after 1820. How did this work in frantic real-time in January 2020, with hospitals overflowing, fear widespread and knowledge incomplete?

Policy

After spending my first five years in China trying to figure out its economy, I thought I should try to understand how its politics and policy formulation worked. I live not in the national capital Beijing but in the commercial capital Shanghai, where few paid any attention to politics. Most were too busy making money.

One day I had lunch with a friend married into a political family, so I asked him about how China's politics worked. Rather than relate insights from his in-laws, he replied he had just asked the same question of a long-time business friend, who two years earlier had become a party member.

"What was the answer?" I asked eagerly. Presumably he could provide one. After a long pause, my friend replied that he could not tell. "All I know is that they talk a lot and for a long time". Discussions up and

down the party membership of some 95 million are extensive, following a familiar route. In a crisis, this has to be done very quickly, initially just among a few top experts.

First, define the issue. Then collect as much information as possible (*yanjiu*) before exploring possible solutions. Discussions may include non-party experts from home and abroad. Policies can then be sketched, debated and designed for further refinement. When there is agreement, the policy is taken and explained to party members to gain their understanding and acceptance: buy-in. An exhaustive, extensive process, it is as well that Chinese are good listeners. This is a big difference from the West.

"Chinese listen, whereas Westerners interrupt when a new thought occurs to them. Conversation is like a painting. You have to start somewhere. The beginning might not be the ideal place but it is a start. There is confidence it will be a good conversation", Swiss Ambassador Uli Sigg, who negotiated the first Chinese-Foreign industrial joint-venture in 1979, said in 2019. The last four sentences are very instructive: re-read them.

Apart from listening, China has a traditional, "distrust of adversarial debate", wrote Hans van de Ven, professor of modern Chinese history at Cambridge University. "Throughout Chinese history, the written word, reflecting considered opinion, free from passions of the moment, has been highly regarded". This was not the experience globally in 2020–2022. The exception was among medical specialists and other scientists across the world, who very largely communicated in a collegial, professional, measured way.

Chinese medical experts from COVID's front-lines began the process, rapidly writing research that advanced real-time global understanding. Everything, from identifying problems to discussing remedies and implementing policy, had to be done in double quick time in a country of 1.4 billion.

In Practice: In a Crisis

Traditional approaches provide the policy process. Three very different things are relevant to handling crises like COVID. Regrouping assembles basic ideas and information to correct course. Recognising the limits of knowledge anticipates the likelihood of unexpected problems: unknown unknowns. Vision and information must be communicated clearly. Altogether they reach a solution.

Regrouping

Those responsible for initial setbacks, alongside experts not involved, have to analyse the main mistakes, then outline corrections. Many are very basic things but easily missed or forgotten in a rapidly unfolding disaster: McNamara's Fog of War.

China's top leaders regrouped. After gathering information from the ground, they sent a small team of leading medical specialists to assess Wuhan. This then recommended a lockdown on a scale never attempted before in world history.

Swiftly, some 38,000 medical personnel plus materiel, from China's other 30-plus provinces and regions, poured into Hubei province and its capital Wuhan. Another 4,000 followed soon afterwards, along with almost 1,000 administrators.

The National Health Institute's deputy director responsible for this mobilisation identified in May 2020 five basic ideas: none complicated. Co-ordinating all five simultaneously was the challenge:

- **Mobilise large-scale resources to focus on one objective:** Something well understood in the land of the Great Wall and the Grand Canal. Kill the virus.
- **Provide food and means to all people to survive a lengthy lockdown:** Again mobilise large-scale resources, reaching down to the last person.

- **Stop further infection by separating mild cases from the seriously ill:** Establish separate hospitals for COVID patients. Keep functioning non-COVID-affected hospitals.
- **Masks are only needed in crowded public places:** Not necessary in parks.
- **Keep a balance between health and economy:** That said, the first priority is to save lives and kill the virus. Otherwise no one is safe, causing the economy to suffer anyway. As Dartmouth assistant professor Erin Bromage wrote, "If you don't solve the biology, the economy won't recover".

Unknown unknowns

US Defence Secretary Donald Rumsfeld was once ridiculed for talking about "unknown unknowns". Such an idea doesn't baffle Chinese at all. The concept existed almost three millennia ago in the *Dao De Jing, The Way*, the heart of Daoist philosophy, especially of strategic thinking.

A very Daoist insight came from WHO-China Joint Mission Chinese leader Dr Liang Wannian's warning at the February 24th press conference that, "The new corona virus is very cunning and tricky. Our current knowledge is not sufficient" — cunning, tricky, knowledge not sufficient. Unexpected consequences, surprising developments, change of direction, they all happen, including variants: be prepared. Only the specifics cannot be known in advance.

Long COVID sufferers would wish Dr Liang had been heard in the West. So would employers who found significant lethargy, absenteeism and prolonged illness among their workers for many months or even years afterwards. Many, especially young people, did not take the virus seriously. If they caught it, recovery was assumed: no worse than flu, no long-term effects. Long COVID could not have been predicted exactly but the risk of underestimating the virus certainly could.

Long COVID brought debilitating fatigue, headache, shortage of breath, weak muscles, low-grade fever, brain fog and hair loss. Mental health problems, damage to the lungs and heart were suspected: so too strokes. It would have been better to be prepared, to admit the limits to knowledge and be ready for anything, as China did.

Vision

Vision was clearly communicated. First, basic measures were laid out. Then by May 2020, Zhong Nanshan together with a few other top medical and health specialists explained the likely future (see the next section: *Elite*). There was good news. COVID in China was fully under control. Vaccines were on their way. September could see the first ones seek official approval. By year end, vaccines could be available to the general public: all good.

However, this came with a large dose of caution. Constant vigilance was needed. Viruses usually last three years or so before they peak, the public was told. There could be variants that would strengthen if society dropped its guard. That now was the greatest danger. Mitigation measures were still very necessary.

When the Delta variant wreaked its havoc outside China in 2021, Zhong Nanshan was again on television to explain what could be done; and to brief on China's progress in new vaccines. These were rare appearances. Everyone knew they should listen carefully when he spoke, and should follow.

These are basic ideas, applicable anywhere — where there is political will and social cohesion. That of course is the problem. Whereas East Asia has similar thought systems, not all Confucian incidentally, the West has too many societies divided by cultural or political fault-lines, preventing agreement on COVID policy.

In politics and much of Western media the word adversarial barely begins to describe the often toxic language used. This contributed very little to genuine understanding or progress, as debate is meant to do.

Indeed, toxicity impeded both. COVID Didn't Have to Happen in the West but it did.

Elite

The elite, key people, is the third strand of China's policy process. Scholar officials are the foundation of its administration. 110 years after Wu Lien Teh ended the Manchurian Plague, Zhong Nanshan led China's fight against COVID.

Similarities between them are remarkable. Both had independent minds, paid close attention to science and possessed courage. These shaped their ability to overthrow conventional wisdom, cut through red tape and get things done.

Zhong, like Wu, was well-connected in international medical circles. After qualifying at Beijing Medical University, Zhong studied between 1979 and 1981 at St Bartholomew's in London and at Edinburgh Medical School. He went on to advise the WHO on Smoking and Health. Like Wu, he published in *The Lancet*: winning *Paper of the Year Award* in 2008. At home he was president of the Chinese Thoracic Society and president of the Chinese Medical Association.

Both Wu and Zhong exemplify modern-day mandarins: an elite first established by the reforming Han Dynasty (206 BC–220 AD), which sought the most able people to fill its ranks. The Sui Dynasty formalised this in 605 by introducing the Imperial Examinations to select officials, purely on merit, not by birth or connections. Strong administrative capacity made China's most revered dynasty the Tang (618–907) prosper.

Today, for every policy subject in China there are three or four recognised experts, as financier Jim Stent observed. None hold formal positions, though many are found in academe, specialist institutions or even retirement. When a major decision or solution is needed the party consults them, informally. For COVID, a small but broad group was assembled, headed by Zhong Nanshan.

During an enquiry, the authority of such experts ranks above government officials and even some senior party members, depending on the author of the remit. No one welcomes a visit from experts with a mandate from the Central Committee, as Zhong Nanshan and his team of experts possessed during their January 18–20 Wuhan visit. Nominally given as advice, their writ is more like a decision to be countersigned by the Central Committee or government authority that commissioned the enquiry.

I once asked someone who knew the answer why the government favoured a private sector firm over a state entity to buy the Volvo Car Group in 2010. Indeed, Chery, a state company had sought support first but privately owned Geely received the nod to bid; and a $1.8 billion bank loan.

I was told that one of the recognised auto experts asked both companies the same question, "Why could it succeed where the existing owners Ford had failed?". The implication was what could a Chinese company know or do that a world leader could not. Geely gave the better answer — and has more than justified the decision.

Confucianism stressed the importance of the elite, its role, education and integrity. "The *junzi*, the noble minded, are clear about duty", Confucius said. Fan Zhongyan in the 11th century talked of "a tower of orderly administration" The elite's goal, orderly administration, remains the same today.

The elite's duty was to be, "the first to worry and last to share joy", Fan wrote in *Memorial to Yueyang Tower*. In modern Asia, no one epitomised this more than Singapore's founding Prime Minister Lee Kuan Yew. He and his administrations worried about everything, from the very long-term down to immediate small details. In Chinese public health circles that is Zhong Nanshan.

Zhong earned his reputation in 2003 when he spoke out against prevailing official thinking. He proposed a cure for the deadly SARS virus. As director of the Guangzhou Institute of Respiratory Diseases, in the city at the epicentre of SARS, he and colleagues had identified an "atypical pneumonia" in more than two dozen patients.

Backed by the provincial health department, he told the media that the frightening new disease could be cured and was preventable. A combination of non-invasive ventilation to increase oxygen and cortisone could cut deaths among the seriously ill, whilst speeding recovery (remember Donald Trump had cortisone).

Politically, this advice was very dangerous. The Chinese CDC, which ranked well above Zhong's institute, had already ruled that antibiotics were the only legal treatment for "atypical pneumonia". Cortisone was illegal.

Guangdong province and Zhong saw the benefits cortisone could bring to SARS patients, so continued to argue for its use in moderate quantities. In time it was approved and became standard treatment. When the WHO visited, it endorsed Zhong's analysis of SARS, recommending the treatment worldwide. All this made Zhong Nanshan China's Anthony Fauci. The only difference was that Zhong's leaders listened, as they did again in 2020.

In early January 2020, local officials were the problem. In Wuhan, they had told Zhong that everything was under control. Still heading the same institute, Zhong saw in Guangdong province signs that this might not be true. As with SARS he continued his research, treatment and advocacy.

At Beijing's behest, Zhong went to question Wuhan's officials and doctors on January 19th. He took a small team of leading specialists, with full powers to investigate and to make recommendations.

The team concluded that Wuhan was underestimating COVID. This was reported to Beijing on January 20th. That night, Zhong went on national television to repeat the conclusion; and to announce that human-to-human transmission was likely. This was the key moment. The audience knew action would follow, the fix was in.

China's public trusted Zhong for his no-nonsense, direct approach: he never had to correct himself. Whenever he appeared on television, everyone knew it was important. People listened carefully, especially as alarm, fear and confusion are the natural response to any mysterious disease.

Zhong was the public face of important government messages after Wuhan's January 23rd lockdown. He had been very active in the background even earlier, helping bring China's public health policy back on track by working behind the screen in government, like a traditional scholar-official. In this area, Zhong was the acknowledged and respected expert.

Zhong even subsequently spoke on television with unconcealed emotion about the needless deaths of unprotected doctors, nurses and hospital workers, including "whistleblower" Li Wenliang. Zhong spoke up for experts and expertise, which some bureaucrats and politicians had ignored for their own ends, putting the public at great risk.

Plenty of other expert work was done by other parts of government. This ranged from communicating speedily with foreign bodies, like the WHO and countries including the US, to discovering and sharing worldwide the genome sequence of the virus in record time. The central figure was Zhong Nanshan.

Zhong's authority and experience changed the course of COVID in 2020, helped greatly by the approach and a wide range of experienced colleagues. All had acquired much knowledge from SARS. Lessons learned were applied in China's health institutions and systems, whose deficiencies SARS laid bare in 2003.

After SARS 2003: Long-Term Thinking to 2030

After bringing SARS under control, China saw it did not know nearly enough about such diseases. Long-term thinking and elite officials' education required a remedy. Fortuitously, an opportunity presented itself. The WHO Assistant Director of Communicable Diseases post fell vacant in 2003. China nominated Hong Kong's health chief Margaret Chan, who was selected; and subsequently headed the WHO from 2006 until 2017.

That meant China was abreast of all latest trends, thinking and best practices in global communicable disease control: familiar with all the key players, epidemiologists and scientists. Chan's knowledge helped China better understand how to cope with 2009's H1N1 bird flu. Vaccine development advanced with China in 2014 working with the US on an Ebola vaccine. Even though a Canadian citizen, Chan still advises Beijing.

China, after SARS, sent officials to Harvard Medical School to understand better how to control epidemics. William Haseltine, Professor of Public Health Policy confirms this. Following up, Harvard sent experts to Beijing to brief the Central Party School, whose principal remit has been to look for long-term threats to the Party's continued rule and advise on mitigation policy.

Exposed by SARS, China's health system gradually became a high government priority. China lacked the basics, even beds and buildings. Expectations grew with personal incomes, yet the system was inadequate for the mounting burdens placed on it. China was still an underdeveloped economy in 2003. However, China was less poor than it had been, so the political decision was made to spend more on health.

Priorities began to change. Spending on healthcare as a percentage of GDP almost doubled between 1995 and 2015. From 2009 to 2012, China spent $124 billion on community health centres and hospitals. Treatment of life-threatening conditions started to be subsidised heavily. It was not just about money but new systems too. That posed a problem.

There was no appropriate Western model to follow. China had to figure things out for itself. A comprehensive plan was needed. Top of its agenda were ideas to drive down drug development expense, minimise costs and retail prices, target disease prevention, reduce bills for long-term illness, discover breakthrough drugs and develop new treatments: a very long list.

China could though tap into its own resources, especially scale and new technology. Over 80,000 Chinese with Western PhDs worked in life sciences abroad in 2009. China began to establish life science parks to attract back talent; by 2022 there were 160.

China's scale is a great advantage and magnet. With a long tradition of collecting data and a new era of Big Data, it can link patients' medical records to enable large-scale research. Genomics has greatly expanded what is possible. Previously, there were only 3–400 "drugable targets", now DNA sequencing raises the potential to more than 30,000. China's BGI, formerly the Beijing Genomics Institute, has the world's largest sequencing capability.

On the funding side, China has created an investment ecosystem with research, early-stage funding and government support for drug and medical device development. This long-term thinking has laid the foundation for an improved health system. Now the focus is on healthy living to keep down healthcare costs before they explode: mitigation.

A Healthy Action Plan for 2019–2030 has 15 detailed campaigns to promote healthy living; and to control major diseases, especially the diseases of affluence like cancer, heart attacks and strokes. The focus includes improving awareness of balanced diets, fitness, smoking, alcoholism, mental health and a healthy environment. Targets are set for healthier eating — less sugar, salt and oil — 500 grams of vegetables and fruit every day. An apple a day keeps the doctor away and all that.

If China can get things done and make them work, why cannot the West? That is the subject of the next three chapters.

Western Failings

Chapter 15

Politicians and Society

In a freedom-loving country ... It is very difficult to ask the British population uniformly to obey guidelines in the way that is necessary.

Boris Johnson 2020

Five hundred deaths a day is unacceptable. ... There has been a lack of discipline.

Angela Merkel 2020

What explains why Western societies so often mishandled COVID? Three groups failed the West: politicians, society and the media.

Most politicians were too frightened of their base or wanted to play to it: choosing to follow rather than to lead. Not all of society is to blame but enough were hostile to adopting measures that worked in China. Few in the media gave enough timely detail. This was perfectly possible, as the medical and scientific media showed. The rest of the media was often uninformed, ill-informed or ideologically motivated.

None of the three groups acknowledged what China did to bring COVID under control. Few were even interested. If they had been, they could have learned a great deal, sparing their societies much suffering.

Unable to Follow Forebears Who Copied China

Why couldn't Western politicians have followed China and the rest of East Asia? If they had, there might have been only hundreds, not even thousands, let alone some two million deaths in the West and nearly seven million worldwide. A few did, partially. The rest didn't at all. Like startled rabbits staring into oncoming headlights many froze. Mesmerised, unable to act, they could only repeat irrelevant dogma and blame — pure incompetence.

The mystifying thing is why not? Strict policies worked. Governments that adopted these policies showed competence: a proven vote winner in the early days of facing COVID, from South Korea to New Zealand and Singapore. Blinded by old mantras, many couldn't even see that. Instead Western politicians dithered, dissembled, winged it; and the rest is painful history. This didn't have to happen. Western failings are its own.

The irony is rich. Political and social will today is lacking. Yet in the 19th century a younger much more self-confident, successful West had no problem with learning from China. When faced with a major problem, Britain didn't think twice. It was open to good, practical ideas from anywhere, including other cultures thousands of miles away.

At the height of its imperial might in 1855, determined to remain global leader, Britain borrowed very deliberately from China. Britain's most troublesome administrative problem was its increasingly overwhelmed civil service. This was burdened by ever-greater demands, enfeebled by geographic overreach, as well as weakened by corruption and nepotism. Administrative ineffectiveness and incompetence threatened the British Empire's continued growth.

The answer was simple. Introduce meritocratic entrance exams for the civil service. Make it open to all, not just to the privileged. Whitehall called this the "Chinese Principle", after the idea's originators, some 1,250 years earlier. Most of the West did the same, spreading the idea to the rest of Europe, North America and Australasia, even parts of Latin America and Africa. This helped underpin Western dominance ever since.

Today, Britain cannot even copy its own adaptive past. In a world of muddled thinking, rather than do the logical thing to learn from initially very successful East Asia, politicians in the US and UK in particular, tossed and turned in 2020, stopped and started, hoping to find the right electoral formula: without cost to their jobs. They only managed to pile up dead bodies; and eventually their own, politically.

British Prime Minister Boris Johnson explained that in "a freedom-loving country … It is very difficult to ask the British population uniformly to obey guidelines in the way that is necessary": hot air not policy, let alone leadership or successful action. Crises need leaders, expertise and an informed society. Britain, the US and much of the West lacked at least one of these, often two and sometimes all three.

Chancellor Angela Merkel sounded much more of a leader than did Johnson or Trump, when she said, "The most important key to us successfully fighting the virus is the responsible behaviour of every individual and the willingness to cooperate". Another time she said, "Five hundred deaths a day is unacceptable": full stop.

Johnson must have skipped the British history chapters about the 1855 "Chinese Principle" or about British cities in 1940 braving the Blitz, let alone the whole nation coming together to accept six wartime years of food rationing and a limited amount until 1954. He gave no thought to the freedom-loving COVID policy that terminated the lives of almost 200,000 Britons, five times the number the Luftwaffe killed in the Blitz. These are facts not words. Words though are cheap, easy and quickly forgotten, as many Johnson colleagues demonstrated.

Conservative MP Desmond Swayne railed against face masks, a "monstrous imposition that threatens our fundamental liberties". Masks are no more an imposition than seat belts, speed limits or fire regulations:

they save lives. Future generations will laugh at Swayne, as we do today at King Canute.

In a similarly pompous and empty vein, Tory MP Daniel Kawczynski, tweeted: "Each MP must be accountable for their vote in such a massive civil liberties/economy/jobs/ mental health/issue". He made no mention of physical health let alone life itself, surely the most fundamental of human rights?

President of the Bundestag Wolfgang Schäuble provocatively commented Germany needed to weigh better the social and economic costs with the desire to save lives: decisions should not be left to virologists alone. "The massive economic, social, psychological and other effects need to be weighed up", he said, "To just bring everything to a halt for two years can also have horrific consequences". Indeed it can but East Asia showed so clearly nothing like this is necessary.

Two to three months of strict measures and constant vigilance can bring COVID under control, if done from the start. That is the evidence from East Asia. Such a response also ensures a faster economic recovery, as China proved in the second half of 2020.

German society instead, tired of controls, reopened its policy discussion: the result? While the economy remained in recession, a record number of new cases, hospitalisations and deaths mounted in the winter of 2020, to be repeated again in 2021. The same happened throughout Europe and North America, pushing back the global control of COVID by at least another year and giving new, more dangerous variants time to evolve and multiply — as then happened with Delta and Omicron.

Schäuble, former finance minister, then left his economics perch, saying he did not believe that the first clause in the German constitution, stating that "human dignity is inviolable" meant preserving human lives at all cost. From the man who previously considered Greek debt repayment a "moral issue" this was an interesting take on both morality and basic human rights. Which was more important, money or lives?

Some saw the merits of both cases. British Transport Secretary of State Grant Shapps did, declaring "I am both for lives and livelihoods". Think about it. Both at the same time are not possible. Which is the priority, which comes first the horse or the cart? One must, which one he did not say: confused, lacking logic.

People completely missed the fact that China's approach was to kill the virus. That was the top priority: do that first. Stop giving the virus more time to mutate into ever-more dangerous variants. Then all the other non-health problems, especially the economy, can be managed. Instead the UK and US plunged into the worst of both worlds, time and time again, wave after unnecessary wave. It might have helped if they had known of some economic research using Randomised Controlled Trials in China.

This found, unsurprisingly, that the fewer confirmed COVID cases there are the higher people's GDP growth expectations. Consumer sentiment, the major part of Western economies, will be stronger, driving consumption. Therefore cut infections to bolster positive consumer expectations and spending.

That way, biology will lead to a permanent economic recovery not another lurch into stop-start. Simply do this by containing the disease's spread, recommended author of the research Cornell PhD economist Dr Yan. Restarting the economy on its own would never be enough, as many states in the US and countries in Europe found to their cost.

The final word should go to the two adults on either side of the Atlantic. Chancellor Angela Merkel pinned blame for the second German wave squarely on the "lack of [social] discipline". It was as simple as that. In the US, Anthony Fauci merely stated the obvious, "there is personal responsibility and there is societal responsibility". They both matter; and are not mutually exclusive.

Society's Responsibility

Western society has not known such a challenging global health crisis since the "Spanish Flu" of 1918–1920. A century of improvement in public and personal health has followed. Not all shared in it fully but most people appreciated it greatly.

Consequently, experience of danger generally declined in the West. Even war, after 1945, has been fought elsewhere, on others' soil and often with others' lives. The Cold War was a long, thin icy chill but no one died, directly, in the West; and Western economies not only recovered but boomed. The world went to the brink over Cuba in 1962 but found the political wisdom to step back from global destruction. A long increasingly comfortable period of peace, at home anyway, nurtured complacency in the West.

COVID was a reminder not to take anything for granted. Lulled into a false sense of security by a century of improved health, most people and their societies in early 2020 took time to wake from their slumber. That is not too surprising and does explain why the initial response was so slow: human nature perhaps. People should not be castigated too harshly for that.

Society though has to shoulder some responsibility: notably for its hostility to strict measures and refusing to make killing the virus the goal of public health. That had been proven right in East Asia.

COVID fatigue is no excuse, only a partial explanation. Inability to conduct proper test and trace regimes merely speaks to incompetence. Politicians and parts of society toyed with the idea of herd immunity, of learning to "Live With the Virus", without mentioning that 1.1 million could die in the US or more than 200,000 in the UK due to COVID. This only gave the virus time to survive, adapt and mutate: for stronger variants to evolve.

Blaming the political class is easy but the reality is societies get the politicians they deserve. Decades of growing individual disengagement from national and local politics, as well as from other communities within nations, leaves fault at society's door.

Progress does not move permanently in a straight line, as many in the West like to believe. That is why the West should pay attention to Sir John Glubb and Paul Kennedy (Chapter 4: *The Power Equation and the Decline of Empires*). Decline is not inevitable but, if it is to be avoided, renewal must occur. Even that is not guaranteed, as all regimes, empires and dynasties eventually have proved.

Glubb's Six Stages of Empire ends with the Age of Decadence: not the decay of morals but of institutions. Not just the visible facades of buildings to provide justice, health and education but the invisible glue that holds society together.

Governance is one such pillar. Moreover, appreciation of public service and its value has declined, undermining government effectiveness. This is where it is fair to talk of a failure of the political class, though, as mentioned, society-at-large in democracies is ultimately at fault.

Western bureaucracy is a related area of decay. This is where comparisons with East Asia are fair. A dose of Western 19th century self-confidence to copy the relevant parts of the Confucian blueprint would not have come amiss.

Nor would detailed knowledge of what had worked in East Asia. From Japan to Singapore, experienced Asian administrators and politicians have shaped policy to develop strong economies to deliver improved wealth, health and education. Not just to a few but, through inclusive philosophy, to an increasing majority. Inclusion reflects a more meritocratic, collective and community-based approach to life than the individualistic 21st-century West can accept. That though is what it is.

There is plenty of rigor and competition in East Asia but also much more social cohesion, as Ian Johnson noted in his accounts of Wuhan; and after his bad experience in the UK. Accepting strict measures in Wuhan, he judged, was overwhelmingly voluntary and personal. Not because they were imposed by those some Westerners dubbed authoritarians or even totalitarians but because society knew it needed them.

Such collective thinking is hard, if not impossible, for some to accept in societies like the US that exalt rugged individualism. Similarly with those individuals who seek their version of personal freedom as the ultimate destination for society. Even many others in the West, with less clear-cut ideology, feel uncomfortable with what they imagine China to be — which is why China and East Asia need to be much better understood by the West, for its own sake (Chapter 21: *Understanding In a New Era*).

Political participation has generally declined in the West. Membership of traditional political parties is down markedly, and remaining members often spend more time fighting each other than battling purported opponents. This suggests new parties must form or new ways of conducting politics emerge. Coalition politics are one area into which many countries in Europe have stumbled, so far imperfectly.

The decline of the two-party system is symptomatic of the malaise in new thinking. The two worst Western performers among major economies during COVID have been the two countries where two-party politics is still most entrenched: the US and UK.

The worst decay of all has been trust in expertise. Populism used to be largely an anti-elite position but now has been harnessed by splinter groups within the elite. Some among elites see it as the best way to reach the top in politics: for personal advancement not principle or country.

In recent years, first came Brexit, then Donald Trump, fuelled by similar anger, disappointment and fear. Confused ideas about taking back control are the deadly sirens of the 21st century. Distrust of expertise, let alone experience from foreign lands and alien cultures, undermined the West's initial response to COVID: populism's latest scalp.

The ultimate cancer of populism is that it requires no evidence. Merely sound bites and charged emotion in relentless campaigning to spread and reinforce unproven assertions. It does not listen to the evidence of others. In the "New Cold War", hostility towards China gives Chinese evidence no credence at all. That undermines any informed discussion. That is society's loss; and responsibility. The media though cannot escape responsibility either. It is the third leg of how decisions are made.

ABC, Words and Fu Manchu's Ghost

Western politicians, society and journalists often coyly refer to successful measures coming from "Asia". China is rarely mentioned by name, even though, as WHO mission head Dr Bruce Aylward had pointed out early on, "the vast bulk of early COVID experience and data was from China".

Indeed China was, "the only country to have turned around serious large scale outbreaks". Yet, initially in 2020, Western media and government credit was rarely given to China. Instead it went to Anywhere But China (ABC). China was cancelled, its world lowest death per million counts ignored. In its place, other Asian experience was readily quoted.

That was until early favourites Singapore, South Korea, Australia, New Zealand and Hong Kong lost control and staying power. They were quietly dropped as exemplars for the West. Respectively, after almost three years of COVID, they had suffered 286, 588, 614, 661 and 1,398 deaths per million compared with mainland China's 3.61: repeat 3.61.

In 2020, Washington and its media were pushing the idea that the WHO had much to learn from Taiwan about COVID and must be heard. This meme died a quiet death. For by December 2022, Taiwan had recorded 616 deaths per million — 170 times worse than China, hardly a good example. By June 2023, Taiwan deaths neared 800 per million.

China was talked about in a very different language. Words became weapons. Powerful negative images were conjured into explanation. A whole coded language developed that would make dog whistlers proud, connecting with their followers, unheard by others.

"Draconian" was the word to describe China's COVID lockdown measures from the very start. Everyone knew what that meant: no need to spell it out. This only faded out of use when democracies like South Korea and New Zealand introduced similar measures, parts even stricter.

Not worthy of us said Australian Prime Minister Scott Morrison of China's measures: implying not applicable, not our values. That was shortly before he had to acknowledge Australian Special Forces blooding rites of passage included murdering young, defenceless Afghan boys: values? Here Be Dragons (Chapter 11: *Challenges*).

Racist word imagery even made it into the local letters pages. *China finds new way to invade* ran the headline in New York's *Riverdale Press* above a letter to the editor in 2020. Invasion, like hordes, is a graphic word used by racists from the US to the UK, from white suburbs to the Brexit referendum.

Politicians and media have a language all of their own. Insufficiently called out or fully confronted, it hides racism. Even before COVID was known, *The New York Times* carried a story on December 5, 2019 entitled *The Chinese Roots of Italy's Far-Right Rage.* This led one Asian American to complain about dog whistling after it wrote that Italian far-right leader Matteo Salvini, "offered a rudimentary solution to Italy's travails: Close the gates.... Denigrating Islam, and warning of an "invasion" that threatened Italians with "ethnic cleansing…". Excellent exposure for racist tropes, reported without direct challenge let alone rebuttal.

The word targeted carries a hidden sense of menace. The sub-heading read, *When China first targeted small textile town.* The town was Prato, highlighted earlier (Chapter 12: *This Didn't Have to Happen*)

Politicians and Society   183

Sub-editors usually write the headlines, sub-heads and section headings. Therefore the writer may not be to blame but that does not absolve the paper's editors from responsibility. Presumably this is acceptable language at *The New York Times*.

Why is the sub-head so wrong? Apart from the title indulging at the very least in borderline racial insensitivity, the words "China first *targeted*" could not be more wrong. The facts are plain wrong. The sub-head reeks of a Chinese conspiracy: part of a grand Chinese plan to take over the world, starting with this small and hence very vulnerable Italian textile town. Wrong on all counts, the facts are these.

Those Chinese that came to Prato are largely from Wenzhou in coastal China, famous for its private sector. *Wenzhou Ren*, Wenzhou people, are known for their entrepreneurial acumen and energy. A disproportionate number of China's most successful entrepreneurs, including Jack Ma Yun of Alibaba and Li Shufu of automaker Geely, have roots in its distinctive business culture.

Traditionally, Wenzhou people have kept their distance from government. After 1949 Wenzhou had very little state industry. Indeed it became something of a backwater, partly because of its pre-Communist past which for a time, like Shanghai, gave it pariah status. *Wenzhou Ren* are the last people to spearhead a targeting of Italian small textile towns for the Communist Party of China.

To complete the sub-head's comedy of errors, Wenzhou had strong Catholic connections going back many decades. The Catholic Church assisted early Wenzhou migrants to France in the 1920s. Some of these went to Italy, especially Tuscany where Prato was then a suburb of Florence: long before the Communist Party came to power in China. These were undercover Communist agents and shock troops for the Yellow Peril?

It is not just China that is demonised but others too. However there is a special language it seems for China, which some Western liberals slip into far too easily: especially mentally but sometimes even in public. They would be mortified to be told this is the century-old language of *Fu Manchu* movies, with the slit eyes, drooping moustache and inane sayings, before shrilly pronouncing "Confucius he say" in high-pitched nasal tones, complete with fingertips squeezing the nostrils — but it is.

Authoritarian or even totalitarian constantly describe China's measures, even though as Harvard's Dr William Haseltine pointedly said they were simply public health measures. Reading in the next chapter Dr Ewelina Biskup's first-hand account of the crisis in Shanghai is proof of Haseltine's assertion. Her March 2020 podcast was published in the *New England Journal of Medicine* but carried no further. It was all out there but the mainstream media found no interest in it.

The media is another institution in decline. That is why I devote the next two chapters to it. Largely because the media is the institution I have known longest, first from my training and then the application of many of its principles to investment and economic research. Other major institutions may have followed similar paths to decline but my rule in life has always been to write only about what I know well. Hence I shall examine the media as a major example of declining standards and growing incompetence in Western institutions.

Chapter 16

Media and COVID

How did China control COVID? The media here is not covering it sufficiently for me to know.

Miss Lam, Calgary, December 2020

It is unrealistic to expect that any country could have stopped this particular virus at its source ... I tend to take a charitable view of countries that are at the beginning stage of epidemics.

Dr Jennifer Nuzzo, Johns Hopkins, October 2020

What responsibility do Western media bear for COVID's worldwide spread? This may seem an outrageous question but it must be asked.

Surely it could have reported in much greater depth what had worked in China? The WHO spelt that out on February 24, 2020 (Chapter 12: *This Didn't Have to Happen*). This was crystal clear well before COVID took off on its murderous journey in the West.

To be generous, people, including the media, can be slow learners. Presumably, they would soon learn. That was common sense. The media would provide news and information to help people manage COVID. Giving hope to people around the world struggling with disease, lockdowns and fear would seem an obvious story.

Whether it was the news of no more COVID deaths in China by May 2020 or 650 million people travelling around China during the October 2020 week-long national holiday, without a single outbreak, surely these would qualify? Good news, proof positive the WHO-endorsed blueprint worked. A better life lay ahead for societies that followed strict mitigation measures.

That would have given hope, reinforcing other public health messages. More people in the West would have accepted basic health precautions, including mask-wearing, social distancing and strict compliance. This would reduce infection later in the winter and thereby save tens or even hundreds of thousands of lives: indeed eventually millions.

Only once did I hear in the Western media of the no China holiday outbreaks story; and that was from Don Lemon of *CNN*, who has his own distinctive take on what is news. This could not have been missed: the holiday lasted a whole week. Every China correspondent knew of it, was probably enjoying it, and would have been watching for the outcome. If even a few outbreaks occurred, we would have heard.

Instead, no bad news about China again meant no news. Evidently, a COVID-free week-long holiday did not fit in with the mainstream media narrative. Shortly afterwards, a Wechat message in early December 2020 brought home to me the Western media's abject failure to inform adequately its consumers.

The Need and Right to Know

A remarkable 95-year-old was asking for news. Miss Lam wanted to know how China had brought COVID under control. She asked because her media was not covering it in any depth or clarity. Curious and vulnerable at 95, she needed to know. This was in December 2020, almost one year after the outbreak.

Miss Lam wasn't enquiring from the middle of the Amazon or Congo, she was asking from a G-7 country experiencing a surge in new cases and deaths. The death rate was then 332 per million people (1,260 by December 2022), compared with only 3.6 per million in China by December 2022.

She was not the only Chinese in her country: 5% identify as Chinese. This was a country that prides itself on the values of an informed, well-educated liberal democracy, which included being supposedly a leader in world health. It also championed transparency, a free press and the right to know.

This was Canada. Miss Lam lived in Calgary, Alberta, with a population exceeding 1.5 million, yet her media had not told her how China conquered COVID: keeping its death toll at the time under 5,000. Canada had already seen more than two-and-a-half times more people die in a population nearly one-fortieth of China's.

A refugee from mainland China, normally not very interested in her birthplace, she wanted to know how China had done it. This was more than her Canadian news editors seemed to think was necessary or even interesting. Their attitudes differed little from the standard Western narrative on China's COVID: draconian measures and blame, with silence about anything good.

The gaping difference in deaths per million people was airbrushed out. Like something from Orwell or Kafka: inconvenient truths simply ignored. Frankly to a former journalist, brought up on *Reuters'* insistence for accuracy, balance and perspective, it was breathtaking; and very depressing.

The acerbic tone of much foreign reporting was present at the February 24th WHO-China press conference, one month after Wuhan's lockdown. "The story" of Chinese culpability and deceit had already become part of the Western narrative. Constant, unquestioning repetition of assertions, not hard evidence in clear context, created the storyline that many others followed uncritically: a deadly mixture of half-truths and no hard evidence.

The WHO-China press conference in Beijing should have been a pivotal moment in COVID's history. The perfect time to correct misconceptions: to reset the story, educate and head for recovery. It was not too late. Indeed it was early. There was a proven blueprint to stop the virus, bring it under control and then kill it. This was February 24, 2020, a whole month before COVID became well-established in the West.

Bruce Aylward and Liang Wannian provided more than enough information for all countries to avoid China's fate (Chapter 12: *This Didn't Have To Happen*). The rest of the world, especially in the yet largely unaffected West, South Asia, Africa and Latin America, did not have to suffer like China.

With great lucidity and detail, Aylward urged other countries to act upon China's experience. He then invited questions. The first went to the *BBC*, whose motto is "Nation Shall Speak Peace Unto Nation".

After a few polite pleasantries about what China had done, the *BBC*, on behalf of its worldwide audience, quickly moved on to ask just one question. Preceding this was a statement, "We also need to understand what went wrong". The correspondent then asked, "[To] What extent do you think public censorship played a role in allowing the virus to accelerate?"

Aylward replied that the mission's task was to find out what had worked. This question was outside its remit. However, he did not duck it, frankly admitting he had not considered it, which is very revealing in itself, i.e. unusual levels of censorship were not a primary cause, otherwise, anyone would have noticed it. Aylward did though list half a dozen improvements, neither an indictment nor a whitewash but lessons from which others could learn — the mission's purpose.

Speed in decision-making topped his list. Aylward believed it saved the rest of China from Hubei province's fate. In every outbreak, everywhere, he said there are always delays in acting on alerts, "because you're not thinking of that disease in that place" (presumably here of earlier cases such as SARS or flu). This was part of McNamara's Fog of War. Aylward had been in this fog many times during his almost three-decade-long career as an epidemiologist. No foreign journalist in the room appeared to have been in such fog.

Otherwise, they would have realised that a much more useful question for a worldwide audience would have been, "Can you elaborate on the three best things countries around the world can do to ensure COVID does not lead to millions of deaths?" That opportunity was missed: political propaganda point-scoring won the day, and nearly seven million have died.

The foreign media was slow on the story, not too surprisingly. In under-resourced China bureaus, China's health was not of interest, politics and business were. Lacking China-based journalistic experience of epidemics meant the first foreign correspondent's question about COVID at the Foreign Ministry's daily press conference was only asked on January 17th, according to *Xinhua*.

This was two weeks after China's Centre for Disease Control and Prevention (CDC) director Gao Fu on January 3 had called his US counterpart Robert Redfield with news about the virus, a fact the US Congressional Research Service recorded. On the same day China informed some other countries and the WHO, as well as Hong Kong, Macao and Taiwan.

That means the first foreign journalist's question only came two full weeks after the US government was informed and just one week before Wuhan was locked down on January 23rd: certainly not 20:20 vision.

The New York Times was fast enough though to come up with a political narrative, only one week after the Wuhan lock down. In double quick time, under the heading *China's Old Habits Delayed Fight* on February 1, it had established that, "At critical turning points, Chinese authorities put secrecy and order ahead of openly confronting the growing crisis and risking public alarm or political embarrassment".

To protect people right away, what matters most in a pandemic anywhere? Simply, what is it? China discovered the answer within two weeks on January 11th by establishing the virus's genome sequence in record time. Essential for finding a vaccine and other medical treatments, the genome discovery was immediately shared with the world. This is hardly a sign of secrecy at critical turning points. Focusing on politics revealed the *Times'* priorities and limitations.

From such political platforms spread other narratives that blamed censorship, suppression of free speech and other ideological memes: none medical or scientific. That was covered largely from panicky social media posts and dramatic videos of crowded Wuhan hospital corridors. Very similar scenes would appear in New York a couple of months later: superficial and designed to stir emotions, not understanding so people worldwide could be prepared and spared.

Media obsession with Western ideological memes in its China coverage greatly contributed to fatalities when COVID did take off in the West in late March. People were not equipped to handle it. They did not know what to do nor how seriously to take the virus. Were any in the West prepared by their media for that, medically or economically?

For anyone believing China hid crucial COVID information or misled the US and world community, stop to think for a moment about two things. First, didn't China's dramatic overnight lockdown of 11 million people in Wuhan indicate something was terribly wrong? This was unprecedented in world history. Second, the rest of China instantly took extensive mitigation measures to try to contain the spread. They took it very seriously. Again that was remarkable, in the literal sense.

What more did anyone need to know to be prepared? Certainly not in East Asia or the Chinese diaspora from Prato to London: someone in Western governments must have picked up that. The unfortunate truth is that most of the Western media and its users did not take the health risk seriously. There was a sense that it could not infect them.

Two Experienced Views

Blame China became the media narrative. No mention of their own shortcomings that left people worldwide with insufficient information to take seriously the preventive measures WHO had prescribed on February 24, 2020.

Instead, focus on the origins, which no foreign journalists had done at the time, even though China had informed governments, beginning with the US, in the first week of January; and swiftly shared the genome sequence and other data with the medical community worldwide in the second week.

Querying whether the blame game was realistic, Pulitzer Prize Winner Ian Johnson wrote a dissenting opinion in October 2020. Having had half a year to reach a well-considered and balanced judgment, he wrote that, "a counterargument is that these concerns were initially vague. Taking concrete action required reliable knowledge about a new virus. It took experts time to figure out that it could be transmitted from person to person".

The work had to be done thoroughly not based on initially vague concerns or unreliable knowledge. Otherwise, there could be unnecessary panic, effort wasted and time lost from overhasty rushes down dead-end rabbit holes. Ian is the *doyen* of Western China journalists, with more than two decades under his belt. I have known him well since the mid-1990s and would trust his assessment over those that rushed to judgment with neat, instant analysis, within two weeks of belatedly asking the first press conference question about COVID.

Life isn't like that, as any objective, experienced journalist knows. A complex story is like a photographic print. Only slowly does it take shape in the developing solution, just a few unrelated spots at a time until it is finally identifiable, though still not complete. It all takes time, often much time.

Ian was not uncritical. Bits of the print negative disturbed him. "Some of its [China's] responses to the pandemic were troubling: separated families unable to reunite for weeks on end because provinces set up travel restrictions, villages barricaded like medieval fortresses, and housing compounds run as if under martial law", he wrote.

However, he concluded, "the crucial public health measures … the focused lockdown at the pandemic's epicenter, the clear government directives, the masks and social distancing — *were effective and became standard procedure around the world"*. Mitigation measures worked. China got things done.

In Ian's opinion, the measures worked partly because, again contrary to the consensus narrative, "Compliance in China was overwhelmingly voluntary. Beijing's streets were empty not because people were forced to stay home (as was the case in Italy and Spain) but because they mostly accepted the leadership's message". It was the same in Shanghai during SARS. People knew their history, and saw it being repeated. Therefore, take personal action, trust the government, stay at home and have as little contact with others as possible.

Furthermore, "The feeling I got in China was that after initial panic most people accepted the government's efforts, especially as reports of the pandemic came in from abroad, where the bungling was many times worse", Ian Johnson wrote, "by March critique of government censorship seemed *passé*".

Peter Hessler, like Johnson, is another veteran China observer. His words too should be noted. Standing out from the Western pack, he has written the best English reportage set in modern China since the mid-1990s. He also has an interesting insight into what experts in pandemics thought.

Unlike generalist journalists, experts "weren't focused on the government's early missteps", Hessler found when he spoke with them outside China. "It is unrealistic to expect that any country could have stopped this particular virus at its source", Johns Hopkins epidemiologist Jennifer Nuzzo told Hessler. She went on to say in October's *New Yorker,* "I tend to take a charitable view of countries that are at the beginning stage of epidemics". Wuhan was par for the course.

Another expert, Wafaa El-Sadr, director at Columbia University's global-health centre, pointed out to Hessler that Chinese scientists had quickly sequenced the virus's genome and made it available to researchers worldwide on January 11th. "I honestly think that they had a horrific situation in Wuhan and they were able to contain it", she said. "There were mistakes early on, but they did act, and they shared fast". Shared fast? That was not part of Donald Trump's revised version or the standard Western view, which blamed China for hiding information and not sharing.

A rule in good journalism is "Don't jump to conclusions". In the blame game, it is the opposite. Jump in fast to shape the story before facts emerge or people get bored. First impressions count: control "the narrative". Some did with an interest that was not in discovering the truth.

So who to believe? Generalist journalists with no medical expertise or two globally-recognised experts each of whom said the same thing and were interviewed by two leading experienced China writers? Shouldn't we believe the scientists? Of course, we should, not for their scientific work alone but for communicating it clearly to the rest of the world.

The medical media did much good work, in stark contrast to most of the mainstream media's coverage of China's COVID. Some was very fast indeed. Editors like Richard Horton of *The Lancet,* founded in 1823, and Eric Rubin of the *New England Journal of Medicine,* founded in 1812, brought all the expertise and trust they had with Chinese doctors to provide the highest quality ground-breaking research, which then became the news, for those who wished to listen. *The Lancet's* two initial papers in late January provided enough detailed information for generalist journalists and readers to grasp what was happening: by the end of January 2020.

Epidemics spread rapidly but knowledge unfortunately builds only slowly. To combat this, the medical and scientific media has done sterling work since January 2020. Not just in print but also on television and social media, providing information, interpretation and clear advice. Far from being incomprehensible and dull, it provided gripping instalments of the decade's greatest murder mystery.

Front-Line Reporting

One front-line account came from German doctor Ewelina Biskup of Berlin's Max Plank Institute, who has worked in Shanghai's Tongji University hospital since 2011. What makes her March 24th podcast (subsequently published in the *New England Journal of Medicine*) especially interesting is that it is not about what happened in Wuhan. The Wuhan angle had been covered to death, though generally not in much depth.

Biskup talked about the response in the rest of China: specifically in Shanghai, barely 400 miles downstream from Wuhan on the Yangzi River. That was original, most informative and critical to understand what could happen next.

Why had the virus not ravaged the rest of China, where lived another 1.38 billion people. That was the big question. The answer was not just critical for China but for the rest of the world: to know that the spread could be prevented and how.

For Western readers, viewers or listeners, the podcast could not have been timelier. As a Western doctor, with unique access, experience, insight and trust, she talked about the mechanics of China controlling the virus, day-to-day. This would answer Miss Lam's question in full, if anyone in Calgary or the rest of Canada were listening.

Surely journalists and their editors were following COVID podcasts and certainly the world-renown *New England Journal of Medicine?* By then, I was: not even a journalist but a tourist in Bali. Chinese media regularly carried interviews with it, as they did with *The Lancet* and other peer-reviewed scientific journals. Ignoring the specialist media was like anyone in finance or economics ignoring IMF or OECD reports in a crisis — unthinkable.

Dr Biskup said, in my edited summary:

"In Shanghai everybody was under quarantine and strict social distancing. This gave doctors a lot of comfort to know that there was little chance of being infected by patients. Even if there were any suspicion, patients were immediately transferred to COVID-designated clinics. Physicians not in the front line or who did not treat designated COVID-19 patients had barely any contact with those even suspected of infection. There were designated clinics in the town, well advertised; every potential patient, every citizen, knew them.

All other clinics worked pretty much routinely. Even if a patient arrived at the clinic there were several gatekeepers — literally — to check again temperature and basic symptoms. Patients then saw a nurse, who did more intensive epidemiological and symptomatical analysis. Only when everything was negative did patients see a doctor about their non-COVID condition.

Clinically, doctors were well-informed. Communication from the government down to physicians, potential patients and society was effective. Clinical guidelines were developed and updated constantly. We receive through social media and our own channels (specific medical channels on *WeChat*) updates almost every day.

We were not allowed to leave our homes without a mask, let alone go to a show or any public space without a mask. Every entrance to every public space and residential area was protected by temperature checks, registration and our electronic QR code that we have to update every week. This QR code allows us into specific places. There is a whole algorithm behind it.

(Continued)

(Continued)

Doctors were free to choose if they wished to help at the front line or not [again voluntary]. Many of them did; we saw huge solidarity.

I did a study of 450 physicians who were under constant fear of infection. They were not on the front line but supported the rest of the population medically, with quarantine or treatment. About 20% stated they needed psychological support during that time, and I was happy to see that 18% answered that they actually used it.

The *panic and mass hysteria observed all around the world was not very present here* in China. This helped healthcare professionals work systematically, allowing them to focus on patient care.

The use of digital medicine and telemedicine increased. Many of the follow-ups and consultations were immediately transferred into digital tele-bases. These had been used before but were much more exploited during the crisis. Some 45% of doctors said that they see telemedicine as a good alternative in the future, so this is a positive development."

The podcast aired on March 24, 2020, the very week US and UK cases first skyrocketed. Could more have been said? Reread it and ask whether by the end of March 2020 you knew all this detail, let alone how to control and prevent COVID? Miss Lam, like billions of others, would have been better informed and spared more than half a year of anxiety if journalists had used Dr Biskup's on-the-ground expertise.

Her account however hardly went viral. It barely registered outside medical circles. The global general public was largely left in the dark. This was not the first time the public had been poorly informed about China.

The right to know cuts both ways. The public is entitled to know from both governments and media. Balance was once a pre-requisite of every story. Apart from giving a much better all-round picture, the idea was that even if some media were economical with the truth others, from another perspective, filled in the missing angle or information. As the mainstream media has narrowed, so has diversity of news sources. Credence is given to those within the consensus information universe but not to those outside it.

Then there are the false alarms. From my observation post in financial markets, I lost count of how many Chinese property market collapses, banking and other looming crises the Western media predicted, which never happened. Although it still failed to anticipate China's one major property collapse in 2007–2008! Indeed inadequate reporting had been increasingly common in the last decade, and for some since Gordon Chiang published *The Coming Collapse of China* in 2001. So why did much of the mainstream media inform its audience so poorly about COVID?

Chapter 17

Media Changes

Nation Shall Speak Peace Unto Nation

BBC Motto 1927

Long gone are the days when *BBC* Director General Lord Reith talked of such lofty principles. The *BBC's* motto of "Nation Shall Speak Peace Unto Nation", was his creed, especially relevant after the First World War: peace not war. The mission was to educate, entertain and inform. To bring together people from different classes, regions, religions, occupations, educational backgrounds, nations and worlds: to inform and create understanding.

Almost one century later, veteran investigative journalist John Pilger asserts that, "Journalism has surrendered. It has given up trying to set down the record accurately. China — where is the evidence of Xinjiang etc? We must have the evidence". Just as truth is called the first casualty of war, so too is evidence in the era of opinion journalism.

Journalism has changed: a reflection of society itself. Newspapers have become Viewspapers: views not new facts lead. This is what used to be called editorialising, and strictly limited to the editorial page. News was news, it should be impartial, accurate and complete: not selected to support a partisan viewpoint, that is propaganda.

199

Public broadcasters now must compete with much more heavily funded partisan private channels. These have no interest in balance, objectivity or even often accuracy. To sell advertising, they want clicks, likes and followers.

Papers of record, like *The Times* of London, record no more. They have become weapons in political and cultural wars. The *Daily Telegraph*, once respected for breadth and quality of news, no matter its ideological editorial stance, is now largely partisan. In the opposite direction, fake news migrated from politics to mainstream journalism and especially social media.

What has changed in reporting? The basic standards of accuracy, balance, perspective, context and news judgment have changed. Old strict rules have been ignored.

Rules

Reuters News Agency stayed in business as an independent firm or trust for more than one and a half centuries. That was because of an obsession with standards, rules and accuracy. Now it is the second name in the North American-owned and increasingly run *Thomson Reuters*, though still called *Reuters* by many journalists, a tribute to earlier traditions and standards.

Drilled into new recruits at six-week boot camps, *Reuters'* Rules and culture were reinforced by constant retelling of *Reuters* folklore, passed down by one generation to the next, often imparted with cutting asides never forgotten. A taste of what lay ahead came during my first week in Fleet Street.

The gentlest of the Four Horsemen of the Apocalypse, as the four editors who ran the *Reuters* "file" 24/7, 365 days a year, were known, announced at the boot camp we would first learn what makes a good *Reuters* story. His gentle manner belied a very serious and steely intent.

Each of the four had very different personalities but all shared a fanatical devotion to *Reuters* Rules. They guarded them with their lives.

The Horseman read out a story from that morning's *Daily Mail*, complete with breathless prose, colourful adjectives and speedy adverbs about the glamorous Davina Sheffield, then the current companion of Prince Charles. "Was this a good story", he asked? "Oh yes", one overexcited trainee exclaimed. The rest of us shrank: we suspected not by *Reuters* standards.

"Really?" the Horseman replied, more as a statement than a question. He stopped. "This", pausing for effect, "is a great story". He continued slowly, "Just six words long". Further pause: "Dallas, Nov 22 — US President John F. Kennedy Shot. That was a world beater. The best story I have ever read. Being first on the big stories requires training, great experience and application. It isn't luck, though you will be very lucky if you ever get the chance to write such a story".

Intimidated into silence we became aware of how much we had to learn and how few, if any, could truly succeed. Humility was not a quality we nine graduate trainees possessed in much measure. Steadily, relentlessly humility and professionalism were drummed into us.

Cutting comments on the sub-editing desks introduced the finer points of reporting. One unfortunate trainee sourced his story to a "usually reliable source". With withering sarcasm, Hong Kong desk head Barry "Bazza" Simpson asked if that meant the source was sometimes unreliable and that all others were unreliable.

My own very public lesson was Frankfurt Gold. The whole of the 4th floor of 85 Fleet Street seemed to fall silent and prick up its ears when the finance desk editor Mike Cooling was on the prowl. He stopped behind my chair at the long editing desk. "Who did Frankfurt Gold?" he growled slowly and very deliberately. "I did", I barely squeaked as I shrank into my chair. "Put out a correction", he ordered. A correction was a humiliation for *Reuters*, and especially for the journalist concerned.

I had mixed up the dateline, slug (title) and numbers of takes (pages) on a report I had sub-edited from Frankfurt about a gold conference in Berlin by a US paper out of Bonn. All very confusing but no excuses were allowed. Accuracy means accuracy, I quickly learned: double check every small detail. *Reuters'* credibility for accuracy was on the line. There was much to learn.

In the search for accuracy, information had to be corroborated by at least one other source: accuracy above everything. *Reuters* also required that every line should be easily understood; and not just in London, *Reuters'* long-time home, but also by the New Delhi housewife, the Idaho farmer, the Santiago milkman and one other diverse citizen of planet earth, whom I have forgotten. This was news for a global audience.

Gone were the days when British cyclist Tommy Simpson would head the *Reuters Tour de France* report. Even when he finished 59th in that day's stage, while France's Jacques Anquetil, despite seemingly setting records day after day, only appeared in the second paragraph: parochial.

In similar vein, when Marilyn Monroe exclaimed she "felt like a million dollars", the London sub-editor, who inserted into the story the currency conversion in pounds sterling, to two decimal places, was told to stop being so parochial: well that was a polite translation of what was said. Everyone knew what a million dollars meant by the early 1970s. This was the end of empire and the start of a global journalism, not just of reporting but of readers and viewers.

I trained at *Reuters* in the 1970s. Each word was carefully scrutinised, potential meanings examined to eradicate any confusion, redundant words eliminated. *Reuters'* Rules were considerably harder to follow than those of competitors but saved many a slip and red face. Credibility had a high market value: literally *Reuters* could charge more for its services. We would joke about having to go the extra mile to establish the facts of every story and each statement but our motto defiantly was, "Last but Right". Not that last was acceptable either.

The Holy Grail was accuracy: at speed. Everything had to be checked and double checked: at speed. Unless a named source with a direct quotation appeared in the first paragraph, two sources were needed.

Guarding against manipulation was paramount. Fact-checking alone was not enough. Much of what passes for news is clearly self-serving, only a favourable opinion or view seeking an audience. This isn't news it is propaganda. So are planted stories.

Named sources were the cardinal rule of *Reuters*. Even after Ian Mackenzie and Peter Griffiths in Beijing received a rare "Herogram" that read, "Story leading all world papers this a.m", meaning very well done in restrained, terse *Reuterese*, a few minutes later they received a stiff warning: "Never again send story without named source in first para". They had broken 1976's top world story. The Gang of Four, including Mao's widow Jiang Qing, had been arrested. *Reuters'* Rules applied to everything and everyone, never forget. There are rules, for a good reason.

Rules though are also made to be broken in exceptional circumstances. In this case, the news had to be smuggled out of China through a trusted source: it could not be sent over the open wire or telex. Far too sensitive, it could spark regional fighting, even plunge China into another civil war — as *Reuters* almost did in Nigeria. The censure was a warning not to get into the habit. That was drilled into us. The clear message was we should never even dream of doing such a thing.

Errors, News Judgment and Sniff Tests

Balance and the sins of omission were equally important. During COVID three good news stories managed to evade most Western media. Was bias involved? Was it selective, partisan or blinkered in what it published? Poor news judgment, certainly thorough scrutiny was lacking.

The origins of COVID obsessed some Western governments and media. Therefore when the US CDC reported in *Clinical Infectious Diseases* that research showed COVID was present in the US by December 13, 2019 it should have been picked up and followed, for this was two whole weeks before China said it knew of the virus.

The US CDC report raised all sorts of questions about the origins of the virus. This didn't mean it hadn't originated in China but it did mean the virus had been in the US more than one month before the first US case had been reported, maybe even earlier, possibly earlier than in China. The *Wall Street Journal* ran an article but it never became part of the mainstream story. It didn't fit?

A second instance has been mentioned in the last chapter. Some 650 million Chinese travelled throughout China during the national holiday week: there were no new COVID outbreaks. There was no blip let alone spike in subsequent new cases. These remained flat as a pancake for the rest of October and November.

Imagine if that happened in the US or Europe over Thanksgiving or Christmas. It would be front-page news, leading all TV news bulletins, trumpeting the rewards for taking strict measures. Surely this was useful information to people everywhere deciding whether lockdowns were worth the trouble?

A third misjudgement is that no Chinese caught COVID in Prato, Italy. That should have been worth a look in early 2020. In fact *Politico Europe* did. However, *The New York Times*, which presumably knew Prato, as it had run a recent, long story from Prato on December 5, 2019, missed this European vindication of Chinese traditional mitigation measures, so did everyone else.

Finally, there are Sniff Tests. In financial markets there is a constant flow of information, deliberate misinformation, half-truths and rumour. Journalism is no different. Old Hands know to apply the sniff test to anything that looks irregular. Does it smell strange? Is something odd, out of place, missing or does not add up completely? With much inexperience in Asia and especially China, sniff tests are often all there is to detect fake from truth.

Errors of judgment existed long before COVID. A couple of relatively recent ones raise the question of how did either of these ever get broadcast, let alone become stated as facts. Was there ever a sniff test?

In 2019, a group of 39 people suffocated in a container from Zeebrugge in Belgium to Essex in England. *BBC's Newsnight* said the dead were Chinese. It went on to speculate why 39 people would want to "escape" from such a "regime" (China). It also explained there was no news from China as the victims' parents would be too frightened to report it to Communist officials.

There was absolutely no evidence the victims were from China, except for the police "giving a steer". Facial looks were not a valid criterion in *Reuters*. Bazza Simpson, a burly bear of a man, would have gone berserk if that had been offered as a source: an unnamed police officer "giving a steer"? They looked Chinese! Goodness this is lazy journalism at its most ignorant and irresponsible.

The serious journalism question is why hurry and rush to judgment? Why even raise the question of motivations behind the "escape" before the facts were known. Maybe the *BBC* should dig into it first? Usually, that not only establishes greater accuracy but unearths new information, so no need to worry about falling behind on the story. It may help get ahead. Would viewers be any poorer for awaiting the truth to emerge?

The dead, it turned out, were not Chinese. All were Vietnamese — and the victims' families had not been afraid to report their suspicions to Communist officials.

My instant reaction was to query the report but dismissed this as my frequent response after years of seeing inaccurate reports about China. Why my doubt? Simply put, China just isn't that poor anymore. This was 2019. Yes, in similar circumstances 58 Chinese perished in Dover in

2000 and 23 drowned cockling in Morecambe Bay in 2004 — but in 2019's China people were much better off. I doubted if any were still taking such risks.

I did wonder if the migrants might be Vietnamese, Laotian or Cambodian, whose incomes were very low like China's in the early 2000s. However, I don't know Indo-China well enough, so could not judge.

Was anyone at *Newsnight* qualified to judge whether the people were Chinese, let alone whether this was likely in today's booming China where unemployment is not normally an issue and incomes much higher? Did anyone have the nose to sniff? Did anyone stop to think?

The *BBC* was not the last to mistake Vietnamese for Chinese. *CNN* did the same in 2022 when Michael McCaul, the future chair of the US Congress foreign affairs committee, lambasted the Chinese delegation for not standing to applaud Vlodomir Zelensky's address to the World Economic Forum in Davos. McCaul posted a video he took at the meeting showing three or four seated officials, while all around him stood.

CNN's headline ran "McCaul: Chinese Delegation Refused to Clap for Zelensky". McCaul's tweet carried the charge and said that, "They have blood on their hands and we cannot let them get away with this". There was only one problem with the story, the officials were not Chinese but Vietnamese, including a Deputy Prime Minister.

If its journalists did not know any of the delegates from China or Vietnam, surely *CNN* could have checked before reporting the claim? In the 21st century believing "they all look the same" is no defence, even if still a common Western reaction to East Asians. The second *CNN* example is even much more damning.

Live ammunition, petrol bombs and water cannons mark violent escalation in Hong Kong protests. That was *CNN's* headline on August 25, 2019 about the latest in three months of protests that had "rocked the city". Despite being in the headline, there was only one mention of petrol bombs in the entire online version. Their significance seems to have been minimal, to the point of disappearing but it was a great headline, which is what most people read and retain.

"Petrol bombs" did not appear until the very end of the fourth paragraph. Along with the words that a "smaller group" of protesters "threw bricks and petrol bombs into police ranks", as if that made it of little consequence, barely enough to get a mention. The obvious unanswered question was who acted first. Nothing was said about who acted first.

Next day, *CNN* issued a correction, after taking until almost 6 pm Hong Kong time to correct the story. The formal correction only appeared at the foot of the long story, not at the much more read top, which is where it appeared in the first place — bad practice.

"Correction: A homepage headline referring to this story and posted briefly on Aug. 25 *inaccurately said Hong Kong police had used petrol bombs. In fact, police deployed water cannons and drew guns; protestors threw petrol bombs*".

It did not say which occurred first — protesters threw petrol bombs or police used water cannons? To say the least, this was being economical with the truth. The word "briefly" seemed a stretch: it appeared for almost a whole working day. The corrected story made no sense, if this were a full correction.

Apart from dropping the words "Live ammunition", in favour of the catchier opening, "A gun shot", the headline remained the same: *A gun shot, petrol bombs and water cannons mark violent escalation in Hong Kong protests*. Still leading the story were the words, "A Hong Kong police officer fired a live shot into the air as protesters squared off against police armed with water cannons". A new top photo showed, "police officers points (sic) a gun as clashes between pro-democracy protestors and police escalated on Sunday evening".

The second and third paragraphs of the original story were removed, for reasons not explained. The deleted paragraphs had said, "Four police officers were filmed drawing their guns after demonstrators were seen chasing them with metal pipes, according to *CNN* affiliate iCable". This would sound like important details to an experienced, objective journalist, not something to be cut, indeed well-worthy of prominence.

A new sub-heading was added. This said, *Hong Kong protesters use petrol bombs against police,* but the story's only other mention of petrol bombs was at the very end of the fourth paragraph. There was no more detail. It did not explicitly say that water cannon and tear gas were used only after protesters threw petrol bombs at the police. Read that sentence again. There was no other reference to petrol bombs in the 1,200-word *corrected* story. It did add the police saying that 21 officers were injured: 21 police injured. If that had happened in London ..... This still left many important questions unanswered.

Watching in London the original report, I was shocked. I had assumed throughout the protests that Beijing was trying to avoid at all costs such an escalation from peaceful demonstrations to deadly violence. This was precisely what China's enemies would want to provoke, raising spectres of 1989 and charges of "a regime killing its own children": a propaganda field day.

Fortunately, the world did not have to rely only on *CNN*. German TV *DW* and maybe others picked up news agencies' copy. A few others provided some of the detail to understand better the *CNN* story. Below the heading, *Shot fired, water cannon deployed after petrol-bomb attack* (note "*after* petrol-bomb attack"), *DW* reported that on the night of August 25th", A hardcore group then took over a major road in ... Tsuen Wan district, erecting makeshift roadblocks and digging up bricks from the pavements. Some also threw petrol bombs at the police. To try to regain control, authorities hoisted large banners to warn protesters of the impending use of tear gas and water cannon".

Confirming this, in a section entitled *Molotov cocktails thrown*, *DW* used a *Reuters* photo. Under it, *DW* wrote, "Police responded with water cannons after protesters threw petrol bombs". The photo showed two long plumes of flame, with a billowing cloud of smoke at the head of each and a long tail of fire.

So what was the story that most people would need to know? That a surrounded policeman had fired into the air one warning shot, which hurt no one, or that some protesters threw Molotov cocktails at the police in a major violent escalation of the protests?

Reuters' Rules would have led with the most significant news — police were fire bombed. In any country that would have been the lead. In the *Reuters* pyramid of sequencing, with the most important information first, fire-bombing police would definitely lead, a warning shot would follow. But it didn't when it happened in Hong Kong, China. That though was not the end of the story.

China formally protested. *CNN* investigated. *CNN* had to admit it was wrong and the *opposite* was true. Diesel bombs, the term *CNN* used on air, Molotov cocktails according to *Reuters*, had been thrown at police: quite an error, not the other way round.

To make sense of it all, it fell to *China Daily* on August 29th to cast light on the puzzle. It wrote, "*CNN* has apologized for its "erroneous" reporting after *falsely blaming* Hong Kong police for the actions of protesters during the illegal protest in Tsuen Wan, Hong Kong on the night of August 25.

In a letter to the police, *CNN*'s Hong Kong bureau chief Roger Clark admitted that a news story headlined, "Police use petrol bombs and water cannons against Hong Kong protesters" on the *CNN* website was "erroneous" and said that it was later "replaced".

The petrol bombs, as revealed later in an original video clip, were hurled by protesters at police officers. *CNN*, in its letter, failed to disclose how the mistake was made.

In a daily news conference on Wednesday, Kong Wing-cheung, senior superintendent of the police public relations branch, referred to a "widely circulated tampered video suggesting petrol bombs were thrown by police in the direction of protesters". That is presumably the video I saw on *CNN*: fake news.

Imagine if this had been in the West. Would petrol bombing the police be taken so lightly or such media coverage tolerated, say in London or Washington? Yet, no Western media took *CNN* to task. As for *China Daily's* accuracy, I saw no challenge. As a former journalist in Hong Kong, I was still puzzled. Plenty did not add up, including two key questions. (1) *Cui bono*, who benefited from the fake news? (2) Wasn't anyone at *CNN* qualified to do the sniff test?

Deception and Plants

During COVID, three stories in particular caught the eye — The Wuhan Lab Theory, *Bloomberg's* Unseen Classified Report and Three Anonymous Officials Story and the *ABC-Channel 12* NCMI Cataclysmic Event Story. All looked fishy to me. Nonetheless, they all received plenty of coverage, successfully planting negative ideas about China that could stick forever. The Wuhan Lab story most of all. Yet that had to be disowned.

US intelligence agencies evidently feared the lack of proof about the Wuhan Lab was undermining their collective effort against China. Allies were getting nervous. Veracity was being questioned. Frankly, they were making fools of themselves.

Falling in line, the main Wuhan Lab promoter US Secretary of State Pompeo dropped the idea. Quietly, he told *Breitbart News*, co-founded by Steve Bannon Donald Trump's former chief strategist, that COVID's source was not a Wuhan Lab. Choosing the alt-right's leading website, rather than the mainstream media and over the weekend, worked.

There were no hostile questions and not many journalists around that day to dig into it. Few in the mainstream even highlighted the reversal as evidence of US skulduggery. Basically, it was buried with no consequences or cost but with much credit in the Bank of Conspiracy Theories.

Indeed, many mainstream journalists had bought into the idea, which they sought to perpetuate. *CNN*, while reporting Pompeo's correction, reported that (again unnamed), "experts still believe the virus began in China, it just wasn't in a Wuhan Lab". Again there was no source, no evidence, a mere unsupported assertion.

This was hardly surprising coming from Pompeo, the former head of the Central Intelligence Agency (CIA), part of the US intelligence community that in 2003 had misled its own Secretary of State Colin Powell to tell bare-faced lies to the whole world at the United Nations. US intelligence gave Powell knowingly fake mock-ups of weapon carriers and circumstantial evidence to prove that Iraq had weapons of mass destruction. Iraq had to be stopped, it must be invaded.

This vital evidence, we now know, was false. After this, one would think no self-respecting journalist or media outlet would trust any intelligence agency without hard proof. However, the Colin Powell lesson was forgotten when it came to COVID assertions and China.

The highpoint of journalistic error, by *Reuters'* Rules that is, was *Bloomberg's* March 2020 story that US intelligence accused China of playing down the COVID crisis. American officials reportedly "believe" China has been underreporting the total number of cases and deaths. Anything is possible, so where is the evidence, the proof? That is classified information. Hmm! Names, none. Hmmm, hmmmm: the name is Bond, James Bond. Scrape Bazza off the ceiling someone. Yet it was taken seriously.

The *Guardian* reported that these were the, "conclusions of a classified report from the intelligence community to the White House". These were "revealed to *Bloomberg*" by not one or even two but "three anonymous officials": obviously very thorough reporting. The officials "declined to detail its contents".

Oh dear. No named source, no evidence detailed but a willing media hungry for a scoop. This was repeated widely as truth because it came from "intelligence sources". In decades past, this was not a term used by credible journalists, who cared for their reputations or integrity. They did their own investigations.

No matter its origin or veracity, some US politicians sought any data or information to cast doubt on China's COVID numbers and account. They actively did the rounds with the many US intelligence agencies, urging them to look harder (or more imaginatively). There was no need to mention the rewards of promotion and larger budgets for favourite projects or causes.

This bounty hunting presumably alarmed some in US intelligence. They had learned the danger of "sexed-up" intelligence, as Tony Blair's adviser Alistair Campbell called the exaggerated "information" before the invasion of Iraq. Subsequent decisions could be made based on such faulty information: keep it real, otherwise it could backfire.

No more was heard from the three anonymous officials, though another fake story was even bolder. When the blame game over COVID first started, major US network *ABC* and Israel's *Channel 12* splashed the news that the US National Center for Medical Intelligence (NCMI) had been aware of the virus since the second week of November. That was more than six weeks before China warned of it: quite a splash.

Furthermore, the NCMI, medical intelligence, had published the details of the Wuhan outbreak in an intelligence report. That clinched it, an intelligence report. There was more.

"Analysts concluded it could be a cataclysmic event", a source said. Great adjective cataclysmic: instant emotional engagement, fear tingling. Early November, long before China recorded its pneumonia of unknown origin: second week, convincing detail.

Proof positive China had long covered up the virus and the deaths. There must be more cases, some possibly earlier still, things could be out of control. Great story, with "cataclysmic event" an even greater sound bite: there was only one problem. This was all fake. How do we know?

In a bizarre announcement, the US Defense Department issued a statement from Colonel R. Shane Day, Director of the NCMI saying, "Media reporting about the existence/release of a National Center for Medical Intelligence Coronavirus-related product/assessment in November of 2019 is not correct. No such NCMI product exists". Complete fabrication, no such product, it never existed: a total lie. Who is so brazen as to invent a NCMI report?

Unsurprisingly there was no comment from the White House. Much more disturbing was the absence of any detailed media investigation into what had happened. Why not? What was that all about?

The simplest explanation is that the people who actually have to fight wars, the US Defence Department, pulled rank. They declared these stories fake, presumably as they undermined US security and credibility. Potentially they could stoke the fires of future conflicts if left unchecked. This was serious and required direct rebuttal from the very top.

Did any of the confirmations of fake news raise doubts with the public about other stories? Did they trust their media any less? Most likely not: anyway the fakes had served their purpose, they had planted more seeds of deception. Those who wanted to believe them probably still did; and with it their negative views of China.

Control of the media story is but one part of a widening battle between the once dominant West and the re-emergence of previously major civilisations. Lord Reith's words that "Nation Shall Speak Peace Unto Nation", which became the *BBC's* motto, have never been more necessary since the Cold War. Yet they increasingly sound distant, arcane and naive.

The solution to fake or misleading news is obvious. Return to the much stricter, self-imposed reporting rules of leaders like *Reuters* and the

BBC half a century ago. Otherwise do not use the story: dig deeper. What are the chances today? Too much is at stake, both for media owners and journalists to change.

Former US Labor Secretary Professor Robert Reich pointed to the problem in the US, "Top editors and reporters, usually based in New York and Washington, want to be accepted into the circles of the powerful — not only for sources of news but also because such acceptance is psychologically [and financially] seductive. It confers a degree of success. But once accepted, they can't help but begin to see the world through the eyes of the powerful".

COVID added fuel to the fire of Western concern about China but was not the cause. This had been building for a couple of decades, breaking out into occasional flames under Obama and becoming a full firestorm under Trump. The only remaining question is What Now?

What Now?

Chapter 18

The Real China Threat

Our allies aren't following us.

Jeff Immelt, former GE CEO 2021

There is no other China in the whole world.

European executive 2022

Unintended self-arm is the real China Threat to the US. Contested attempts to "Decouple China" technologically and economically, presented first by President Donald Trump and pursued with different language by President Joe Biden, could well boomerang back to hit America in the face not with an economic recession but a global depression.

"A depression like the 1930s but with bells and whistles on it", is how the Professor of Political Economy at King's College, London Shaun Hargreaves Heap described the worst outcome when I first discussed with him the economic reemergence of China, India and the Rest. "If the US and China fail to establish a new world order with the result that all economic decision-making takes place against a backdrop of major and increasing uncertainty there would be dramatically bad economic effects. In other words, the key issue is the orderly management to a new world order".

218 *America as No. 3: Get Real About China, India and the Rest*

Orderly management to a new world order looks less and less clear, to many unlikely, but still not impossible. Whatever the precise road to America becoming No. 3 by mid-century, it is is likely to be very bumpy; and unable to avoid the destination the OECD has predicted.

Like King Canute, the US has ordered the advancing tide to halt. China must encroach no more on US primacy. Wherever it wants, the US will set the rules, starting with high-end technology. The decoupling image is clear.

The China wagon must be unhitched from the US locomotive. Strong arms must detach the troublesome problem, once and for all. Everyone must rally round or face US consequences.

Dangerously, this image of the world economy is very out-dated. China is now so much more than a wagon. The US is no longer the global economic locomotive. Instead, since the 2008 Financial Crisis, China has been the locomotive, responsible for almost one-third of all world economic growth in the decade after the crisis: China contributed to global growth twice as much as the Old World, the US, EU and Japan, combined.

US decouplers' fundamental error originates from believing that their economy is much stronger than China's. Therefore the US can impose its will untrammeled. In their minds, there is no doubt. That has been their belief since young; and has not changed with the times.

Washington only thinks of the damage it could do to China. Not what the harmful consequences could be for the whole world, including America. The China Threat comes not from China but from the damage the US does to itself and the rest of the world through misunderstanding the reality of its actions against China: shooting itself in the foot. Self-harm is the real China Threat.

The Cost of Decoupling

Half a trillion dollars a year: $500 billion is real money, even for a $22 trillion economy. That is the 2021 figure the American Chamber of Commerce in China (Amcham) put on the cost to the US of decoupling China. This assumes half US direct investment in China is withdrawn or impaired. Of course, it could be worse if retaliation escalated, as it likely would in a hot war.

Not only collapsing sales and profits but crippling write offs on US or other Western balance sheets. Total foreign investment in China by 2018 was an estimated $2.1 trillion: maybe one-quarter American. Is that the price the US really wants to pay, another $500 billion?

In Amcham's *least* pessimistic case, US companies' share of world sales would fall 18%. Imagine what that would do to profits, the Dow Jones stock market index, firms' ability to raise new capital and pensions. An 18% hit to sales would hurt greatly immediately but the real damage would be long-term. More about that a little later.

Full or even substantial decoupling could be a watershed, both for the US and its competitors, especially in Asia. From the ruins, it would accelerate the emergence of the New New World that is already underway.

The world's biggest market would largely be lost to the US and others that decoupled China. Asian and other non-Western firms would very happily replace them. Yes, China would lose much too but that is not the point if one's concern is what happens to the West. Sharing deep pain is presumably not the objective.

The immediate impact would be felt in China's retaliation. Not just to US manufactured exports and China sales but US services. Everything from tourism-related hospitality, entertainment and travel to finance, consulting and education (in so many university towns).

Apart from losing their exports to China, firms will suffer the added cost of replacing cheaper Chinese goods. These have helped keep down US inflation and production costs for two decades.

Many are intermediate goods, which go unseen into an increasing number of US-made products. Such details do not feature in the minds of politicians and media. They can only imagine replacing stacked-high, large cardboard boxes full of Made-in-China finished goods, with Made-in-US products: their American Dream.

This overlooks the countless numbers of small Chinese components that the global supply chain delivers to cut costs inside Americans' everyday-purchases. Disrupting supply chains much more than COVID, by removing the unseen cheap Chinese intermediate goods, decoupling would be a silent killer. There is another.

The long-term and potentially terminal threat for US industry is declining Research and Development (R&D) spending. For R&D is the foundation of future corporate growth and competitiveness, which depends mainly on profit, cash flow and sales. As these fall, so, most likely, would R&D spending. For this is the easiest way to cut costs to buttress quarterly financial profit results and company share prices. Yet this is most short-sighted. It is eating one's own seed corn.

On top of the hit to R&D, China is many US firms' best market. They earn in China higher profit margins than anywhere else. It is also the main future growth market for most Western firms: some 70% by one 2021 estimate. There is more bad news.

US loss would be their competitors' gain. If the US went it alone or sanctions were avoided, as they usually are, then revenues and profits would go to competing firms. These would mainly be in Europe, East Asia and China itself: strengthening all.

Those are the corporate losses. What about for ordinary workers and their families? Amcham calculated 167–225,000 US jobs would be lost directly; and of course many more indirectly. Lost aircraft sales alone could be $38–51 billion, annually. Europe's Airbus and China's COMAC would be delighted. Their profits and R&D budgets fattened, making them even more competitive globally.

Boeing estimates the world's largest aircraft market China is worth, up to 2040, some $1.47 trillion. Boeing's considerable share is at risk. Politics have again entered airline purchase decisions. As US–China relations deteriorated in 2022, China increased orders from Airbus, leaving Boeing out in the cold with zero new orders.

Boeing described its outlook as "difficult", even without mentioning that a direct narrow-body short-haul competitor from COMAC is now approved to fly in China. For the first time, a Chinese manufacturer can capture a significant share of the largest aviation market, not to mention those abroad: difficult indeed.

What of the vulnerability of US IT companies like Intel, Texas Instruments and Qualcomm? Respectively they derive 26%, 55% and 60% of their revenues from China. Chinese profits are also very consequential for GM, Apple and US farmers. How much protection will they require and at what cost to taxpayers? Already $51 billion has gone to semiconductor giants, largely Intel.

The knock-on effect to allies or neutral parties in Europe and Asia could be very damaging. Especially in Southeast Asia where Singapore, Malaysia, Vietnam and Thailand are particularly vulnerable.

The numbers speak for themselves. The four countries' exports, as a percentage of GDP, in 2021 were respectively 185%, 131%, 106% and 58%. The world average is 43%. Even the advanced economies would be hit. OECD members Germany and South Korea were 47% and 42% respectively. The target China would be much less affected.

China had only 20% export dependence, well below its 2006 peak of 37% and likely to decline further, while India has a rising 13%. The US has only 10%. They all benefit from being continental size economies with large domestic markets on which they can rely in tough times.

The US decouplers though may not have the last laugh. In the rush to decouple, hawks ignored one cast-iron fact. Previous Western embargoes on the sale of military equipment, space technology and vaccines only made China much stronger: more competitive in the long-run. Why repeat that?

Are big hits to revenues and profits, along with tax subsidies, a price worth paying for an ideological policy that mainstream economists dismiss as ill-founded and very dangerous? Didn't Smoot Hawley's protectionist tariffs, which led to the global disaster of the 1930s Great Depression, teach anything?

Commercial Reality

Decoupling was Trump's signature policy, aiming to defeat enemies and coerce allies to follow. On paper this may seem easy. In fact, it is very difficult. Despite being US policy for five years, quite the opposite has occurred.

Responding to China's bulging economic muscle, Trump imposed bans, fines and tariffs on Chinese goods. The promise was to create more American jobs. This was the greatest attack on free trade since US protectionism in the 1930s or Britain's ban on Indian textile exports in the 19th century.

Trump's ghost still haunts White House China policy. Joe Biden may speak in different tones but words are not matched by major deeds. To distance himself from Trump crudities, he talks of intensifying competition, yet with further bans on Chinese companies Biden acts like Trump; and increasingly more so.

This not only angers Beijing, which wants mutually agreed multilateral trade that has been the cornerstone of world growth since the 1950s but also confuses many US firms. They think they have competed strongly with China for decades. Naturally, they want this to continue. Considerable success is seen from cars and planes to power-generating equipment and avionics, from consumer products to agriculture. Services are the latest sector to open more, yet hostile US–China policy threatens US firms' positions in this largest economic segment of all. There are alternative providers.

Some 210 of the world's largest 250 listed companies operate in China. Most have prospered. Profit margins for high-quality foreign goods in China tend to be fatter and growth rates faster than elsewhere, certainly than in mature low-growth Western markets. China is where the best future growth lies. There is nothing like it in the whole world.

Familiar US names feature prominently among the top 25 foreign firms in China, by stock market value. These include Honeywell, GE, P&G, Dupont, Coca-Cola, J&J, GM, IBM, Prudential, Cisco, Pepsico, Microsoft and Caterpillar.

Europeans Philips, HSBC and Siemens are the world's top three foreign firms in China. Other European and Japanese firms follow: Danone, Estée Lauder, Nestlé and Unilever to SAP, AirProducts, Sony, Honda and Abinbev.

KFC sells more chicken in China than in Colonel Sanders' native land. General Motors in 2021 sold 46% of its vehicles worldwide in China, some 2.9 million compared with 2.3 million in the US. Cummins sells roughly 40% of its engines in China. China is Apple's third-largest market, accounting for a growing 20% of revenues. They are all there for a good reason.

Foreign firms' revenue growth in China is expected to be more than anywhere else over the next three to five years. So said 70% of Shanghai American Chamber members in 2021. Not only US, European and Japanese companies benefit increasingly from China. So do many others. China's largest independent mobile advertising network is a joint-venture by India's first unicorn start up InMobi. Southeast Asian agribusiness giant Wilmar made half its 2020 edible oil sales in China: some $28 billion.

Foreign presence in China continues to grow, though some paused in 2022 after the US responded to Russia's invasion of Ukraine with trade sanctions, while cutting off the country from the global financial transactions system SWIFT. Some feared China could be next. Many cannot believe this is happening and await further developments. Some consider other locations — though few can match China, except at the low value-added end of production where even Chinese firms are relocating to lower-cost countries or automating with robots.

Guangdong province alone had 179,300 foreign registered enterprises in 2019. Nationally there were one million: why? "Who could afford to lose this market that will be home to 800 million middle-income consumers by 2035?" a Chinese official explained. Withdrawing from China comes at a cost: for some far too great a cost. Only foreign governments' law would force most to withdraw.

Disentangling all threads of trade and investment is nigh impossible; and certainly not cheap. Made-in-America products would simply be more expensive, adding to Americans' cost of living. Tariffs on Chinese goods (many made by US-owned companies) are either largely passed on to American consumers or profit is taken away from shareholders. This is what Trump imposed and Biden has largely retained.

US manufacturing has fallen behind in many areas. Heavier investment by others is the main reason. Firms, notably from China or Southeast Asia, have upgraded to the latest and most efficient technology. Often, the US did not; and simply has to accept there are some things it does not make as cheaply or even at all anymore.

After COVID and Ukraine, strategically important goods understandably will be made more at home: everywhere. These though should not be a long list, if limited to genuine security concerns. Again, they will probably be at prices often much higher than competitors and consumers pay in the rest of the world.

Think 5G where Huawei equipment is an estimated 30% cheaper than that of its two European competitors. Then consider 6G, where Huawei is already a leader in patent registration. Exclusion is a hefty tax on consumers. How many such surcharges can voters bear in times of higher price inflation and stagnant or no incomes? Politicians should take note. Let go, and enjoy the cost benefits of free trade instead of expensive self-harming protectionism.

There are some 70,000 US firms in China. That number is unlikely to shrink considerably simply because the US President and Congress so wish. Not judging by the immediate corporate reactions: government fiat and coercion will be needed to enforce decoupling. Why? Without access to the China market's scale, lower costs and dynamism, foreign firms are at a competitive disadvantage globally.

China, the Workshop of the World, has the largest manufacturing base, the most skilled workers and the most industrial clusters: all-powerful magnets. Present in all 360 industrial categories, unlike the US or Europe, China now has everything, starting with the legendary China Price: significantly cheaper than the West.

China's private sector innovation and competitiveness can offer prices impossible to ignore. In newer fields, China's manufacturing costs can initially be only half those in the West: 30–40% cheaper is not uncommon (Prologue: *China Cost*). These much-lower prices give buyers unbeatable value, building China's market share at Western expense, a self-reinforcing loop.

Chinese suppliers have long worked on razor-thin margins, even accepting initial losses to get a foot in the door to prove their mettle. Indeed it is a centuries-old Chinese business strategy. Thin profit margins cut prices. That might seem like bad news but not when they create a significant entry barrier that deters less capable, ambitious or daring firms. Demand then increases; and with it long-term profits.

The equation is simple. Foreign firms get lower prices while Chinese suppliers learn global best production practices: a free education. These then create ever-improving quality, which generates even more business and profit for both: symbiosis. Few competitors can match either foreign leaders in China or its suppliers.

All now worry about supply chain disruption. The impact during COVID and then the Ukraine war is nothing like what would happen if the US made it illegal to manufacture or use significant numbers of products or parts from China. Certainly, if China responded with sanctions on Western firms or if Chinese consumers boycotted their goods.

Consumer Boycotts

This is not an imaginary threat. Individual boycotts have already happened. The Japanese auto sector in 2014 lost 20% share in the fast-growing China market when the sovereignty dispute flared up over some barren rocks, called the Diaoyudao Islands in China and Senkaku in Japan. Japanese firms have never recovered fully what they lost. This helped Volkswagen topple Toyota as the world's No. 1 auto maker.

South Korean car brands' have fared even worse. Sales in 2021 were a mere quarter of their 2014 share: down 75%. Some of the acute shrinkage coincided with South Korea allowing, against strong Chinese opposition, US advanced THAD missiles to be based on its soil. These put China's provincial capital of Shandong, Qingdao, only 380 miles from Seoul, well within range: Beijing is less than 600 miles away.

In 2022, leading sportswear makers Nike and Adidas were hit. After announcing they would not use Xinjiang cotton, their China sales fell 19% and 24%, respectively. As Chinese consumers' perceptions of US interference in China's affairs and outright bullying increased, popular feeling towards America and the West has hardened. The same is beginning to happen among the estimated 60 million overseas Chinese, who are usually much wealthier than the average mainland Chinese.

China has a long history of consumer boycotts. American discrimination against Chinese immigrants led to the 1905 Chinese Boycott of US goods. This followed the original 1882 US Chinese Exclusion Act, which was only repealed in 1943, leaving long-lasting bitter Chinese sentiment towards the US. Part of what China calls its Century of Humiliation from 1839 to 1949.

That had its roots in 19th-century foreign invasions of China. The West principally took special privileges, economic and government, as rights under what China calls the Unequal Treaties. Most heinous of all was the forced sale of opium, directly against Chinese government edicts, under the banner of free trade.

Along with slavery, forcing market opening to sell opium was the high point of British hypocrisy during its "civilising mission". Karl Marx dubbed it, "the free trade in poison", as the Executive Director of the UN's Office on Drugs and Crime, Antonio Maria Costa recalled.

Opium, from its Indian colony, was the only thing Britain possessed to pay for all the 19th-century British imports of Chinese silk, porcelain and tea. Balancing Britain's great trade deficit with opium emptied China of much of its silver: then a major store of wealth, like gold today.

Maintained literally by gunboats, this forced trade was followed by indemnities that cleaned out China's treasury. Eight foreign powers in 1900 — Britain, US, France, Germany, Austro-Hungary, Italy, Russia and Japan — invaded China and made it pay for costs and losses in what the West calls the Boxer Rebellion.

Few in the West are aware of this history, let alone the scale in money and lives. An internal British government report of 1910 stated that 10% of male adults in Sichuan, one of China's largest provinces and opium growing areas, were addicted to the drug. There was no national figure but it would have been in the millions. The UN estimated that worldwide in 1906 there were 25 million opium users: maybe half of them in China at the dawn of the new century.

Japan colonised increasing amounts of China in the first half of the 20th century. Oxford's Rana Mitter estimates the number of China's civilian war dead at 12–20 million during Japan's invasion from 1931 until its defeat in 1945. Another two to three million soldiers were killed or wounded. The Chinese Nationalist government at the time gave a higher total number. Only Soviet losses were greater in World War II, yet today China's losses or even involvement is largely unknown in the West let alone acknowledged with gratitude.

Little to none of this is covered in any detail in Western school history books. Some Western commentators even dismiss the Century of Humiliation as communist propaganda or suggest the past is the past and should be left there. That ignores history. Not only did the idea originate before the Communist Party was born but the facts are undeniable and explain current sensitivities, so should be known.

The most accessible Opium Wars account in English is by Indian novelist Amitav Ghosh, whose *Sea of Poppies* was shortlisted for the 2008 Booker Prize. This illustrates that China's history during foreign dominance is still remembered throughout Asia, if not in the West — and should not be forgotten either by foreign politicians or firms. This brings us back to the potential for Chinese boycotts of Western goods and services. Foreign amnesia and ignorance are part of the real China Threat.

Who has the greater staying power in a boycott? China, Chinese consumers or Western firms with quarterly earnings reports to make and share prices to protect? China has more choices and an ace in its hand: market size. As one European executive put it, "there is no other China in the whole world". Meaning only China can deliver the profit, scale and corporate growth that foreign multinational companies need; and not to be lost, if at all possible.

Retailer H&M, with over 500 Chinese branches in its fifth largest market, knows all about this. In 2021, the Swedish retailer announced it would stop using Xinjiang cotton. After nine months China sales dropped 41% on an annual basis. H&M quickly sought to "regain trust in China". After 16 months H&M returned openly to Alibaba's on-line Tmall platform. In the meantime, H&M continued to invest in China through its other brands: principled? Most are more practical.

Leading Japanese retailer Uniqlo simply said it had found no instances of human rights abuses in Xinjiang and had no plans to leave China. Most large foreign companies now employ world classification leaders like SGS and DNV to investigate local suppliers and their practices.

Human rights criticism is not new. The iconic blue jeans maker Levi Strauss quit China in 1993 citing, "pervasive violation of human rights". Yet by 2010, the same Levi Strauss celebrated its 501st China store opening. In 2020, there followed the very latest "NextGen beacon store". That's business; and a demonstration of corporate will power, with an exceedingly sharp commercial focus on profit not values.

Ericsson's CEO threatened to move the telecoms equipment maker from its 145-year-old Stockholm home if the government banned China's Huawei from bidding for business in Sweden. Ericsson feared being treated the same in China. This is not an idle threat. China did not retaliate against Apple for instance when the US banned phone maker Huawei but who knows after the "intensive competition" the Biden administration promises? Everything is connected in the New New World: coupling not decoupling is what makes the world go round, without it things could breakup or in the new word fragment.

Unintended Consequences

As with many complex problems, simplistic solutions are offered. Rarely though are simple solutions successful. Failing to understand the complexity of manufacturing, supply chains or the 21st-century economy will cause much trouble for the US. All too often, measures create both short- and long-term unintended consequences — shooting one's self in the foot.

Very little public debate occurred once Trump broadcast his simplistic idea. Jon Bateman of the Carnegie Endowment for International Peace wrote that, "neither Biden nor any other senior US politician had made a serious effort to educate the American people about the costs and risks of decoupling".

October 2022 is when the US ratcheted up its pressure by proposing rules to limit the export to China of advanced semiconductors, chip-making equipment and supercomputer components. These apply to other countries too: extraterritorial in legal jargon, long-arm reach in the vernacular: a practice widely condemned in principle. This was heavy artillery, with guided missiles.

Bateman declared that the, "zero sum thinkers who urgently want to accelerate technological decoupling" had won, "China's technological rise will be slowed at any price". Even stronger, broader measures could follow, including in biotechnology, manufacturing and finance. *Foreign Policy's* headline read, *Biden Is Now All-In on Taking Out China:* the sub-head concluded, *The US president has committed to rapid decoupling, whatever the consequences.*

The US did this without fully consulting its allies: potentially an expensive mistake. It may backfire as the US needs solid support from its allies and well-coordinated strategies to decouple China, as they used against Huawei.

The hasty decision, just before the G-20 Bali Summit, allowed China to complain, under World Trade Organisation rules. As Bateman wrote, "Much of the edifice of US techno-nationalist policy — from export controls to tariffs to blacklists — runs more or less counter to the WTO's general bar against country-based discrimination …. The 2019 WTO decision concerning Russia and Ukraine cast real doubt on the US interpretation (for a successful case)".

Prophetically, Bateman concluded the *Foreign Policy* article by saying, "for now, Washington must wait to see how others play their hands". The answer came swiftly enough, and probably much faster than the White House expected or welcomed.

German Chancellor Olaf Scholz, whose government was already in a one-sided war of words with Washington over the price Germany was paying for US gas, was very direct. He stated bluntly that Germany would not decouple China: see the later section *Refusing to Decouple*.

Scholz quickly followed that up with a one-day trip to Beijing to see Xi Jinping and Premier Li Keqiang, accompanied not by his foreign minister but by a dozen leading German industrialists. Several, like two global major industry leaders BASF and VW, in chemicals and autos respectively, had very recently started or announced more multi-billion dollar investments in China.

French President Emmanuel Macron put on an even more impressive display in April 2023 when he spent four days in China, along with 60 business leaders. These included firms from aircraft manufacturer Airbus to the world's cosmetics leader L'Oréal, water company Suez to energy and automation company Schneider Electric, all very active in China. Macron also spoke of the need for European autonomy and the refusal to follow the US in decoupling China.

While those headaches are for Washington to resolve, Beijing has its own. For in the short term China would be hard hit, though so would the US. However, China has had five years to prepare for decoupling, preparing people, firms and government for it. Meanwhile, US firms largely ignored the possibility until 2022 and, like many in Europe, still believe or just hope extensive decoupling does not happen.

The early warning sped a slew of policies in China, including the wonderfully ambiguous and flexible idea of a Dual Circulation economy. This has many interpretations, baffling binary commentators. Time revealed the main intent. Namely to strengthen further China's domestic economy, develop more economic and technological self-reliance, yet still open up its market, where that is advantageous. This may not be enough immediately but it is a start to meet a whole raft of challenges in a fast-changing world.

Not least of the challenges will be a global economic depression if the US continues to underestimate China's ability to adapt, survive and rebound. Especially, while ignoring America's vulnerability to the consequences of decoupling.

Refusing to Decouple

Markets, jobs and profits from China, let alone consumer boycotts, are largely absent from most Western media coverage. So is Germany's core long-term industrial strategy Industry 4.0 (Chapter 8: *China's X-Factor*). This is a major omission that will lead to harmful decisions unless the West learns and changes.

By late 2022, German strains with Washington and some of its allies appeared over a growing number of issues. With the US, the government criticised publicly the price of US gas sold to Germany. France had done the same. They then moved on to attack US subsidies that discriminated against EU firms.

With the EU, Berlin caused anger by acting independently of Brussels: unity and solidarity were ignored. Germany subsidised its consumers for energy directly. Rather than going through the EU, as it had on earlier collective policies such as the green transition fund and refugees, Germany asserted its own sovereignty, and in the process cut out other EU members.

Despite constant repetitions of US–Europe unity, after Russia's invasion of Ukraine, Berlin declared publicly in November 2022 that it would not decouple. Apart from a few criticisms of Chancellor Olaf Scholz's visit to Beijing to meet with President Xi Jinping, the silence from the US and the rest of the EU was deafening: trouble deferred as President Macron proved less than four months later.

Europe's leading economy was not decoupling. Allies were not united on everything. That can be the problem with alliances. Other countries have competing interests; and not always the same priorities. Top of these for Germany is Industry 4.0.

Designed in 2011 to protect German manufacturing long-term from its two declared competitors, the US and China, Industry 4.0 looks out many decades. When China understood its potential and what China could offer Germany, Beijing pushed hard to persuade Berlin to collaborate formally. This it did. For it is all about the Fourth Industrial Revolution, impacting the future for as far as the eye can see: no small matter, both can benefit.

To secure its leading position as the world's high-end manufacturer, Germany wants and needs 4.0 to become the global manufacturing standard in the age of AI: 5G, Internet of Things and all that comes next. For that Germany requires many 4.0 adopters: manufacturers in Germany alone are not enough. Substantial market size is needed, and growing access. It also helps to have very demanding consumers to keep firms on their toes, forcing innovation and better service.

After de-industrialisation and slower economic growth, the US no longer offers that. Especially after its increasingly unpredictable politics, treaty reversals and a common determination to Make America Great Again.

China is the obvious answer. German companies can then apply globally their China-gained 4.0 edge. This corporate strategic consideration, as well as supportive government in China, comes up frequently when talking with foreign firms in China.

Germany and China are an unbeatable manufacturing duo, leaving the US and Japan to find their own competitive strategies. Not just market and manufacturing size: China has the necessary supporting infrastructure, built by a very adaptive, entrepreneurial private sector.

Major German firms like VW, Bosch, BASF and Siemens have extensive experience and investments in China. Often going back three decades or more, China is very familiar territory. Just as China is a "second home market" for American firms like Honeywell, GM and GE, so for German manufacturers: game on inside the West. Do not lose sight of that.

234 America as No. 3: Get Real About China, India and the Rest

After Ukraine, Industry 4.0 takes on another complicating dimension. There is no mistaking the fact that long-term German high-end manufacturing survival is at stake, not to mention for politicians jobs and votes. Leading companies are playing their cards behind the scenes, and now publicly after accompanying Chancellor Scholz to Beijing.

Plenty of Asian and other firms would welcome the chance to take Germany's China market share, should it follow US decoupling. The fact German firms will not give them the opportunity should send a loud signal to Washington. US business is well aware. Scholz's Beijing visit would have come as no surprise. Macron's trip may have been much more forceful and consequential than expected.

Is corporate Europe backing the US in its trade conflict with China? Is it heck? Jeff Immelt, formerly CEO of global conglomerate GE and Chair of the US Business Council, told the *Washington Post* in 2021 that tough trade policies on China would *not* make the US "better off". Competitors from other countries would benefit. That is the real China Threat: self-harm.

Immelt said bluntly, "Our allies aren't following us". He should know. He calls China GE's "second home market". If tensions with the US persist, China may be the second home market too for more and more European firms.

Not to mention Asians from Japan, South Korea, Southeast Asia and Australasia, who have decades of experience in China; and varying degrees of cultural affinity. All joined together in 2022 to trade through the Regional Comprehensive Economic Partnership (RCEP) (Chapter 9: *The New New World*). The US withdrew from negotiations to join RCEP after it failed to contain China. US Asian allies went ahead without the US. Asia keeps trade separate from security, ever sensitive to realities.

What may the US do? What are its options?

Chapter 19

Old China Hand in the White House

I believed in 1979, and said so, and I believe now that a rising China is a positive development, not only for the people of China but for the United States and the world as a whole.

Vice President Joe Biden, Sichuan University, Chengdu 2011

President Joe Biden has been learning about China since being the junior senator on the first US Congressional Trip there in 1979. He recalled in 2011 that the group of 30 had spent, "several days of business with then Vice Premier Deng Xiaoping. It was a very different country then, but what was absolutely clear to me was that China was on the cusp of a remarkable transformation".

China's potential and importance Biden saw from the start of its reform era, as he tells it. Moreover, Biden later spent several days with Xi Jinping, both in China and the US, before Xi came to power. Vice President Kamala Harris said Biden's approach to foreign affairs is to know countries and their leaders through relationships. What that means today is the unanswered question. What now?

The US–China Roller Coaster

Biden admitted to the Chengdu students that his 1979, "first visit came amid a debate in the United States of America similar to the one that exists today [2011] about how to view China's emergence". Nothing changes, only the details. Years later, Trump took aim, branding him Beijing Biden.

The China Debate has come full circle. It began with McCarthyism and treason allegations in the early 1950s made against Old China Hand diplomats of "Who Lost China?" As if China were anyone's to lose, except for the Chinese themselves to enemies. Now, again, US hostility to China is widespread and another McCarthy, the House Speaker, is in the picture.

US–China relations have been on a roller coaster ever since Nixon met Mao in 1972 and US diplomatic recognition in 1979. The last two decades have been a wild ride, not that the early 1990s were smooth. Quick snapshots of relations in 2001, 2011 and 2021 reveal much:

2001: This was the best decade for relations. China had looked to the US for some advice and emulation in the 1990s after Deng Xiaoping rebooted China's Reform and Opening Up in 1992. Beijing learned many lessons in economics: from the Federal Reserve System to macroeconomic management, from commercial banking to capital markets. Chinese firms began to learn best practices. Some of China's brightest students attended Ivy League schools, including Harvard's Kennedy School of Government.

After 9/11, much sympathy for the US poured in from around the world, including China. Islamic fundamentalist violence in Xinjiang prompted China to be the first country to join the US War on Terror. Some from Xinjiang had fought in Afghanistan against the US coalition and had been captured in Tora Bora. They vowed to destablise China. The US sent some 21 Chinese Uygurs to Guantanamo Bay detention camp. Both countries saw eye-to-eye on this top priority for each.

George W. Bush appointed his Yale fraternity friend Clark "Sandy" Randt as Ambassador to China. This may seem odd but in Asia the most important thing in an ambassador is to have their leader's ear and confidence: very few do. Singapore's Lee Kuan Yew was so insulted by having a lightweight political donor, with limited access to the White House, thrust on him as US ambassador that if Lee had anything important to communicate or discuss with the US he would fly to Bangkok to see the region's leading US official.

Randt not only had the Bush ear, he spoke fluent Mandarin. After 18 years experience running the China practice of a leading US law firm in Hong Kong, he was an expert on Chinese commercial law: well qualified. He became the longest serving US ambassador to Beijing. Relations were very good, both for the US and China.

More to the point, the US economy in 2001 was eight times bigger than China's. It was no threat. Even in 2010 the US GDP was two and a half times China's. The gap's shrinkage for most was not a worry. Many in the US believed in the Coming Collapse of China or doubted China's rapid growth could be sustained. They assumed US economic superiority was permanent. Frankly, they did not understand China or economics: including their own.

2011: Biden's warm words in Chengdu were the last. Three months later President Obama made his Pivot to Asia Tour: to Hawaii, Australia, Thailand, Myanmar and Indonesia. The tone and content was very different from Biden's in Chengdu.

Obama pledged to maintain US military spending in Asia and to promote democracy and human rights, whatever the budget cuts. "Other models have been tried and they have failed — fascism and communism, rule by one man and rule by committee. And they failed for the same simple reason: They ignore the ultimate source of power and legitimacy — the will of the people". He felt comfortable saying this in Australia. For good measure, Obama agreed to station 2,500 marines in Darwin, only 700 miles further away from China than Guam and more than 2,300 miles nearer the Chinese mainland than Hawaii.

Obama's core message was, "America is going to play a leadership role in Asia for decades to come". That was the assessment of Bill Clinton's former China Man, Professor Kenneth Lieberthal, who became senior fellow emeritus at Washington's Brookings Institute.

Lieberthal then struck an unmistakably critical note, writing that, "Obama and [Hillary] Clinton talked in Asia as if Asians did not view the global financial crisis as "made in America", as if the American system of democracy has recently been performing splendidly [Lieberthal had said, "political meltdown over raising the debt ceiling in August 2011 did enormous damage"], and as if the American military had all the resources necessary to sustain any type of deployment Washington wishes across the vast Pacific region. *But none of these is true*". Ouch: from a recent Senior Director for Asia at the National Security Council; and from the same party. The words are even more salutary to read a decade later.

Lieberthal added that Obama's, "Asia-wide strategy and some of the rhetoric accompanying it played directly into the perception of many Chinese that all American actions are a conspiracy to hold down or actually disrupt China's rise". The implication was that Obama and Clinton were neophyte amateurs out of their depth in global affairs.

2021: Trump finally broke China's trust in America. Problems had been growing with Obama and Hillary Clinton but Trump was too much. His shadow hangs over the future, making the rest of the world, especially China, much more cautious in their dealings with the US for fear of what might come next.

Regard in China for the US has largely been lost. US COVID incompetence played out constantly in the news. So did racial tensions and violence, including attacks on Asian Americans. Democracy was dealt a very visible blow on screens in real-time at the Capitol. Soft power was crumbling at the edges.

Sparks flew in Anchorage in 2021 when top US and Chinese foreign affairs officials met. China's Yang Jiechi told Antony Blinken that, "We thought too highly of you." The US can no longer, "speak to China from a position of strength", meaning moral superiority, Yang added.

Yang, usually very diplomatic in public, spoke like a stern teacher after Blinken said there was rising global concern over Beijing's human rights record, "We hope the United States will do better on human rights. The fact is that there are many problems within the United States regarding human rights, which are admitted by the US itself", Yang countered.

Yang went on, "China will not accept unwarranted accusations from the US side". He added that relations had fallen, "into a period of unprecedented difficulty" that "has damaged the interests of our two peoples". The gloves were off.

Xi Jinping merely told a group of lawmakers in Beijing that, "China can already look at this world at eye level". No longer does it have to look up to anyone — for the first time in two centuries. Everyone should treat each other with equal respect, as he had told UNESCO in Paris.

Only time will tell how much of this was for domestic consumption but US lecturing and condescension were finally too much for Beijing. This was not 2001 when the US economy was eight times that of China's. Nor had the US demonstrated much competence in 2020: time to drop the moralising Exceptionalism and understand China's new weight. This was 2021.

US Domestic Lessons

Much has changed since Biden spoke in 2011 to the Chengdu students. Could Biden have changed his thinking permanently about China? That is the open question.

Biden may feel he must trim his sails to US political reality. Almost across the political spectrum America demands Something Must Be Done About China. Two different domestic forces have come together around a common idea, the economy and jobs. Each has a different concern but together they have made common cause: the perfect storm.

Voters have largely seen flat real (adjusted for inflation) incomes, even a decline for some, along with growing uncertainty. This has been going on for a quarter of a century but became more pronounced after the 2008 Financial Crisis. Two groups of US voters are increasingly unhappy, white blue-collar workers lacking tertiary education and former local white elites resentful about losing their inherited privilege.

Initially, there were still differing responses. The mainstream academic, economic and major business establishments were not worried. China, for Multi-National Corporations (MNCs), opened new opportunities to drive up profit growth and lower costs.

They were not wrong. US exports to China have risen 500% since China joined the WTO at the end of 2001, five times more than to other countries. Deflation had helped improve US living standards by making many goods cheaper. This was very positive for both the US and China.

The first institutional group to push back against engaging with China was in the military and intelligence communities, along with their supporters. Frankly, it raised their importance, budgets and career prospects. The military-industrial complex, of which President Eisenhower warned so strongly in his 1961 farewell speech, was alive and waiting.

The more the economic gap shrank, the more the military and civilian allies could see US dominance challenged. China one day as the world's No. 1 economy: that was unacceptable. In practical terms, besides being a growing threat, it gave an unmissable opportunity to lobby for higher military and intelligence budgets: more weapons, profit and jobs.

Wars are not just fought on battlefields. Indeed, Sunzi's *Art of War* 2,500 years ago said the greatest success was to achieve one's objectives without resorting to arms: gaining enemy compliance without firing a single shot. Neither was Sunzi the first in human history to discover the benefits of psychological warfare or dark arts (Chapter 17: *Media Changes*).

Military and intelligence attitudes began to harden towards China in 2009 (Chapter 10: *The New China–US Equation*). Domestically, after the financial crisis, they harnessed rising individuals' fears: stress and uncertainty. Steadily these helped change the narrative on China.

Think tanks and media found a gold mine. Plenty of topics to gain funding for think tanks and academe. Endless stories for the media to print and follow: easy work.

These pumped out growing negativity about China (Chapter 16: *Media and COVID* and Chapter 17: *Media Changes*). This was even before Donald Trump arrived with hopes of pulling off the Deal of the Century but in the real world could not even get North Korea's young leader to comply with his wishes: reality TV is not reality.

The US has swung sharply away from Biden's decades' held view of engagement. He will need all his skill to craft a successful China policy — especially with the Congress he faces and a country that, whatever it thinks about Trump as a person, believes he has a good point in Make America Great Again. Politicians steadily joined the anti-China bandwagon.

The bipartisan-supported contest was declared officially at Biden's first presidential press conference. After some words of praise or warning for China, choose your interpretation, Biden, with an eye on his domestic audience, threw down the gauntlet. America's mission was to show that democracy works better than "autocracy".

This presumably is measured by competence, welfare and quality of life in the widest sense, not by high flown rhetoric. After the US, government and society both, bungled the COVID public health and economic responses, witnessed deadly insurrection on Capitol Hill and never mentions again the disastrous 2019 Johns Hopkins forecasts of pandemic readiness that ranked the US 1, UK 2 and China 51, the US has no reason to be so confident. Definitely it is game on.

No Self-Confidence for Chinese Lessons

A confident 19th century West did not hesitate to solve its greatest governance problem by learning from China (Chapter 15: *Politicians and Society*). First Britain in 1855, then the rest of the West, copied China's 1,250-year-old open exams that decided admission to the civil service. With meritocracy, they established much more competent bureaucracies.

There was no such self-confidence to learn from China about COVID, either in America or most of Europe. A grisly and unnecessary death toll resulted. There was no assumption that China was competent, even though the WHO spelt out that Chinese approaches worked and should be copied — pure Western hubris, arrogance and failure.

Biden privately must have recognised this; and a lot more about China from four decades of contact. Not just eye-catching high-speed rail but China's whole approach to administration. Admiringly, Biden's Economics Advisor Brian Deese spoke of China's "meticulous thinking" about strategic investments: doubtless the president's view too. Coming from the country that raises free markets and free enterprise to a sacred creed, Deese seemed in awe of such state achievements.

I would not have expected Deese's words before I read them. It seemed like the modern equivalent of Lincoln Steffens saying, after visiting Moscow in 1919, "I have seen the future and it works". The only difference is that China is going from strength to strength more than 70 years after modern New China began and a century after the Communist Party of China's foundation. Not just two years after a revolution when no major cracks in the system were apparent to Steffens.

Without any sense of awkwardness, the US is even embracing statist Industrial Policy. This puts taxpayers' money behind investments too large, risky or long-term for the private sector to do alone or too reluctant to fund at all. American free enterprise believers regard it as pure poison.

Industrial Policy has long been one of the main charges made against China's "unfair" competition by all previous US administrations. The EU and WTO have rules restricting or even banning it. Yet Biden asked Congress for some $50 billion for semiconductors; and $110 billion in all, without a hint of doubt or discomfort. That was a major break with the recent past.

The Missing Piece

So far, something very important is missing. Biden is not thinking aloud about the China and Asia of 2035, let alone 2050. He ploughs ahead as if his actions can stop any relative change in power.

Yet what might the Power Equation look like in 2035? Considering China's economic momentum, rising education levels and population size it could look very different. That is the 2035 question to answer publicly now.

What of mid-century, the 100th anniversary of the Communist Party coming to power, by when it hopes to have completed China's full modernisation of its billion plus people? US politicians will lose no votes for ignoring 2035 or 2050. Stop! That is the wrong way to look at it. Like climate change the long-term must be addressed before it is too late.

What will that mean for Biden's great grandchildren? Shouldn't everyone be prepared? Not exploited by a rallying cry to pass immediate domestic legislation but so people can adapt long-term to the New New World and ease the coming birth?

The problem is that Biden is looking backwards. In the wrong direction, just as British guns did in Singapore in 1942. Build Back Better is a clear slogan, even if a bit clunky. The only problem is having a very 20th century ring to it. Biden has an enormous domestic task on his hands, to fix last century's problems: politically he has no choice.

This necessary domestic focus hobbles the US in handling the future. Merely building back better will take up most of Biden's energy, time and political capital. His eye is mainly on what worked in the past elsewhere, especially China, not what the world may look like in 12, 30 or even 80 years from now in Asia and most of all in China.

That is where he and Americans should be looking: a Pivot to the Long-Term Future. To provide real leadership Biden should focus on this crucial question in much more honest detail: not just in empty slogans and sound bites.

The immediate problem is that Biden and the Democrats are placing much faith in government and democracy. Yet Congress is seen as not working. Its approval rating in October 2022 was down to just 21%: 21%. A 2020 George Washington University poll found 54% believe the presidency is ineffective. Furthermore, 85% in an *AP-NORC* mid-2022 poll believe the US is going in the wrong direction — and that includes almost 80% of the president's own party.

Strong headwinds: not an easy time for any president, anywhere; and with faith in democracy eroding worldwide. Some 58% of people were unhappy with democracy, according to a 2020 global study by Cambridge University's Centre for the Future of Democracy. All very unnerving for those knowing of Sir John Glubb's final stage of empire, institutional decay, the Age of Decadence.

Ironically, the Alliance of Democracies Foundation, headed by a former NATO Secretary General no less, found that 71% of Chinese believe China has the right amount of democracy. Only people in Norway, Switzerland and Sweden ranked their countries higher: quite a finding. Governments anywhere must deliver, and not everyone believes they do.

What has happened to American self-confidence that in the 1960s put a man on the moon within a decade? How does it compare with China's? British financier Stuart Sinclair observed that, "Chinese people have confidence that every problem has a solution. Americans used to be famous for that!"

"Indeed, when we went to live there [China] in 2004, I was amazed at the scope and quality of public administration, at least in the realms of construction, road maintenance, utilities and suchlike. Later travels to Gansu, Harbin, and the like underlined what a massively audacious and well-administered amount of infrastructure growth has been achieved. In the UK we manage shabby and costly projects".

That is almost two decades ago. There are now far more reasons for Chinese to feel confident: not least incomes, health care and education but most of all economic performance. At this stage of China's development, it really is The Economy Stupid. Instead of looking for a durable long-term relationship with China, the US has confronted China. That is looking in the wrong direction.

A confident West, in the 19th century, benefited from looking to China for ideas, while an intellectually curious, self-confident Western society travelled the globe for knowledge and understanding. Today's historians, writers and scientists should again help chart new maps to explore the rest of the world and its common future, so as to help rekindle change at home where it is much needed.

Chapter 20

What Can the West Learn From Itself and China?

We seek a relationship with China based on friendship, cooperation and mutual trust, comparable with that which we have, or seek, with other major powers ... [But also] We ... need to measure our actions carefully so that we do not give the Chinese the impression that we are careless of our own interests.

Australian Prime Minister Gough Whitlam, 1973

Physician heal thyself.

Luke 4.23

The West can learn from its own experience and history. Be it from Australia, post-imperial Britain or US recoveries after the Civil War, Great Depression or the Vietnam defeat, the West can learn from its past. It could also learn from China but can it?

The most powerful thing the US and West could do to restore global strength and soft power after the 2020/2021 disasters of COVID and Afghanistan would be to make its democracy work much better. So observed a Chinese critic.

Displays of incompetence, some directly related to democracy, erode US soft power. Most importantly, democracy's self-appointed leader needs to look competent to the outside world: no easy task after the recent twin disasters.

A renewed political focus is required at home — as Biden identifies. Fix mounting domestic problems, before they overwhelm. Every country knows its to-do list, so I shall not itemise them specifically only consider how.

Review everything: prioritise, as China does. Budgets are not limitless, including for the military. As President Lyndon Johnson learned, it is impossible to have guns and butter forever. Decide how to pay, where to cut, what to increase; and Just Do It. Though do it without the distraction of "foreign entanglements", of which George Washington warned. This domestic focus could take a decade. If not done, the US may sink deeper and deeper into chaos, struggling with sluggish economic growth.

No quick fixes exist. That has to be accepted. Neither to the West's problems nor the increasing hostility between some in the West and China. No single silver bullet can solve all problems. There are great shocks: more lie ahead.

These are the cards we are dealt. Many are challenging but that cannot be helped. The longer a start is avoided, the harder it will be. With sufficient goodwill and common sense all round, they can be managed. Begin with some Australian lessons.

Australian Lessons

How can the West get along with China, to *huo lu*? Australia has provided good lessons in how to manage relations with China: both well and badly. That is where they reached in 2022 under Prime Minister Scott Morrison: very bad. Now there is a fresh chance to improve them, though the Australia, UK and US AUKUS agreement for nuclear-powered submarines, clearly aimed at China, is not a good start.

To be Australianised is a new term on Chinese social media, meaning punished, marginalised, ignored, left last in line. This is so different from almost half a century ago when Australia became the first Western nation to establish full diplomatic relations with Beijing. A breakthrough for China, it brought decades of economic benefit to Australia.

After four very amicable decades, Canberra changed course in 2018 when Prime Minister Malcolm Turnbull banned Huawei equipment for no other apparent reason than to please the US. There was no evidence that Chinese telecoms equipment provider Huawei had ever interfered in Australian affairs. We know because Turnbull wrote in his memoirs there was "no smoking gun".

Solid foundational advice for relations with China came from Prime Minister Gough Whitlam who established Australia's full relations with China in 1973. He wrote to his new Ambassador Stephen Fitzgerald, "We seek a relationship with China based on friendship, cooperation and mutual trust, comparable with that which we have, or seek, with other major powers".

Whitlam then counseled the need to look after Australia's own interests; and be able to say "No" to China. Both sides should respect what China calls core interests and red lines, not to be infringed or crossed. Today that would be all issues of Chinese sovereignty, from Taiwan to Tibet, Xinjiang to Hong Kong and the South China Sea.

However, Whitlam continued, "We ... need to measure our actions carefully so that we do not give the Chinese the impression that we are careless of our own interests. They are themselves hard-headed realists, and it would be unnatural of them not to take advantage of us or hold us in contempt for apparent weakness".

Whitlam bemoaned the, "failure of [Australian] governments to implant in our education the study of China and Chinese. If they had, it would have given us what's missing at the top of our political and other institutions — a critical mass of leaders who know China, who understand Chinese thinking, who can imagine a Chinese world and not be intimidated by it, who can themselves think in Chinese".

Think in Chinese: imagine a Chinese world and not be intimidated. That was written half a century ago. It seems a million years away today.

With more than four decades of China experience behind him, Fitzgerald, now Australia's elder statesman on China, argued in 2017 that, "China must be given the highest priority. Many analysts, and President Xi Jinping himself, have suggested China currently offers more prospect for stability, predictability and continuity internationally than any other major player. Given the non-democratic nature of the Chinese Party State, this is a disconcerting irony. But a screaming priority for Australia must be to encourage, buttress and if possible enlarge China's resolve to continue this way".

Four lessons from Gough Whitlam for the West stand out. (1) Establish equality of treatment, the same as with other major powers. (2) Be a friend at court, trusted to talk truth to power, not to pursue narrow national interests. (3) Educate society, especially its leaders, about China. (4) Be able to think like Chinese and share mutual benefits.

Post-1949 Chinese leaders from Zhou Enlai onwards learned Western tongues and scripts. Through it they gained some understanding of the West. Even Mao Zedong quietly learned some English, from his Australia-educated doctor. To whose advantage was that?

Words, Rules and Realism

Words matter. Saying as President Obama did that, "The world has changed. The rules are changing with it. The United States, not countries like China, should write them", may sound acceptable in the US but not elsewhere.

As Fitzgerald noted on the writing of rules, "China is one of many countries that have urged more inclusive, representative and equitable rules. But China has also said it is not seeking to overturn the existing order, only to reform it". Reform not overthrow is completely consistent with what China has done in finance and trade for decades.

Fitzgerald concluded that, "there's no doubting China has moved decisively into rules making, on a scale that is potentially game-changing for the international order". This can put other countries in a bind but, "the big issue for Australia ... [is] whether China's grand design is ultimately for the general good. [This] depends on the degree of its accommodation to principles and liberal ideas evolved within the existing international order and embodied particularly in the UN. That makes a goal, for Australia, of close involvement with China's rules-making not an idle option but fundamental".

In fact, China considers the UN to be the most important institution through which to resolve global problems. China gives the UN institutions, from development, intellectual property and trade to health and ecology, a public prominence the West does not. Chairing the UN COP-15 to achieve the 2022 landmark Kunming-Montreal Global Biodiversity Framework, considered by many the equal of the Paris agreement on climate change, illustrates China's involvement and ability to get things done, against the odds.

Engagement is fundamentally important, to be a friend at court to speak truth to power. A more recent Australian ambassador to China Geoff Raby called for "constructive realism" in relations with China. Ideological stances achieve nothing, as Donald Trump's administration proved.

Whether it was ending the US–China trade deficit (it widened), stopping China's technological advance (checkout quantum communications and Huawei's progress in industry-changing photonic chips: read Harvard's Graham Allison) or China's growing influence in Asia (neither South Korea nor Singapore joined the Quad to contain China. With them, it could have been a much more powerful Sextet): ideology failed. New shiny ideas, of the sort Kissinger decried, all failed.

Stop before actions do more self-harm. Might there be lessons from history for an enduring global US role, different but still influential?

The Right History

Look to history but use the right history. Comparing today with Germany's challenge to British world leadership in 1914 ignores the most basic realities. Those were two similar-sized economies and populations. Even the US and Soviet Union were much more evenly matched than the US and China are over the long term.

The US–China 1:4 population difference in this transition is much more like the US replacing the UK a century ago. This played out over several decades, though the eventual outcome was never in doubt. Population size and economic potential were too different.

Also, recall that although the US and UK were related by blood and culture the transition was far from smooth. There was tension, before and after the US became the undisputed dominant power. In economic policy the US followed its own interests, from Bretton Woods in 1944 and the creation of global economic institutions to dollar supremacy. In foreign affairs the US forced Britain, France and Israel to end their attack on the Suez Canal in 1956: great ignominy for Britain, former ruler of Egypt from 1882 and once one of the jewels in the imperial crown.

Compounding this was US Secretary of State Dean Acheson's stinging description of Britain having "lost an empire but not found a role". Like a whiplash that stung.

This time it is the US at a major population disadvantage: more than four times smaller than the overtaking country. The same goes with India. Furthermore, China has enough economic momentum and endowments to build an ever-growing advantage for two or three decades. From that will flow further economic, political and military capability.

Can the US give way as the UK did, peacefully? Not happily for sure but recognising what drives wealth and military power — population and eventual economic size — it may not have any easy alternative, short of war, which it may not win.

Look to Post-Imperial Britain

There is one thing the US has not considered. It could look to the UK. Maybe it could find a role, just as Dean Acheson once said Britain had not found? Ironically, the previous global empire's history could instruct its successor: should it wish to be advised.

Twice, in phases, under two different prime ministers and two different parties, the UK took tough decisions that right-wing politicians opposed vehemently, still in love with dominance, national pride and empire. Each time those looking backwards were defeated and Britain advanced, stronger into a new era.

In 1947, Labour's Prime Minister Clement Attlee ordered the end of British rule in India. India was the Jewel in the Imperial Crown. Victoria had been Empress of India no less but economic realities not sentiment proved decisive. Britain, after not one but two very costly world wars, had to admit that it could no longer afford the financial drain. Even war leader Winston Churchill could not stop it. Britain and its resources were exhausted.

What mattered most at home, after winning the war in 1945, was to address Britain's high unemployment and grinding poverty of the 1930s Depression. Britain started to withdraw from the empire to focus on building a fairer society with a welfare state and mixed economy at home. Health, housing, education, pensions and full employment were the main concerns (not unlike some in the US demand today).

In the second example, Conservative Prime Minister Harold Macmillan in 1960 told the white South African parliament in Cape Town that the Wind of Change was blowing through Africa. The message was that *apartheid* South Africa should prepare for change. Within the decade, Britain withdrew its forces from East of Suez, back to Europe and Blighty, from where its world-dominating imperial navy had set sail for two centuries.

As more African and Asian countries became independent, so Britain built up the Commonwealth of Nations, the Commonwealth, which now has 56 members: four were not even former British colonies. That could not compare with Britain's previous position but it gave Britain a stage, something to lead: important psychologically.

The US should find something similar to retain influence and pride in the 21st and 22nd centuries. Maybe it is not through politics or government but companies and universities. Not media, not by decoupling or excluding but by including and building bridges: rebuilding soft power. These were part of the original US soft power, before US government, politicians and media tarnished it.

Economics and markets are unsentimental. They respect only numbers, performance and cycles. No longer are these permanently in the US's favour. As the US approaches its 250th birthday, neither Sir John Glubb nor Paul Kennedy would have been surprised by current relations deteriorating. To them it was predictable. That though should not stop the search for acceptable solutions, either from West or East.

China's experience is millennia older than the US. Meaning it has had far more time to make mistakes, as well as good decisions, from which to learn. Societies that advance often borrow ideas from others. There is no shame in it, indeed it is a strength.

Governance and Policymaking

There is no need to adopt China's system wholesale, just adapt parts learned from COVID and other examples. Notably, two things: how to get things done and how to help avoid or mitigate the next disaster. We don't want to be saying ever again, "This Didn't Have to Happen".

Begin with policymaking. Biden's economic advisor Brian Deese is right about China's "meticulous thinking" but there is much more to it than that. Chapter 14: *How China Works* and Chapter 8: *China's X-Factor* cover this in detail. Consider the major Western problem of adversarial politics, followed by Chinese solutions.

China abhors public adversarial politics, traditionally and since the 1960s Cultural Revolution. Political infighting is conducted "behind the screen" in much of Asia, with consensus sought before making changes publicly. That focuses attention on finding solutions not playing to the gallery or crowd, which is demagoguery.

In the US it led to Donald Trump, though the extreme US version of adversarial politics began much earlier in the 1990s when government itself was shut down by a hostile, partisan Congress. Four-year political cycles or even two-year cycles drive this. There is little room for long-term thinking or compromise. Winning the next election is top priority.

"US politics are about selling not governance", former CGTN Washington correspondent Tian Wei observed: very telling. The amount of time spent on policies for campaigns rather than governing varies but is an unhealthy imbalance for sure.

The written word, not adversarial argument, is sacrosanct in Chinese policymaking. That has been the traditional view for millennia. Clever debating tricks, glib slogans or lies do not make good policy. Only well-considered thought, written without emotion, can devise good policy, away from the noise and pollution of adversarial politics. Start with evidence.

The best way to make good policy is with strong, credible evidence. In the West this is not always the case. Australian Prime Minister Malcolm Turnbull even admitted there was no evidence, "no smoking gun", of Huawei interfering in Australian affairs. He said he acted against Huawei when posed with a hypothetical question: "Could it?" Try using that in a court of law when the evidence is against you. Good luck.

The hard evidence was that Huawei had not interfered. Who said so? The British Government's Communications Headquarters (GCHQ), responsible for intelligence monitoring, did. For, at the company's request, GCHQ had access to Huawei's code for eight years and found nothing malevolent. A major component of the Anglo-Saxon Five Eyes intelligence sharing network, GCHQ had said so publicly for years, until the UK bent to US pressure to ban it, regardless of the evidence.

There are technological ways to stop interference. However, these are of no interest to those politicians or military and intelligence people, whose *modus operandi* excludes evidence. Instead, emotion, lies and fake news are their stock in trade to pervert healthy public discussion and policy (Chapter 17: *Media Changes*).

This is very dangerous both from a security and an economic perspective. Australian firms and workers have already suffered, as have Asian Australians from hate attacks, just like their Asian American counterparts.

The idea of innocence until proven guilty by the evidence is central to the rule of law, a fair trial and respected judicial system: in mob rule it is the reverse. Otherwise, courts become meaningless — and justice denied.

A strong sense of accountability exists both in traditional and modern Chinese thinking. China's system of inspectors, assessors and disciplinary censors goes back a couple of millennia.

Just like Western corporations, China has targets, performance indicators and regular appraisals. Indeed Singapore, which has drawn both on traditional Chinese and Western thinking, is often called Singapore Inc. China too has many of the characteristics of a modern corporation. As a partial description, China Inc is not far wrong.

Whenever people talk about democracy and China, I always suggest they should use the A word not the D word. Imperfect as accountability can be, as the need for China's anti-corruption campaigns illustrates, it explains an important part of what Deese says about Chinese governance.

Generally, real accountability works. It is practical, pragmatic and non-ideological. Judging by the number of senior officials dismissed, individual accountability seems more common in China than in today's West.

Daoist Thinking

After focusing on Confucianism (Chapter 11: *Challenges*), the emphasis here is on Daoism, its forerunner which has much to teach. First, start with the Big Picture.

Go West Young Man: that exhortation set up two centuries of US growth and mobility. Now the picture is on a very small screen, resulting in paralysis or costly division. In the land of the Great Wall and Grand Canal, China never forgets the importance of the Big Picture: vision.

After vision, provide a sense of place, proportion and perspective. In the universe, big things can be small, small things big. This is relevant for everything from foreign relations to the environment.

Respect nature: this is now understood all the way to the top in China. The elite still learns from Daoism, which places great importance on nature. As a corrective to the super-rapid economic growth that created so many environmental problems, China was scheduled, before COVID, to host the 2020 UN Biodiversity Convention to, "build a better future in harmony with nature". Xi Jinping introduced the concept of Ecological Civilisation, having promoted strong environmental awareness in the booming Zhejiang province during the early 2000s.

Humility is essential. Pride comes before a fall. People must learn they cannot control everything: COVID taught that. Pandemics and biodiversity are much easier to understand with a sense of Daoism. So are countries and cultures.

Ambiguity works in tight spots, much better than in "your face" words or rash actions. Strategic ambiguity over Taiwan has served China and the US well for four decades. Ending it could open a Pandora's Box of disastrous unintended consequences.

Virtue signalling and ideology can ultimately come at a stiff price. Some 98% of diplomatic disputes are managed not resolved, as one US ambassador pointed out sagely. Ambiguity is very helpful in dispute management.

As for conflict itself, policy adviser and karate Black Belt Lawrence Baum, an American ironically, has an interesting take on different approaches to conflict. When the US punches, Russia punches back; Japan blocks with karate; and China moves slowly to let the energy pass, by opening up. Float like a butterfly, sting like a bee.

This very Daoist approach, grasping flow's critical importance, is pretty much what China has done with its economy since it joined the World Trade Organisation in 2001. Moving slowly, China bought time to strengthen itself and change. Nonetheless, the world flowed forward steadily in the desired direction: all sides benefitted.

The concept of flow and fluidity bring us to the book's front cover.

Yin and Yang

Yin and Yang (shown in the *taiji* diagram on the book's cover) underlies much of Chinese philosophy. The whole is one but its relationships are always divided into two.

Two forces, one negative and female, the other positive and male, merge to create the universe and drive the world. Their flows of energy explain long-term cycles and the dynamics within them.

This applies to things large and small, from world history and the economy to family and personal relations. The knowledge enables people to find a balance where otherwise there would be conflict.

When these two types of energy combine they create one body with two natures. These are constantly in motion, changing.

Overall one expands and the other shrinks but the bright dominant force can never occupy the whole body, while the declining part does not disappear altogether. It may be hidden in the shade, the dark, but its roots remain. The two energies propel each other forward, generating momentum.

As one type goes to the extreme, the other loses energy and momentum, so has to give way. This makes the rising force stronger and stronger until finally it reaches its zenith. Then, in turn, it begins to wane.

Things may go to the extreme but eventually they reverse. The aim is to maintain balance between the two energies. If not, ultimately they break up with both sides the loser.

Intriguingly, similar patterns are found on silver, bronze and pottery in other countries including Iraq, Greece, India, Asia Minor and Syria. This is not to suggest they were linked to China or the Yin and Yang. Only to suggest that other civilisations living with nature and the cosmos could understand the world in similar terms.

What is their relevance today? Apart from the fact this interpretation of the world is strong in China, partly because it is seen fitting in with modern physics, it also stresses, especially in a time of conflict, the importance of harmony and cooperation. Better to have opposite forces, negative and positive, combine than split apart. In a nuclear era the latter is more than uncomfortable.

Other Traditional Ideas

Four ideas — priorities, long-term thinking, time and the 360-degree view — are central to making policy. Some have been featured in Chapters 8 and 14 but merit expansion.

A clear sense of priorities is essential: constructing a mental hierarchical pyramid of importance. Without priorities there will be gridlock or at least clashes that slow action. Either way, it is costly. During COVID, China's stated priority was to kill the virus to save lives. Everything else flowed from that single idea.

Short-termism is the bane of Western governments and firms. Taking the long view provides enough time for complex problems to be untangled and addressed gradually, in the best sequence, so better policy emerges.

The basic unit of time in Chinese policymaking is a decade. I never understood this initially but finally comprehended when I saw it in action: a powerful tool and insight. Sequenced, long-term policy is very different from the Western limitations of four or five-year political cycles, with insufficient time to achieve their goal.

Some major Chinese policies have been spread over several decades. Eliminating extreme poverty is one, ending illiteracy another. Making China the world's leading manufacturer by 2050 is a 35-year project, broken into three stages. The West, seemingly unable to grasp or take seriously such a long project usually refers to it as the Made in China 2025 policy. That makes it sound much more immediate. Of political benefit to protectionists, it sounds more urgent more threatening. However, this ignores the fact the West has plenty of time to adapt, join in and benefit from China's policy.

360-degree thinking proved very important during China's COVID. At the outbreak, it captured as fast as possible all that could be known. Silos were broken down very quickly.

In an era of the single silver bullet, the great value of 360-degree thinking must be well understood. Not exclusively Chinese, it exists in other cultures too, like many ideas China uses.

The West's problem today is that adversarial politics look for the single straight knock-out punch or silver bullet. Wham, bang, done: you're out. The Chinese approach is to take the all-round picture. Not just the detail and long-term perspective but to discover a balanced blend of factors to solve the problem.

In COVID's very first weeks, no data proved what worked. Yet by late February 2020, enough key factors were known — hand washing, social distancing, masks, isolation, quarantine, test and trace and, where necessary, tight lockdowns.

From Wuhan, it was still not clear which was the most important factor but together several showed they worked. That was what mattered. Combine all, together they work. Keep an open mind. Refine constantly when evidence appears: regroup, review. Collect all relevant factors from 360-degree thinking. This differed so much from Western single bullet solutions.

For Donald Trump it was vaccines. Blind faith in a magic bullet bet everything on just one idea. The major problem was that vaccines alone were not an immediate solution, at least not without many deaths. It would take a year of scientific research to discover what worked and what was safe. Moreover, virologists and epidemiologists knew variants were most likely, even after widespread vaccination. Before safe vaccines arrived, Trump's single silver bullet in the West excluded wholesale adoption of mitigation measures, central to China controlling COVID.

Therefore don't put all eggs in one basket. Variants may become increasingly contagious, deadly and difficult to counter. China understood the life cycle of a virus; and planned accordingly. Typically it can take three years to control fully. Three millennia of written Chinese history of pandemics teach that.

I shuddered when Trump proclaimed that vaccines were the answer: at least not on their own. US Pharma would ride to the rescue. The cavalry was on its way, the election was in November: time to double up on the single bullet. Just one vaccine before the election and Trump could claim victory. He never mentioned how many would die before a vaccine was widely available: more than half a million Americans, even with some mitigation measures, as it turned out.

Some Europeans, including the UK's political advisers, chose herd immunity as the silver bullet — again without any hope of quick success. Before 70% of Britons became immune, half a million of the herd, it was estimated, would die: half a million. That figure shocked the politicians into changing tack. In the end 200,000 still died largely due to lost time and policy incompetence.

Ironically, I first learned the value of 360-degree thinking at the leading US brokerage research firm Merrill Lynch in the mid-1980s. At Merrill, investment strategy was headed by Investment Hall of Famer Bob Farrell, whom *Institutional Investor* ranked best market timer for 16 out of 17 years. He missed almost nothing. Every significant factor was logged, assessed and integrated into his 360-degree view. Priorities were identified, short and long-term timing set.

Bob Farrell had 15 people working directly to him, while receiving updated and new input from some 120 of Merrill's company, industry and thematic analysts around the world. They covered the whole 360 degrees, sometimes several times over. Everyone at Merrill was plugged into Bob's thinking and recommendations. There were no silos, only open doors: again a powerful tool.

This all-round American way of thinking went out of fashion in the 1990s when Wall Street enthusiastically embraced the management consultants' dream panacea of a single bullet. It was much easier to "sell" to investors. Terms like New Paradigm tried to justify the unjustifiable, namely excessive overvaluations of dotcom stocks. Other fads came and went but fundamental research, constantly reviewed, updated and adapted, still proved the most useful long-run approach.

All this helps but the real answers to managing the challenges, which a changing world brings, lie with the West. It is not principally for others to resolve. It is the West that cannot accept change in facts on the ground.

The West has to do most of the work, for its own sake. By 2025 only 10% of the world will be Anglo-Saxon and white: barely 4% from the US. Existing power disparities will not be sustainable. Get started: work with China's weight not against it. The next chapter explains how. Misunderstanding is at the root of today's problems.

Chapter 21

Understanding In a New Era

The history of Afghanistan we didn't understand at all … We never understood the culture. We never understood the religion. We never understood the tribalism.

US Defense Secretary 2013-2015 Chuck Hagel, *CNN Amanpour* 16th August 2021

The gnarled pine…. That is China… no one has been able to explain why it grows like a corkscrew, just as no one can adequately explain China. But like that tree, there it is…old, resilient, and oddly magnificent… gesture over geometry, subtlety over symmetry, constant flow over static form.

Amy Tan, *Saving Fish From Drowning* 2005

Travel is fatal to prejudice, bigotry and narrow-mindedness.

Mark Twain

No one pretends China is easy to understand, quickly. That probably goes for all unrelated cultures but China seems to present a special mental block for many Westerners.

When Henry Kissinger first met China's Premier Zhou Enlai, Kissinger began by noting China was a mysterious land. Zhou assured Kissinger that as he, "became more familiar with Chinese he would not find China so mysterious", according to the USC US–China Institute research papers. As Zhou told Kissinger, China would lose its mystery; and become simply another reality, just as France became for Zhou after he arrived in Marseille, aged 22.

Chuck Hagel's words say it all. What a damning but courageous confession! Before Afghanistan is airbrushed from Western history, recall what the recent US defence secretary from the Afghan war said the day of the US withdrawal. Re-read Hagel's words. Why should US understanding of China or any other foreign country's culture be any different?

Amy Tan wrote of China being like a "gnarled pine ... old, resilient and oddly magnificent". Its philosophy and art created out of Buddhism (Tibetan, Indian and Han), animism and Daoism is, "an amalgam that is *pure* Chinese, a lovely shabby elegance, a gloriously messy motley that makes China infinitely intriguing. Nothing is ever completely thrown away and replaced ... That is the Chinese aesthetic and also its spirit .... But if you leave too soon, those subtleties will be lost on you". Long-term, deep immersion is needed: a few years are not nearly enough.

The West has much to learn and unlearn. Then solutions can emerge to resolve the inevitable tensions that arise as relative economic sizes reverse. Apart from new policy approaches and ways of rethinking old problems, for those uneasy about the nuclear option they can try non-military solutions.

Go To China

Beyond policy lies one obvious solution. Encourage travel and deep immersion in each other's society, especially among the young. Afterall, Joe Biden's granddaughter studied at Xi's *alma mater* Tsinghua and Xi Jinping's daughter went to Harvard.

Travel though should not be aimed solely at the young or elite. I am constantly impressed by insights older, ordinary Westerners have after visiting China. Often they find things to emulate back home.

For those with open minds China is fascinating and rewarding. Go to China: to see not just the physical infrastructure, with *de rigeur* high-speed rail trips, but also much stunning scenery and how people live their lives: some very different, others very similar.

Go to China; and not just ultra-modern coastal China but less-developed inland China, where the Chinese majority lives. Its needs are increasingly uppermost in Beijing's mind.

Don't be put off by the language: many signs are in English. Younger people have a basic grasp of English. Get one of the new translation devices or just a guidebook.

Better still hire a guide. Not only to get around but for something much more important. A cultural interpreter to describe better what you see. To learn why people act as they do, to gather what is in their minds.

Not only will travellers see China differently and much more richly, they will also view their own culture and country anew, constantly, silently challenged: enlightened. As Mark Twain said, "Travel is fatal to prejudice, bigotry and narrow mindedness". Chinese would say travel can find harmony and knowledge, including of oneself and one's society.

In its latest encounter, China has been learning about the West for more than two decades. No longer passive subjects under a century of foreign domination but as active tourists, the world's most numerous. Chinese have been doing their bit to understand others. Once a sealed state, some 150 million Chinese toured abroad in 2019: making up for lost time to get to know the world, especially the West.

Now it is the West's turn to catch up: to know China and the Rest. Go there, live there, study there, work there. Put aside preconceptions. Forget media stereotypes and demonisation. Trust your own eyes, ears and instincts. Keep an open mind, even on human rights and their evolution: listen.

The Western concept of human rights may start to seem too narrow or not to fit among the top priorities China has chosen. Remember China is governed by priorities. The top priority has been overcoming poverty.

Over time priorities change but for now lifting 850 million out of poverty and wiping out extreme poverty altogether is hard to beat.

Log the array of first-hand images in China for future memory and reflection. Check media accounts against them. Do they sound plausible? Are things presented in the only perspective or are there different ways of seeing the same thing? Maybe some detail or context is missing?

Take on board the West's extensive presence in China, some 6,000 miles or more from home. Not just Westerners in the major cities but their products everywhere. All those Mercedes, BMW, GM and Peugeot vehicles, Marriot, Novotel, Hilton and Hyatt hotels, Walmart, Prada, Zara and Apple stores not to mention Starbucks, McDonalds and KFC. Brands from Japan, South Korea and Southeast Asia often arrived before them. Foreign names have already penetrated the world's biggest growth market with one million foreign-owned firms.

Infrastructure has become China's calling card. Is there anywhere a more visually exciting and pleasing airport than Beijing Daxing that Zaha Hadid designed? Is Daxing (pronounced Dar Shing) even known in her adopted UK home, now self-styled Global Britain? At full capacity Daxing will be by far the world's largest airport.

A country physically transformed: distance-shrinking high-speed rail speaks for itself. Outside the coastal plain, spectacular viaducts, bridges and tunnels against dramatic backdrops capture the imagination. Travelling at high speed through mountainous Guizhou, a friend from India remarked it should be mandatory for every Indian politician and senior official to take the same trip: to see what is possible.

All snapped images provide food for thought about how the world will look in 2050. It is future context for everyone. So, how can government officials and politicians start to understand China better? Apart from the already mentioned Australian lessons they should take business classes.

Business Classes

Academics and journalists once provided largely reliable, seasoned, unbiased insight into China, with long-term perspective. No more, with rare exceptions, it is usually limited at best. Many have been hobbled by domestic agendas that divert funding and time to more ideological areas, derived from fears of Western relative decline since the 2008 Financial Crisis and the subsequent Pivot to Asia. Limited not just by focus but by knowledge too.

I am always surprised at how illiterate, about economics, finance or culture, many are who pronounce on China: including some business journalists and academics. Many only know their own specialities, be it politics, security or one narrow aspect of finance, displaying remarkable ignorance of the broad sweep of China's development or society. They miss the big fact: China's economy is catching up fast.

The mood music too often is the negative narrative of China's Coming Collapse or the latest contextless detail. Not the much greater, broader reality on the ground that points to a very different conclusion.

Much knowledge is out-of-date: overtaken by a rapidly changing and ever-swelling body of information on China. Even before COVID, academics visited much less due to funding and political constraints. Journalists lived in their own bubble, mainly in Beijing, stuck on the 24/7 news treadmill, breathing in each others' fumes, rarely bothering to go outside to the real China of 1.4 billion people: too time-consuming, not requested by editors.

There is a joke among Old China Hands about the typical new foreign journalist. After a week, he or she is asked how they find China. "I could write a book, many books", he confidently replies with great enthusiasm. After a month, he is less sure, even about one book's title. Then, after a further three months, the book idea is "too complicated": instead a long think piece is contemplated. After a year, he is asked how the long piece is going. "I haven't decided what to write yet", is the weary, confused reply.

Commentators and opinion makers in the West find it much easier. They are often not required to have any significant, direct experience of China or even Asia. A friendly returned or retired diplomat will help with "expertise", narrative and usually unattributable quotes. Everything can fit neatly into hermetically sealed world views, Made in the West. Too many in the media prefer to tap intelligence and military minds, with minimal on-the-ground experience: much easier and safer for careers.

Indeed China is complex, complicated and vast, hence hard to understand. However, it can be learned, given time, will and humility. This includes modifying some long-held ideas. First, misconceptions must be set aside. Cut through the lens of mystery, as Zhou Enlai suggested to Kissinger, to find reality: it exists.

How can the West find reality and best learn about China? Do not despair. There is a good answer — its business communities. After two, three and even four decades of China experience, leading Western companies, along with start-ups and pharmaceutical firms, often at technology's cutting edge, have much practical China knowledge.

This is why they succeed, not just in China but globally. They are the explorers of the late 20th and early 21st centuries, the modern equivalent of 19th century Western travellers, historians, writers and artists or even Marco Polo who died almost 700 years ago.

One of the people at our 2004 enlightenment about the intensity of competition in China was Dick Sanderson, head of research at GE Asset Management (Chapter 6: *Sources of Dynamism*). Directing research into listed US companies, he had to worry about their future: just like a good Confucian scholar-official. He had come halfway round the world to understand the competition.

At the end of the workshop, Dick declared himself very depressed. He could not see how US companies could withstand the Chinese competition on the horizon. That vulnerability was now clear to him; and very disturbing.

Many firms were not up to the task immediately but quite a few learned. From them an elite group of US companies rose to the challenge very well. In 2005, one of these elite companies held a two-day conference in Beijing entitled *China 2015*, looking out one decade: very Chinese.

The legal counsel flew in from Washington DC. As the morning's first main speaker, he began with an icebreaker. At least that is what the 200 attendees thought when he instructed them to register immediately, on returning to their offices, all the company's intellectual property in China. Everyone laughed, knowing that was a waste of time: just work around it. Get on with doing deals, there was a whole continent to conquer.

"No", the legal counsel said sharply, in a stern tone — and he was the most senior person in the large room — "I mean it". Everyone stopped laughing. With a jolt they awoke. They listened, they registered: they took China seriously and a decade later that showed in the firm's much improved China performance, across the board.

In Corporate America and Europe, more and more executives rise to the top with direct experience of China or at least of Asia. They have much to teach. They understand China's proven potential, future opportunities and how China works, including how to navigate its potholes and roadblocks. They have lived China. Successful firms Just Do It, get on with it: not complaining, not blaming, simply by understanding. For they know this is reality, and potentially a very critical one for their firms globally.

New New World: End of Western Ascendancy

Business people "get" the new global era. Revenues and profits tell them that the Vasco da Gama Era has ended. That is how the Australian Coral Bell described the big picture in 2007, with "the end of Western ascendancy over the non-Western world ... and the end of unchallenged US paramountcy". Quite a shock, for some: The Times They Are A'Changin'.

Despite such perceptions, many Westerners still cannot see that Asia and the world are no longer controlled by the aftermath of Vasco da Gama's journey around the southern tip of Africa to India in 1497. Five centuries of Western colonisation and domination, especially of Africa and much of Asia, including China, have ended.

The next eight decades to 2100 are hard to imagine but may differ significantly from the last eight. Who, even 40 years ago, would have predicted all three developments — the collapse of Soviet Communism, Japan's lost decades or the rapid re-emergence of China? Be prepared for shocks.

Books of the last quarter of a century predicted the *Coming Collapse of China*, *The Coming War with China* and the *The River Runs Black* (skyrocketing pollution). There were numerous analysts' reports about Ghost Cities, which subsequently magically de-materialised or bank crises, which never happened: stress yes, collapse no. Expect the unexpected, not comforting straight-line continuity of Western dominance or China's apparent mistakes and vulnerability.

Economic tectonic plates have shifted. With them, power equations change. These movements will only accelerate, making mutual co-existence ever more difficult. This will be just when the world must live together if it is to get through the rest of this century in one piece. Fighting climate change, pandemics, water problems, bio-diversity and other pressing global problems cannot be done in a vacuum, certainly not in a Cold War that could become nuclear hot.

We live in a multicultural, increasingly tightly connected, world. Respect others. Don't exclude, include; and When in Rome Do As the Romans Do. That may be all well and good for some but others still want to know "What to Do About China?".

Stopping China is an itch that some must scratch. Lesser dog status, no matter what logic suggests or determines, is unacceptable. Travel to understand China will probably not appeal to them.

Attempts to thwart China will increase. An alliance of democracies may sound plausible but in the long run may not endure, given competing interests among each other and pressure to fix domestic problems first. The Quad (US, Japan, Australia and India) might seem a splendid Australian idea to cloak a military alliance with peaceful intent to contain China and to keep the US in the Pacific.

Yet expecting others to follow policy that principally promotes US interests is unlikely to last long. Japan and Australia have already shown where their economic priorities and loyalties lie by joining RCEP, the world's largest free trade arrangement, along with China: India is still contemplating it and defies the US on Russian sanctions. Can the US accept being overtaken by India's economy or Nigeria's population? Can it agree to one person one vote in global governance: a true test of democracy?

The Quandary

The more the US opposes the re-emergence of China, India and the Rest the higher the cost. This is the root of its quandary. The sooner the West can find ways to work with China, India and the Rest, the sooner it will reap the benefits. If not, trouble lies ahead, deepening trouble.

In 2009, when the post-da Gama trends were already clear, I asked a former US State Department official, whom I know very well, why couldn't Obama acknowledge the reality of great difference in size and lead the US into a more secure future with China? Rather than get into an eternal battle, where scale and time are on China's side, the US could develop a functioning very long-term relationship for mutual benefit, as Nixon and Mao did.

To a post-imperial Briton, this seemed the obvious answer; and one perfectly possible to achieve. Justifying belatedly his Nobel Peace Prize, Obama could bring all parties together to acknowledge the future course of world history; notably, the re-emergence of former regional powers and even global ones in a multipolar world. They could even be a counterweight to China.

The answer both startled and depressed me. That was impossible, I was told. Obama could not afford to go down in history as the president who gave up US global supremacy to China. A repeat of the McCarthy era, under a witch-hunt of "Who Lost China?" could well follow. The hawks were already on manoeuvres. What could Obama do, short of nuclear war, other than obstruct, delay and hope for the best?

Since then nothing has worked. The economic gap has narrowed much more in China's favour. From having an economy 150% larger in 2010, the US GDP is now only 36% bigger and looks set to be smaller still or zero by 2030. Remember, on a GDP purchasing power parity (PPP) basis which is what really matters, China's economy is already larger by some 27%. Only by GDP, the psychologically comforting measure to the West, is it not, yet.

The military equation too is changing. In the Western Pacific it seems to be going, as the economy has, in China's direction. Previously, in 2013, when Xi met Obama for the first time at the Sunnylands retreat in California, Xi noted that the Pacific Ocean was plenty big enough to share: an oblique reference to two spheres of influence that both would respect. The US could not countenance that. Xi's suggestion was ignored.

Obama could not provide true leadership by telling his people the truth. One of the most cerebral presidents became a proverbial ostrich, like many in his nation. His successor did worse because he convinced China of America's true intentions. That gave China more time to prepare in earnest, from boosting R&D in critical areas to adjusting long-term plans in detail.

Since Obama's days, warfare has moved on. The next generation of conflict will involve space. Cyber security tops all agendas. Now it is on Biden's watch. China is suggesting an idea based on Mutually Assured

Vulnerability (MAV) in space: again from Tsinghua's strategic thinker Senior Colonel Zhou Bo.

Already four countries (US, China, Russia and India) can shoot down each others' satellites: time to act before it is too late. Just as a balance of nuclear terror maintained peace during the Cold War, by recognising Mutually Assured Destruction (MAD), so MAV could achieve the same balance in space and cyber warfare.

As with nuclear weapons, the four nations have a vested interest in preventing proliferation: keeping the power advantage safely in their own hands. Worth exploring the chances to reduce risk? Better to be talking than planning destruction, which could prove mutual. Are there non-military options?

Could US–China relations be reset? They were in 1972. Could Joe Biden and Xi Jinping do a Nixon-Mao reset? That is today's biggest question, especially after the US withdrew from Afghanistan, unable to make its vast military might count against less than 100,000 Taliban fighters. In fact it still is the right question even after Russia's invasion of Ukraine, for without a US–China agreement on how to handle the future everything else pales into insignificance. It is time to take stock.

Chapter 22

Taking Stock

Politics is not the art of the possible. It consists in choosing between the disastrous and the unpalatable.

Harvard Professor of Economics and US Ambassador J.K. Galbraith (1908–2006)

Of course, being overtaken in GDP should not be a cause of war let alone Armageddon. Common sense sees that but who can say with certainty what politicians and others may think or do in 5–10–15 years' time? By then it will be too late to change course.

After the relentless US pressure — military, diplomatic, psychological and economic — of the last few years, China cannot afford to take the chance that common sense will prevail. Much has changed in recent years: not just in US words but more importantly in actions. The China–US trust account is virtually empty, relations frostier. Danger has increased. This is not a time to be complacent.

Never underestimate danger, especially in a nuclear age. Most changes in the order among dominant powers have come through war. Future US decision-makers could act very differently, as Donald Trump proved. China cannot afford to pin false hopes on others nor wait for actions to prove or disprove the sincerity of words. First, it must prepare for every eventuality.

Three Unthinkable Changes

Get Real: three seemingly unchangeable things *have* changed in the last decade.

1. Improving US–China relations for almost 40 years have ended. Growing US hostility has replaced what was good enough to get along.
2. Almost all corporate consultants believed US–China trade would continue to triumph over domestic politics. History proved them wrong. Indeed, politics are only likely to intensify. Consultants underestimated the public's and politicians' need for a scapegoat to blame for struggling US real incomes, and grossly overestimated the willingness of US business to argue its case.
3. Experts dismissed containment as generals fighting the last war: the Cold War against the Soviet Union. They reasoned that decoupling would be much more difficult as China was the world's No. 1 trader and foreign direct investment destination, whereas the USSR was insignificant in both. Also, China is more than four times the US population, while the Soviet Union was only 15% larger. Both points are true, yet a Cold War China containment strategy now exists.

Different Perceptions: Abroad and at Home

Do not overlook how much US public opinion has changed since 2008. The amount of think tank and media hostility towards China has grown to the point of demonisation. China is now the enemy in more and more minds: today's Soviet Union. A *casus belli* would be much easier now to sell domestically, especially after Russia's invasion of Ukraine. Naturally, there has been an equal change in Chinese public opinion responding to this hostility.

Pew Research in 2021 found almost half of Americans believed that "limiting China's power and influence is a top priority", while two-thirds described themselves as "cool to China" and 70% were prepared to push China on human rights even if there were an economic cost. One Brookings expert described the numbers as "eye-watering".

The danger is they prepare people for continued conflict and possible war. Only 15 years ago, China had positive ratings. A majority in the US thought well of China. Then the 2008 financial crisis brought jobs and economic stress to the front of US voters' minds, demanding someone be blamed: China was the easy target.

Notwithstanding that Harvard's 2021 Youth Democracy poll found 52% of young Americans, aged 19–29, consider US democracy to be "in trouble" or "failing", while only 7% believe the US is a "healthy democracy", many want to blame China for US ills. Negative feelings, both abroad and at home, are a toxic mix. Irrational populism feeds on them.

In contrast, foreign surveys find Chinese trust in their government at a peak. Competence and the ability to get things done, to deliver, are at the root of what Harvard's Ash Center found in its latest 2019 survey.

The Edelman Trust Barometer, conducted in November 2022, found that little had changed as a result of COVID, despite much media coverage to the contrary. Trust in the central government was at 89%, the world's highest. China also topped the overall trust index rankings for the fifth year running; and in 2022 in the index's three other components of business, NGOs and media.

Former *Financial Times'* Asia correspondent David Dodwell noted perceptively that, "'Regime Theory has long argued that authoritarian systems are inherently unstable ... but the Ash team finds that the Communist Party... appears to be as strong as ever [after 70 years in power]'". Regime Theory about Chinese authoritarianism so far is so wrong: like the Coming Collapse of China. One day either could be proven right, one never knows.

What we do know is that for two decades they have been proven very wrong, encouraging false ideological hopes among some Americans about China's vulnerability. Consequently emboldening ideologues who have helped dig an ever deeper hole for relations. China has only become stronger, yet some American China experts still talk about the

Chinese government's fragility, despite evidence from independent US and other Western sources to the contrary.

Media

Sir John Glubb talked about the final stage of empires being the Age of Decadence (of institutions). Western media is very much a case in point. Reporting standards in terms of accuracy and balance have fallen steadily in recent decades. Society has to pay a price for being less well-informed about how to handle wisely the changing global dynamics.

Hiding in plain sight are the consequences of two future shocks: China's GDP overtaking the US and the non-Western world comprising 90% of the population. Instead of being well informed about either, much Western media falls back on the past and its privileged position. Rewriting history, almost as soon as it happens, the media has "tropes" and "memes" to plant ideas that flourish, even if facts are lacking or deny them.

The *New York Times* still in December 2021 wrote of China having, "navigated the COVID-19 pandemic relatively well [sic] after initially failing to contain the spread of the virus". This was as if discovering the all-important genome sequence, within a breathtakingly short two weeks, and immediately sharing it worldwide did not count. Similarly, as if contacting the WHO and US within five days of confirming the unknown virus showed it failed initially to contain the virus. As for China having done "relatively well", comparing China's far, far fewer deaths with the US's 1.1 million is bizarre: an interesting use of the word relatively.

People often say the world has shrunk over the last half-century. Yet, in some ways, Western nations are just as ill-informed as ever about the rest of the world; and are just as parochial. Some believe more so. Take US media coverage of its president meeting virtually with China's president in their first talk as presidents. The world's two most powerful politicians presumably would lead all news bulletins in the US?

CNN, the most international of US channels, led first with two racially based US murder trials. This was followed by revelations about senior Trump officials Pompeo and Mnuchin talking about their president and thirdly that the Wyoming Republican party cancelled the membership of Liz Cheney. To the rest of the world these were parochial.

Everything is local, especially politics, but that is the problem. This focus can rob the public of what it needs to know. Otherwise how to make informed decisions about foreign relations and even war? To its credit, the *BBC* led extensively on Biden-Xi; and not with government handouts but insightful reports from a correspondent in Shanghai and an expert in Singapore, both Caucasian but well-informed.

Not Knowing How Much China Has Changed

Much knowledge about China is very outdated. Even the facts are not known correctly, as US veteran China fund manager Brook McConnell of South Ocean complains. The extent to which China's quality of life is catching up with the US is not appreciated nor that China's educational foundation and economic base is rapidly improving.

China's greatest attraction abroad is as the world's single largest source of economic growth. For governments and firms alike that matters. Globalisation 2.0 after COVID is unlikely to make much difference. China is still expected to generate 20–25% of world growth over the next decade, some say 30%.

China is now much more than just the heart of global supply chains. More importantly, China is the growing global hub of innovation and knowledge chains. That is simply too strong a magnet to ignore. Whereas six of the world's 10 most valuable listed, and hence older, technology companies are from the US, six out of 10 most valuable unicorns, young pioneering technology start-ups with a value exceeding $1 billion, are now from China: the future.

In addition, absence from China puts firms at a significant competitive disadvantage globally. Limiting themselves to just 80% of the world's market, missing almost one-third of its future growth, hurts. Company's R&D unit costs rise if R&D expenses cannot be spread over the largest numbers. Budgets are cut to fit their cloth. Without sufficient R&D, profit margins are squeezed, while new consumer trends and innovation go unnoticed.

Understanding government policy anywhere is challenging, China is no exception. Its 2021 mid-course economic policy corrections were largely misunderstood, even though most were similar to Western practices. These include pro-competition anti-monopoly regulation (anti-trust), fiscal (property tax), income inequality, affordable housing, education and sports. "Soak the rich socialism" is a lazy, ideological misrepresentation. Combined, long-term, they should strengthen the economy through greater competition, while boosting consumer sentiment.

The extent of China's economic restructuring is not grasped. China has shed many poorly paid jobs, moving workers into higher-value work that pays much better wages. This in turn drives consumption. All is built on China's rising R&D spending of the last quarter century, very substantial education gains and demanding consumers.

The US will be surprised how fast China moves up the value-added curve to compete with the West. Next are intermediate goods — components largely for electronics, computers, machinery and autos: the very jobs the US wants to bring home. In the EU, intermediate goods comprise 40% of all exports: not a small number to emulate.

Equally surprising in corporate governance is that China now handles half the world's intellectual property cases. That is the estimation of a foreign legal consultant, with more than a quarter of a century experience in China. Some 99% are between Chinese parties. Foreign plaintiffs rarely lose, winning a higher percentage than locals.

The environment has seen a similarly striking improvement. Take China's legendary bad air. Stringent enforcement of regulations has cut emissions sharply, especially from coal-fired power plants. On the road China's Standard 6 now matches the EU Standard 6.

Even though annual GDP growth averaged a high 6.6%, PM 2.5 concentration dropped 56% between 2013 and 2021, according to NGO Clean Air Asia. So, even though the economy grew nearly 80%, the total more than halved. Sulphur dioxide concentration in the same period fell even more, by 78%. Water and soil pollution are the next major priorities. Already underway they are a decade or more behind air in their clean up but a start has been made.

All illustrate that China can get things done. On top of that, China's average life expectancy in 2021 rose to 77.1 years while America's fell to 76.1, the US CDC reported.

US Soft Power: Not What it Was

Does the Emperor have no clothes? Increasingly that has been the perception outside the West. The "deligitimisation of US rule", as Singapore-based Parag Khanna calls it, is nothing new to the Rest. It has been happening for two decades since 9/11. Screens everywhere have been full of images of Western-involved conflict and body counts. COVID and the Afghanistan retreat only made it worse.

At home, the US has the world's largest number of COVID deaths; and the related right to life. It failed more than 1.1 million Americans and their families. Human rights violations were exposed by the Black Lives Matter protests, tension and violence. Governance and democracy were eroded by the invasion of the Capitol on January 6, 2021. US soft power took hit after hit.

Abroad, the US squandered much goodwill after 9/11, 2001. The rest of the world watched with mounting distrust the invasion of Iraq on trumped-up charges with fake evidence. Then, with disgust, it viewed images of gross abuse, humiliation and torture at Abu Ghraib prison. Guantanamo detention camp and rendition just made matters worse.

Later the invasion of Libya spread instability from North Africa down across the Sahara to West Africa. One decade on, Boko Haram still murders and takes school girls hostage. ISIL and Al-Qaeda affiliates mushroom in West and East Africa: all unintended consequences but very real nonetheless. Then came proxy wars in Syria and Yemen. Pope Francis deplored that "immense tragedies" in Syria, Yemen and Iraq were "being passed over in silence": silence.

By encouraging regime change à la Arab Spring, at least 350,000 people have been killed in Syria, according to UN estimates. By other estimates, 6.7 million have been displaced internally and 6.8 million fled as refugees: nearly 14 million out of a 2011 population of 22 million, well over half. In Yemen the UN estimates nearly 400,000 people have been killed and more than three million displaced. Blame can be spread widely but some has diminished US soft power among the Rest.

Admiration has dimmed, soft power begun to crumble. Meanwhile, East Asia's self-confidence has grown significantly after controlling COVID far better than the West. This is the 21st century's equivalent of Japan driving out British, Dutch, French and Portuguese colonialism in 1942, dealing an ultimately fatal blow to European empires.

Such turning points do occur, and with long-term historic consequences. Western incompetence may be swept under the rug in the West but will never be forgotten in Asia. Nor will the growing sense of "being Asian".

Hard Power: Also Changing

No one has analysed US military power like former US Assistant Secretary of Defence and Harvard Professor of Government Graham Allison. His assessment of the current and future power relationships of the US and China is contained in two papers that Harvard's Kennedy School, Belfer Center published in 2021.

This was either the military equivalent of strategic realism or a loud wake-up call, depending on interpretation: maybe both. Allison began with three fundamental admissions about power in the third decade of this century, showing how much has changed.

1. The "era of U.S. military primacy is over: dead, buried, and gone — except in the minds of some political leaders and policy analysts who have not examined the hard facts", he wrote.
2. Even though the US is the only global military superpower, "China and Russia in some important ways are its equal". Russia has a nuclear arsenal comparable with the US, while even after a US first strike China can inflict mutually assured destruction from a "fleet of survivable nuclear forces".
3. The US now recognises Russia and China as "great power competitors" that can prevent US dominance along their borders and in adjacent seas. The National Defense Strategy Commission in 2018 stated that by 2024 large parts of the Western Pacific would have become "no-go" zones for US forces.

In a "limited war" over Taiwan or along China's borders, the US would likely lose, "unless it fought a prolonged war that escalated, with unacceptable loss of life and material": Kissinger's "Armageddon-like clash."

Allison lined up prominent defence insiders to confirm his analysis. Former Deputy Secretary of Defense Robert Work said China has, "analysed US capabilities, including war games, more carefully than have many Americans who still want to cling to facts from a world that was".... and is no more. That is quite a turn-around in some insiders' perceptions.

Ironically, it was the US display of overwhelming power in 1991's Operation Desert Storm against Iraq, reinforced by 2003's Shock and Awe bombing of Baghdad, that awoke China to the extent of its vulnerability. China had no overnight solution but long-term thinking began. Like China's economic comeback, set in train many years earlier,

China's military thinking underwent a complete overhaul. The context is very important.

In 2015, Xi Jinping instructed the military to restructure so, in his pointed words, it could "fight and *win* wars". Not having fought a major war since the early 1950s in Korea, it had much to do to win. In 2017, Xi announced the People's Liberation Army's goals were to be fully modernised by 2035 and a world-class force by 2049: China has much more capability to come.

Meanwhile, the US focused most on counter-insurgency and counter-terrorism for more than two decades: largely asymmetrical warfare akin to small-scale insurgencies and guerrilla warfare. Not useful background for fighting a peer competitor. Furthermore, while the US is engaged everywhere, China is focused overwhelmingly on defending its borders, with home team advantage.

Focus has been not just on military capacity but also on related technology. Remember Paul Kennedy's observation. Military strength "is inextricably intertwined with economic power and technological progress". There is no getting away from it.

The most up-to-date assessment of the technological race between the US and China is in the 2021 Harvard Belfer Center report led by Allison and reviewed by industry leaders like Google's former CEO Eric Schmidt. It concluded that,

"China has become a serious competitor in the foundational technologies of the 21st century: artificial intelligence, 5G, quantum information science, semiconductors, biotechnology, and green energy. In some races, it has already become No. 1. In others, on current trajectories, it will overtake the US within the next decade".

The US may continue to lead in some areas, such as semiconductors on which Biden focuses, but not in others of the same or greater significance.

Changing Power Balances: Much Uncertainty

The power equation is changing. Tectonic plates grind and groan ever louder. The US, China and Europe will all soon be of similar GDP size. Each decade after that China will most likely pull further ahead. The existing five BRICS are already larger than the G-7 on a PPP basis. By 2060 they will be 15% larger than the entire OECD. If, as is likely, the BRICS expands membership it could eclipse the OECD (Table 1. Real GDP on Purchasing Power Parity Basis: *Economic Power Shift 2020–2060E*).

This is the New New World. Not just in economics but in military power. The relative decline of US military power in the Western Pacific, recognised by the US itself in 2018, has yet to register widely. It will be a major shock: another unchangeable that changes.

The future holds many, many unknowns as the US struggles through one of its "democracy crisis" periods. Obsessed with domestic political calculations, the danger is that Washington misjudges Beijing's thinking, ignores good advice or is simply too distracted elsewhere. Funding too may be a problem.

US domestic problems will slow handling issues that matter to other countries. Do not assume China and the Rest will let the US dictate global events or agendas forever. Nor that they will accept foreign policy constantly in thrall to US politics, electoral cycles and timing. This may even include some allies. Patience is limited. Deng Xiaoping advised that China should hide its light while building up its economy. That phase has passed.

The West should not ignore Chinese public opinion over sovereignty in Xinjiang, Taiwan, Hong Kong, Tibet and the South China Sea. These are red lines to Chinese, giving their leaders less room for flexibility: not helpful to the US.

Each country or region has new priorities, and legacy issues to resolve. Most countries have a new generation in charge.

In Asia too, power equations are changing for countries, firms and industries. Geography and cultural affinity are powerful magnets drawing the rest of Asia closer to China economically, no matter the geopolitical manoeuvres and sloganising.

Although avoiding unnecessary dependence on China leads to many intricate dances, on all sides, the overall trend is towards greater regional economic integration, as RCEP has shown. "Middle Powers" and strategic locations will play both sides, the US and China, against the middle. They may well require a bit more diplomatic space between the dancers so they can *huo lu*, get along with both, which, for now, is the general choice.

Economically, 80% of Taiwanese businesses have links with the mainland, according to Taiwan-raised venture capitalist Charles Liu. His Taipei primary school counts hundreds of alumni in Shanghai alone. Decoupling from China would be really hard for Taiwan; and impossible for the US to replace quickly the China workplace or market.

Militarily, the *Economist* may headline Taiwan the most dangerous place on earth but China wins 18 out of 18 war game simulations, according to former US Deputy Secretary of Defence Robert Work. Geographic proximity and focus trump hardware inventory. China would have to pay a stiff diplomatic price to recover Taiwan by force but the outcome increasingly is not in doubt.

The danger of nuclear accidents cannot be ignored. President Biden raised it with both Presidents Xi and Putin. He does not know what future presidents might do. What can be said with certainty is never say never in nuclear calculus. Risks are far too great: no laughing matter.

The West is rapidly heading for a point of no return with China. Nonetheless, the *Financial Times* headline writers, reversing John Lennon's call to *Give Peace a Chance*, jokingly made light of the serious issues in 2021 with *Give War a Chance*. Maybe not: it is for the West to think more deeply and decide.

Soon it will be too late. The longer tensions are allowed to build, the more uncertainty rises, economic and military. More dialogue is needed urgently to stop a collision. Reality of China's size and likely future heft must be admitted. Denial will get the world nowhere.

As Nixon wrote in 1967, "We simply cannot afford to leave China forever outside the family of nations, there ... is no place on this small planet for a billion of its potentially most able people to live in angry isolation". This is the time for practical vision: pragmatism.

Understand that China's long history has taught many lessons. From these China draws ideas to navigate today's uncharted waters. US–China history too can teach helpful lessons. It is simply common sense that only a Grand Bargain can reverse the current collision course. All the benefits have been detailed (Chapter 2: *US Foreign Policy*) but it will still be difficult after all that has been said and done.

Galbraith's prescription to solve difficult problems is to choose the least bad option. To reverse his words, the unpalatable beats the disastrous. What might this mean in practice? If there is to be a Grand Bargain, neither side will get all it wants: not immediately, anyway. It may have to concede in some cherished areas. That could be unpalatable but as in any negotiation, both sides will have to compromise.

China may have to give ground on some economic issues. Like any good negotiator, China will have been holding back some concessions, waiting for a bigger bargain rather than be salami sliced to death by individual issues. China has long been ready to open up more its markets but a faster pace may well be required. This should not be hard for China as its firms have been preparing for the day over the last two decades. Indeed, China's economy may even gain from it.

The US would have to give firmer guarantees over the One China Policy regarding Taiwan. Second, it would have to provide assurances not to intervene in China's domestic affairs. It would also have to normalise trade relations through the World Trade Organisation (WTO), instead of taking arbitrary actions outside it or ignoring WTO rulings. Finally, the US will have to acknowledge the long-term economic and demographic facts of the 21st century, agreeing to accept and work with the change not to fight against it.

The need for deeper mutual understanding has never been greater. This starts with boosting people-to-people communications. Not just with the general public but by building academic and media expertise. Psychology is important. Both sides have to understand how an agreement will be received by the other's domestic audience and help to improve its appearance to the other.

None of this is easy but where there is a will there is a way, especially as the clock counts down. The Doomsday Clock is at 90 seconds before midnight. If the will is lacking, the future will be full of deepening antagonism that could approach Kissinger's Armageddon-like conflict and crippling economic dislocation. Any unpalatable solution would certainly beat that disaster.

Chapter 23

Conclusions

Oh, East is East, and West is West, and never the twain shall meet...

*...But there is neither East nor West, Border, nor Breed, nor Birth,
When two strong men stand face to face, though they come from the ends of the
earth!*

Rudyard Kipling, *The Ballad of East and West*, 1889

The West has long misunderstood the East, especially China. Even the best known line in English about East-West relations has been grossly misunderstood. Look carefully at what Rudyard Kipling actually wrote in the poem above, the *Ballad of East and West*.

After the opening line of "Oh, East is East and West is West and never the twain shall meet", the biographer of the British Empire, stated in the third and fourth lines that no gap exists. Not when two strong men from the ends of the earth stand face to face. Weak men are another matter.

Could two strong men be Joe Biden and Xi Jinping, true leaders not vote-counting calculators? I do not doubt Xi could: could Biden or a successor be? Each reader will have their own answer. Anyway, why all the fuss? We shall return later to that very sensible question.

First though, what is China's economy telling us today? What does Huawei say about corporate China? What does China's Modernisation, its latest development strategy, mean for the future?

China's Economy Today

China's economy today has many things going for it. Nonetheless, many in the West are stuck with old mindsets about China. The West ignores today's reality at its peril. Education, technology and consumers are just three defining changes.

Education has expanded markedly over the last quarter of a century. China now has more graduates and professionally qualified people than the US has workers. Backgrounds in STEM subjects provide in-depth scientific knowledge and large numbers to drive corporate China.

Already it leads in new areas of old industries like EVs, batteries and drones, as well as in the critical new frontiers of 5G and 6G communications and nuclear fusion. In both, Chinese firms have registered the most patents. The focus on education has helped create the technology that takes China to the Far Side of the Moon and Mars.

R&D innovation has helped make China globally competitive. This has boosted incomes in a series of reinforcing loops, making workers wealthier, to become the world's largest group of affluent consumers. Their size, curiosity and love of novelty are a retailer's dream.

Yet after three decades of momentum, more than 60% of Chinese consumers still live in the less developed interior. All aspire to the same things standard on the now much richer and more developed coast. China has the world's largest number of internet users, some 1.04 billion. Yet only 72% are on line. That leaves another 28% to follow: more than the total US population. Equally thought-provoking is that only 221 Chinese in 1,000 own a car: in America, it is 890. The great difference is potential writ large.

Opportunity abounds. Firms and individuals, governments and organisations, from nearly 700 million in ASEAN to the World Economic Forum, increasingly engage, learn from and share in China's growing prosperity.

Many Western firms find in China their highest profit margins, biggest overseas markets and largest supply chains. Increasingly, China is their second home. After initial trials, several decades ago, they understand China: unlike many in Western governments and media.

Modern infrastructure and speed — China Speed — get things done faster. High R&D levels create new processes and products. China's spending on basic research, the sort that helps make breakthrough discoveries, has doubled in the last five years. These drove North America and Europe to global dominance for two centuries.

China now has the world's largest banks, deposit bases, pools of private equity and a high savings rate. With these it can finance new industries and expand the old. For instance, China is the world's largest maker of robots. No longer is its great advantage cheap labour. That grainy, grimy picture has changed completely.

Managing change is China's X-Factor. The millennia-old *Yi Jing*, the *Book of Change*, is but one source of traditional ideas that inform Chinese administration, commerce and life. Millennia of experience and philosophy help today's decision makers. History shapes their thinking, from long-term perspective to strict adherence to priorities and constant review.

Competition, driven by all these factors, has built China into the Workshop of the World. That used to be Britain in the 19th century and the US in the 20th. Now China is the 21st century story, with the wind at its back. America faces headwinds, not surprisingly, after a full century as No 1.

This has been a good run, considering America's much smaller population size than China or India; and future numbers similar to Nigeria, Indonesia and Pakistan. The US will likely remain a global power but in a multipolar world. As Sir John Glubb observed, all empires end. On average they last 250 years but never more than 300. Countries usually endure, though not always. However, for some people this is not the same as being No. 1, but here are the facts.

Long-term economic weight is reflected in world manufacturing output. US share has almost halved to 16.8% in 2019 from a 1953 peak of 32%: before war-torn Europe and Japan recovered. The new 21st century leader is China: far ahead at 28.7%. Behind the US is Japan with 7.5%, Germany 5.3%, India 3.1% and South Korea 3%, UN data reports.

US manufacturing jobs peaked at 19.6% of its workforce in 1979 before losing more than one-third to 12.8%. Politicians and much media are stuck in the past's highpoints, oblivious to today's reality.

Ahead lies self-harm if the US stays on its present course, be it of growing conflict with China or inconsistent relations with others. Unintended consequences range from economic decoupling causing disruptive slower growth, even a global depression, higher price inflation and lower US firms' profits to declining trust as America arbitrarily breaks or refuses to sign international treaties. "Forever Wars" erode US soft power. Chapter 18 *The Real China Threat* details the harm for economies, companies and industries.

US self-confidence, which once put a man on the moon within a decade, is no more. With it has gone competence. Only a sense of Exceptionalism and hubris remain, even after the mismanagement of COVID, the 20-year war in Afghanistan and the widespread inability to get things done.

To put this in perspective, China's and India's populations determined the world's largest economies for 18 of the last 20 centuries. Recent Western dominance has been an aberration. Economically, there is no fundamental reason why it should continue, especially with the three great shocks ahead of economics, demography and competence.

Yet that need not be a disaster, except for a few egos and pockets. The West's relatively good life can continue, if it stops underestimating and demonising China and the others. Don't think this will only be about China. Don't think that India, the world's largest electoral democracy, will be spared criticism when it begins to challenge seriously US economic, let alone political, leadership.

There will be plenty of ammunition with which to discredit India. Already on Western radar screens are caste discrimination, religious intolerance and debt bondage: legally abolished in 1976, it still exists. India ranked fourth in the 2016 Global Slavery Index with 19 million in different forms of slavery or modern slavery, as it is now called to include forced labour and marriage.

Huawei

Nothing illustrates China's reality better than Huawei. Targeted for destruction, first by Trump and then Biden, after five years reality was on dramatic display. At the 2023 Barcelona World Mobile Congress, which bills itself as the world's most influential connectivity event, Huawei filled the entire first exhibition hall. Major competitors Nokia, Ericsson, Samsung and IBM were relegated to the second hall.

David Goldman of *Asia Times* explained the prominence. Huawei "has reemerged as the world's top provider of telecom infrastructure, a source of cloud-based artificial intelligence (AI) applications for mining, manufacturing and service industries, and a builder of digital technology for specific industries, especially automotive…[Whereas Western] telecom companies think of 5G mobile broadband as a consumer technology and worry that their market is close to saturation…Huawei thinks of 5G as an industrial technology and believes that the new digital economy is soon set to launch."

Huawei estimates that some 10,000 Chinese firms have dedicated or private 5G networks, Goldman reported. Some 6,000 are manufacturers. That might not seem like many but there are only 171 private 5G networks outside China, with less than 20 in factories. Grabbing leadership in the next stage of development is emblematic of Chinese resilience, speed and innovation.

Now Huawei is ready to introduce 5.5G, with one-third more capacity. This will be another turn of the screw on competitors. Saudi Arabia and UAE are likely early adopters. Goldman concluded that, "China's economic turn to the Global South is probably the pace-setting economic event of the early 21st century. *We are on the cusp of a great new wave of globalisation led by China rather than by the West*, which will draw billions of new participants into the global economy: *the era's pace-setting event.*"

I first heard of Huawei in 2001. Consultant George Baeder, an adviser to the world's communications networks leader CISCO, told me I must visit Huawei when I moved to China. Why? "CISCO calls Huawei the Chinese CISCO": a kindred innovative spirit, packed with ability.

Intrigued, I then asked Nimal Chandaria, whose family was the major investor in Venture, Singapore's largest IT-related company, if he knew of Huawei and its reputation. He replied, "Huawei equipment is very good." "How did he know?" I asked. "We use it here in our Singapore office. Good quality and so much cheaper than competitors," he said. That was enough for me. I went to see someone who worked for Huawei.

The most important person to have appreciated Huawei's culture and ability even earlier was Gao Shangquan, who became known as "China's Father of Economic Reform". In the 1990s, Beijing sent Gao to Shenzhen with a specific mandate: to close Huawei on the grounds it operated in an industry restricted to state entities. State-owned firms had complained to the central government that communication networks were their province, though the real reason was they wanted to eliminate privately owned Huawei's unwelcome competition.

Professor Gao was most impressed by what he found. On his return to the capital, he recommended Huawei be allowed to continue in business, for the good of China's economy. When he recalled this in 2019, I could tell he regarded it as one of his greatest achievements. Certainly he cherished the memory.

This example of China's ability for the government to change basic policy on expert advice added one more reason to my list of why it is time for the West to Get Real about China. China's thinking does not ossify. This is clear in the latest phase of its development strategy. Indeed, China's Modernisation seems to pull together all Xi Jinping's previous thoughts on governance, reform and policy, creating the foundation for the next few decades: much as Singapore did in the 1980s, once it had overcome its first series of steep challenges.

China's Modernisation

The world will be hearing much more about China's Modernisation: Healthy and High-Quality Development too. Not to mention what People-Centred policy and Common Prosperity for All will mean in practice. Social responsibility is one thing, Xi Jinping announcing in March 2023 strong support for the private sector is quite another.

There are many dimensions bundled up in these few words. Together with the earlier announced Global Security Initiative and the Global Development Initiative, China has laid out its stall to ensure sustainable peace and development. Better relations between nations are proposed in the Global Civilisation Initiative.

Previously China played down any idea of a China Model for others to emulate. Now, with a strong track-record of proven development approaches, China is spreading its experience more widely, with good reason. Indeed, the overall 2020 UN Sustainable Development Goals (SDGs) would not have been met if China had not far exceeded its goals. Now, China actively helps others meet their 2030 SDGs, including through UN agencies.

China has much to share on major issues that concern many non-Western countries. These include eliminating altogether extreme poverty, lifting 800 million people out of poverty (850 million by the World Bank's slightly lower definition), dramatically improving air quality by 57% in one decade, managing COVID with by far the fewest deaths among major countries and virtually wiping out illiteracy.

China's development path is neither a replica nor repudiation of the West's. It is though an alternative. China does not have the time to take a couple of centuries to become a fully mature prosperous economy. At most it has one century to go from extensive poverty to high income status.

Nor can it pollute the world the way the West did. It has shown, after its own polluting decades, that developing economies can address and reverse environmental harm, even during periods of high economic growth. That is a great global good, which other poor developing economies are beginning to follow.

China has happily learned from others' successes and best practices, adapting them to local circumstances. Much has been done simply by creating opportunities. Education and opening up the economy created the jobs that lifted most who have escaped poverty. Changing the economic system, with an emphasis on markets and competition was essential but the final 100 million, trapped in extreme poverty, required direct state support. This pragmatic, non-ideological approach has worked.

Two former World Bank China country heads, America-raised Yukon Huang and Dutch Bert Hofman, discussed the real meaning of China's Modernisation, a term that has baffled many, on CGTN with Tian Wei. Huang began by saying that China's concept of development is much broader than the normal definition. It covers living standards and ecology but other dimensions too, ethical and cultural included. These are all the issues China has been addressing for several decades. Only now are they all coming together in a coherent whole under the term China's Modernisation.

China's rejuvenation, as Xi Jinping calls it, is much more than an economic recovery. It is restoration of the nation to its previous standing. Uniquely, in Huang's words, China has collected all the energies of its people in a way never done before, to address social and economic objectives.

Hofman called this widespread mobilisation of people and resources a "whole of nation and people approach". A single problem, be it poverty, pollution, pandemic or illiteracy, can be attacked with a scale and focus never before seen. Latest examples are COVID, bad air, revitalising rural China and spreading the digital hi-tech age to all, to avoid a digital divide. It is how China will meet its 2030 and 2060 climate change targets.

All this is done, Hofman noted, while maintaining "Chineseness". Everything has to consider Chinese characteristics: local conditions, thinking and stage of development. Similarly, other countries must consider their own characteristics before applying any lessons from China.

The all-round, 360-degree approach, taps the energy, vitality and creativity of everyone. The motivation is simple. People aspire to a better life. From their own direct experience they know that poverty, illiteracy or whatever is very ugly, demeaning and painful. This is not confined to individuals but the nation too, from which comes the collective will that in China has proved to be unique.

Global Economic Realities

Back to the question about why make such a fuss? The West's economy will continue to grow: only more slowly than the Rest. The decline will be *relative*. Westerners will still be much richer per person than those in non-Western countries for the next few decades at least, if their governments manage the transition well. The answer therefore is this: there is no need for Westerners to worry. They will simply have to adjust to reality.

If not, they will have to hope their nations' declines do not match China's loss of share in world GDP. This fell from 34% in 1820 to a low of 5% by 1949: India followed a similar collapse. Such things happen, so listen and learn. Don't be arrogant. Otherwise the same fate could befall the West. Bear in mind, China took 150 years before its subsequent recovery began: a very long time.

The real danger is that the West in denial hasn't seen anything yet. Even more painful shocks lie ahead for the US economy in the 2020s, 2030s and beyond. This will doubtlessly generate ever more domestic demands to "Do Something About China".

The numbers are not small: for some, they are terrifying. China will create in the 2020s extra GDP on a PPP basis equivalent to one-third of the US economy's entire size; and another quarter in the 2030s. This compares with only one-sixth in the last decade and nothing in the 2000s.

Nearly three-fifths of the increase in global GDP in the four decades to 2060 is forecast to be in the five BRICS countries (Brazil, Russia, India, China and South Africa), according to the OECD forecast. Already they comprise almost two-fifths of world GDP, while the G-7 mature economies account for slightly less.

More alarming for some in the West, the G-7 will only create one-fifth of the world's extra GDP by 2060. If the BRICS expands, as it intends to do, it could capture almost four-fifths of the world's extra GDP — a Western military strategist's worst nightmare.

The three remaining G-20 developing economies — Indonesia, Saudi Arabia and Argentina — may join next. Indonesia alone could add 10% to BRICS' share of 2060 world GDP, while Saudi Arabia, though smaller, has powerful linkages with the rest of the Arab world, energy producers and capital.

This expansion would have global impacts: economic, political and potentially, very significantly, financial. Reportedly 24 countries have applied for BRICS memberships. If all joined, they would be the new global majority: outnumbering the West. Where will the West's democratic legitimacy be then?

Even without formal enlargement, like-minded non-Western states are cooperating to solve problems. Not just economic and health: out of the blue came news that China had brokered an agreement for long-term rivals Saudi Arabia and Iran to resume diplomatic relations, reopening their embassies. For years other parties had failed to do just that. China obviously had the trust of both countries and the ability to find a solution that had eluded others.

More than a large feather in Beijing's cap, the 2023 signing suggests China's more active role in world affairs, as anticipated by its Global Security Initiative. Top diplomat Wang Yi said, "China will continue to play a constructive role in handling hot spot issues." Hot spot handling: that is music to many ears outside the West.

This came just three months after Xi Jinping visited Saudi Arabia, right after meeting the heads of the US, Germany and the EU Council. He lost no time in announcing to 21 Arab League leaders that plans were well advanced for Saudi Arabia to trade energy on the Shanghai Petroleum and Natural Gas Exchange — in Chinese yuan. The UAE did this in April 2023, using yuan not dollars.

It may also well be a financial milestone in terms of diminishing the US dollar's dominance: a key part of America's economic and strategic strength. Other countries may follow the UAE, which is one of six regionally and economically diverse nations in collective discussions over BRICS expansion.

The UAE already has close and successful cooperation with China to develop vaccines, beginning against COVID. Its Central Bank is working with China's, the Bank of International Settlements, the Hong Kong Monetary Authority and the Bank of Thailand on a digital currency cross-border payments project. This could also weaken dollar paramountcy.

De-dollarisation has entered the financial vocabulary. Not just the IMF but politicians like Donald Trump talk about it, for good reasons. The implications are not just economically but strategically great.

In time, there may well be closer links with countries wishing to join or be associated with the BRICS, such as Bangladesh, Iran and Vietnam. Even OECD members Turkiye and Mexico may want informal cooperation as their world views are similar to those of the BRICS, all former regional powers.

Creating global power for the powerless, BRICS' thinking is non-military. It is all about trade, investment, governance and, increasingly, sustainable development. For a protectionist US this is hard to match when Making America Great Again (MAGA) discriminates against outsiders, foes and friends alike. Offering principally military aid is not enough, especially when expecting to be paid for it.

Aggregate all these likely trends and some in the West will be alarmed. Can this painful economic trend for America be prevented? Yes, the US could embrace a root and branch reform of its economy and foreign policy as China did. Chances though seem slim. Politics would stop it, certainly in the short term. As for China, it could stumble. Though, with more than 60% of its population wanting to catch up with the wealth of coastal China, not to mention the constant upgrading of its industries, new and old, that too seems unlikely. Paths seem set.

Does that mean that what lies ahead is an era of growing misunderstanding that leads to nightmares? Not if all parties make a genuine effort to understand each other much better. Then grasp the real opportunities by cooperating on common problems for mutual benefit.

Understanding

Understanding is what it takes to avoid nightmares; first, knowledge of major global economic trends, then of other cultures and systems of governance. In China, these have been evolving for four decades. They will become ever more important in the next four, not just in economics but also in geopolitics.

Positive perceptions in the Global South of China have, for the first time, overtaken those for the US. So records the 2022 Cambridge Centre for the Future of Democracy survey. French President Emmanuel Macron now worries about losing the trust of the Global South. He speaks as if the South (and himself) has forgotten colonialism, overlooked subsequent neglect, even condescension, and ignored Western invasions: not a good start to regaining influence. Recognising history and behaviour would help.

The West has some serious learning and unlearning to do. Not just about China but India and the Rest too. *Vox* reported that in 2016 the US embassy in Baghdad had only six Arabic speakers among its 1,000 diplomats there. No one in the Rest is surprised.

After all, Biden's "Asia Czar" Kurt Campbell seems not to have lived in Asia nor had any formal education there, according to his profile: unless Soviet Armenia, more than three decades ago, counts. A former colleague of his did not think Campbell had ever worked for long in China and certainly would "not have met any ordinary Chinese". That is why new voices with extensive China experience must be heard, to save the West from its own myths and mistakes — for everyone's sake.

The media is in the same position. It needs to expand its sources and deepen greatly its China knowledge and that of other areas too. As Robert Fisk, once long based in Lebanon and one of the very best foreign correspondents of the last half century, put it, "You can't get near the truth without being there." He could have added, "for several decades, with empathy and detachment". Western mainstream China coverage was aptly described by one Yale Chinese in 2021 as "evidence-light, emotion-heavy".

When experts strongly dispute the accuracy of Western reporting on two of the most recent major China stories the media should take note and learn. One is Hong Kong and the other Sri Lankan debt or the "Debt Trap".

Self-styled old-school journalist and Hong Kong citizen Nury Vittachi, with extensive local information networks, wrote that, "Hong Kong's civil unrest was the most reported news story of 2019 — yet every salient detail presented was incorrect". The media should take a good look at itself, as should its consumers.

Two leading academic experts on Chinese investment overseas wrote, "Michael Ondaatje, one of Sri Lanka's greatest chroniclers, once said, "In Sri Lanka a well-told lie is worth a thousand facts." Americans Deborah Brautigam of Johns Hopkins University and Meg Rithmire of Harvard Business School continued, "And the debt-trap narrative is just that: a lie, and a powerful one." This was written just after the head of Britain's MI6 Richard Moore had promoted it. Phew!

Editors and news editors should check more carefully all their China coverage. Go to China to see it first-hand; and not just Beijing or the major cities. Headline writers should pause before repeating the latest lie or China fiction. Yet story lines on both Hong Kong and Debt Traps continue in the same vein, depriving the West of accurate information or perspective on which to make important decisions.

Would it be too hard to write about US-based eminent Confucian scholar Tu Weiming? His five core points of Chinese traditional philosophy have much to offer (Chapter 11: *Challenges*). He names Concern for others, with sympathy and compassion; a sense of Justice not just law; Civility; Trust; and Humility. These are common to many societies. They are the foundation of much current Chinese thinking such as Common Prosperity and People-Centred policy, much more so than *Das Kapital*.

They also help explain why China will contribute 33% to world GDP growth in 2023, as forecast by the IMF. This is the motor at the heart of Asia overall contributing 70%, with India being a rising 17%.

Tu Weiming's five points would be a good way for Presidents Biden and Xi to begin to discuss the future of the US and China, the West and the Rest. Maybe on a long walk, each accompanied only by his interpreter, the two men would discover how much they have in common, what they both value. It is long overdue; and has never been more important.

The US has ignored Napoleon's advice about China: "the sleeping giant: let him sleep, for if he wakes, he will shake the World." China has awoken: not just recently but steadily for four decades. Everything from Research and Development to economic opening up, especially to the private sector, competition, governance and self-developed technology are rebuilding China. Strong momentum promises even more change and development.

In China's wake will come the Rest: from India to Indonesia and Nigeria to Egypt, Turkiye and Iran. If a smooth transition of global power does not occur, a Clash of Civilisations, in a nuclear era, could well be the price to pay for not trying harder to understand reality and to *huo lo*, get along. All parties would do well to remember this; and to understand what Yin and Yang, along with other traditional Chinese philosophy, can offer all sides to avoid a Clash of Civilisations.

Appendices

Gross Domestic Product (GDP) and Purchasing Power Parity (PPP)

Professor of Political Economy at King's College, London Shaun Hargreaves Heap explains,

> "The issue is what exchange rate do you use to compare US$ denominated GDP with Chinese Rmb denominated GDP. The choice is between market exchange rates ($s per Rmb) or PPP exchange rates (again $s per Rmb).
>
> The market exchange rate is determined by government intervention, trade and capital flows. As a result, who knows what meaning to attach to the market exchange rate at any moment in time.
>
> The PPP exchange rate takes the same basket of goods for both US and China and asks how much does the basket cost in $s in the US and how much does it cost in China in Rmb. The ratio between the costs of the identical basket in both countries then gives the PPP exchange rate. It measures the command that Rmb has over goods and services in China relative to the command that $s have over the same goods and services in the US.
>
> The choice of exchange rate doesn't really change the main point: i.e. China and India will overtake US in terms of GDP (this is demography speaking together with reasonable assumptions about the prospects of productivity growth)."

The core real GDP forecast is on a PPP basis from the OECD, entitled here the *Economic Power Shift*. Since the media and politicians usually report the real GDP, normally from the IMF not on a PPP basis, the IMF GDP data is included to avoid confusion. The trends are very similar.

The PPP basis is the main expression by professional economists of GDP when comparing different economies. The IMF uses this too when making comparisons. The changing list of top 20 countries by population between 1950 and 2050 explains some of the New New World's rise. Eight tables collect the main data needed to grasp these two major global trends. They are well worth digesting before reading the book. Start with Table 1: *Economic Power Shift 2020–2060E.*

Changes in Economic and Population Sizes

Table 1.   Real GDP on Purchasing Power Parity Basis.

Economic Power Shift 2020–2060E							
				$ Extra % of	% Share of Total		Change 2020–60
$ Trillion	2020	2060	2020–60	Increase	2020	2060	
World	101.2	237.8	136.6	100	100	100	% Points
OECD	55.8	101.9	46.1	33.7	55.1	42.9	–12.2
G7	37.4	64.7	27.3	17.8	37	27.2	–9.8
US	19.3	36.5	17.2	12.3	19.1	15.3	–3.8
Euro 17[1]	14	23	9	6.6	13.8	9.7	–4.1
BRICS	39.2	117.3	78.2	57.2	38.7	49.3	10.6
China	23.5	62.1	38.6	28.3	23.2	26.1	2.9
India	8.4	42.2	33.8	24.5	8.3	17.7	9.4

Note: 1. Euro 17 — Euro Area.
Source: OECD. Accessed 013123.

Table 2.   Share of World Real GDP 1990–2027E.

Advanced and Emerging Markets Share						
%	1990	2000	2010	2020	2022	2027E
Advanced Economies	78	78.9	65.4	59.4	56.4	53.4
Emerging Markets, Developing Countries	22	21.1	34.6	40.6	43.6	46.6

Source: IMF Datamapper 011723.

Table 3. Size of Economy Real GDP 1990–2027E.

| | | | | *Size of Economy* | | | | |
$ Trillion	1990	2000	2005	2010	2015	2020	2022	2027E
China	0.4	1.2	2.3	6	11.1	14.9	18.3	26.4
Asia-Pacific	5.5	9.4	12.2	20.3	25.9	31.8	38.9	57.3
US	6	10.3	13	15.1	18.2	20.9	25	30.3
W. Europe	8.9	9.7	16.2	20	19.2	21.1	23.5	29.1
World	23.7	34.1	47.8	66.5	74.9	85.4	101.6	131.6

Source: IMF Datamapper 011723.

Table 4. Annual Real GDP Growth % 1990–2025E.

| | | | | *Growth Leaders and Laggards* | | | | | |
%	1990	2000	2005	2010	2015	2020	2021	2022	2025E
China	3.9	8.5	11.4	10.6	7	2.2	8.1	3.2	4.6
Asia Pacific	5.6	5.6	7.3	8.3	5.6	–0.9	6.6	4	4.4
US	1.9	4.1	3.5	–2.6	2.7	–3.4	5.7	1.6	1.8
W. Europe	3.2	3.9	1.9	2.2	2.3	–6.3	5.6	3.2	2
World	3.4	4.8	4.9	5.4	3.3	–3	6	3.2	3.3

N.B. Average Annual GDP Growth in COVID Years 2020–22 China 4.5%, US 1.3%, Western Europe 0.8%.
Source: IMF Datamapper 011723.

Table 5.   World Population by Region 2020.

Asia Almost Three-Fifths

	Millions	% World
Asia	4,641	59.5
Africa	1,341	17.2
Europe	748	9.6
Lat'Am, Caribbean	654	8.4
N America	369	4.7
Oceania	43	0.5

Source: Worldometers elaboration on UN data.

Table 6.   *Top 20 Populations 2023.*

	Million	World %		Million	World %
China	1,439	18	Japan	126	1.6
India	1,380	17.2	Ethiopia	115	1.4
US	331	4.1	Philippines	110	1.4
Indonesia	274	3.4	Egypt	102	1.3
Pakistan	220	2.7	Vietnam	97	1.2
Brazil	213	2.7	DR Congo	90	1.1
Nigeria	206	2.6	Turkiye	84	1
Bangladesh	165	2.1	Iran	84	1
Russia	146	1.8	Germany	84	1
Mexico	129	1.6	Thailand	70	0.9

NB: India is expected to overtake China in 2023.
Source: Worldometers elaboration on UN data (Retrieved 30th January, 2023).

Table 7.   *Top 20 Populations 1950.*

	Million	% World		Million	% World
China	554	21.9	France	42	1.6
India	376	14.8	Bangladesh	38	1.5
US	159	6.3	Nigeria	38	1.5
Russia	103	4.1	Pakistan	38	1.5
Japan	83	3.3	Ukraine	37	1.5
Germany	70	2.8	Spain	28	1.1
Indonesia	70	2.7	Mexico	28	1.1
Brazil	54	2.1	Poland	25	1
UK	51	2	Vietnam	25	1
Italy	47	1.8	Turkiye	21	0.8

Source: Worldometers elaboration of UN data.

Table 8.   *Top 20 Populations 2050.*

	Millions	% World		Millions	% World
India	1,639	16.8	Egypt	160	1.6
China	1,402	14.4	Mexico	155	1.6
Nigeria	401	4.1	Philippines	144	1.5
US	379	3.9	Russia	136	1.4
Pakistan	338	3.5	Tanzania	129	1.3
Indonesia	330	3.4	Vietnam	110	1.1
Brazil	229	2.4	Japan	106	1.1
Ethiopia	205	2.1	Iran	103	1.1
DR Congo	194	2	Turkiye	97	1
Bangladesh	193	2	Kenya	92	0.9

Source: Worldometers elaboration on UN data.

Acronyms

ASEAN: Association of South East Asian Nations — Brunei, Cambodia, Indonesia, Malaysia, Mynamar, Laos, Philippines, Singapore, Thailand and Vietnam.

BRICS: Brazil, Russia, India, China and South Africa

CDC: Centre for Disease Control and Prevention

CGTN: China Global Television Network

EVs: Electric Vehicles

G-7: Group of Seven Developed Economies

G-20: Group of 20. G-7 plus China, India and others

GCHQ: British Government's Communications Headquarters

GDP: Gross Domestic Product

IFR: International Federation for Robotics

IMF: International Monetary Fund

OECD: Organisation for Economic Co-operation and Development

PPP: Purchasing Power Parity

RCEP: Regional Comprehensive Economic Partnership

SCO: Shanghai Cooperation Organisation

WHO: World Health Organisation

WTO: World Trade Organisation

Acknowledgements

Before thanking all who helped me write *America as No. 3: Get Real About China, India and the Rest* I should provide some context. The central economic idea was obvious to me several decades ago. Major changes, political and economic, lay ahead. As no one had written about it satisfactorily for the general reader, even though back in 2014 the OECD had published its long-term GDP forecasts to 2060, I contemplated a book with the working title of *Get Real: China and the Re-emergence of the Rest*.

First though I wanted to explain how China had recently developed so fast and why this is sustainable. As much as anything, I wanted to force myself to think through all I had witnessed and learned firsthand, then to make sense of it.

The result was *China's Change* that repudiated the Coming Collapse of China thesis, which still today remains wrong, one quarter of a century later. Yet the US idea casts its shadow over much thinking about China, along with the concept of a "China Threat" that has spread throughout the West.

After the publication of *China's Change* in 2018, I was in no hurry to jump into *Get Real*, though by 2019 had sketched the outline. COVID then dealt two cards that prompted me indirectly to start work. I was stuck in Bali; and with plenty of time to think. Even then *Get Real* was not on my mind. Initially, my time was spent in emails and phone calls trying to understand COVID for the simple reason that we needed to know when we might be able to return home to Shanghai.

By the summer of 2020, it dawned on me that the West's failure to learn anything from China about how to contain COVID was illogical. The WHO had endorsed China's policy for having worked and said in February that the rest of the world should do the same. Unraveling the mystery of why it didn't, I found an unexpected reason: competence. *Get Real* already had two great shocks for the West to face — economic and demographic. Competence was now a third.

Get Real suddenly took on a much greater dimension and significance. More work would be necessary to integrate the three great shocks. That proved to be a lengthy process but not an inconvenience. We seemed to have unlimited time in Bali as any near-term return to Shanghai became more and more distant. Bali was most agreeable and we felt very safe from COVID.

The book was only completed in early 2023, with a new title and more dimensions than I had originally conceived. "Future proofing" was needed to avoid the ideas and conclusions being overtaken by events. First I waited for the 2020 US presidential election. That gave me more time to think, read, research, email and write. Then just as the first draft reached completion Russia invaded Ukraine. The publisher World Scientific agreed to put on hold the book's editing until the impact became clearer.

All this delay, in a way, was welcome. For it provided much more evidence for the central idea, especially on non-economic aspects. It gave more time to go into greater depth, while making the structure clearer. The original storyline became stronger, much more timely, and indeed urgent. By March 2023, I was satisfied with the final draft.

America as No. 3 required less input from others than *China's Change* but what it received was even more important. Specialists helped in different ways, giving the expertise I lack as a generalist. Digging deep into COVID, while it happened, was the result of many emails over the three years with two old university friends Katie Abu and Dr Anthea Lehmann. They supplied and explained many medical papers that gave me the confidence to understand COVID, while giving a running commentary on what was happening to policy in the West, especially the UK.

Experts who kept me up to date with China and the rest of the world included Ho Kwon Ping, Benjamin Lim, Andy Rothman, Tjio Kay Loen, Ian Johnson, Andrew Sheng, Luke Minford, William Fu, Chris Lewis, Ma Jun, Simon Ogus, Claire Chiang, Ajit Dayal, Marcus Schütz, Stuart Sinclair, Edward Tse, Gerhard Greif and Chone Sophonpanich. Others shared articles and views I had not seen, notably Brook McConnell, Ramsey Su, Jay Chen, Chris Sherwell, Joe Hargreaves Heap, Andrew Williams and Jim Stent.

I should again thank Professor of Political Economy at King's College, London Shaun Hargreaves Heap for discussing and critiquing all the book's economics, just as he did when we were tutorial partners. Former *BBC* Director-General Tony Hall, with his excellent eye for the real story, helped me understand what would interest Western readers.

Finally, I must thank my wife Tse Oy who lived with the long gestation. Her invaluable knowledge filled many gaps, particularly in Chinese philosophy, history and thinking, not forgetting the daily updates of Chinese social media. Like Western social media this is not always accurate but is definitely part of the bigger picture. It reflects sentiment, fears, hopes and battles for control of the narrative.

To all, as well as those I thanked in *China's Change*, for what I have learned from them over the decades, I am most grateful.

Acknowledging debts, I cannot exclude two great influences that helped me understand developing economies, their societies and politics. My tutors Professors Tony Kirk-Greene at St Antony's and Keith Griffin of

Magdalen both provided academic structure, insight and wisdom to understand all the moving parts. Apart from stressing rigor and intellectual honesty, both valued on-the-ground experience and curiosity as the starting point for real understanding.

Reflecting in Bali, I realised two other formative educational experiences motivated me to write the book. When I was three and four, I was the only British child at a German kindergarten in Hamm, Westphalia, where my father taught at a British army school. To me Germany was normal. Tea with Frau Wieneke was a great treat, especially the Viennese pastries and rich chocolate cake.

Many British memories of the recent war were still strong, and not always so warm, open-minded or forgiving as with my parents. In retrospect, I sense that sending me to a German school was their contribution to international understanding, reconciliation and my first introduction to ideas of a common humanity as opposed to a divided world. Long school holidays took us round the camp sites of a recovering post-war Western Europe for five years from 1954 to 1958, meeting other nationalities, experiencing their cultures and picking up some of their history: learning by osmosis a respect and empathy for others.

Yet something else lies deep in my childhood memory: a dark, empty bombed-out building in the centre of Hamm. This was a stark monument to an unfathomable thing called war. My father had fought in it throughout, as had so many others around us in the British teachers' enclave but this was something very different.

The incomplete deep-black silhouette of Hamm's main church, encrusted by more than a century of Ruhr coal grime, was not part of the sanitised-for-children war story. Without much of its spire and with reduced irregular buttresses, the church bore silent testimony to the very recent past and another side of history.

Germany provided very happy memories. Among other things, it is where, without knowing it, I learned my first thing about economics.

For in about 1956 my German toys were suddenly of much better quality. These were "export quality", now made available to the local market. I suppose the end of reparations, belt tightening or both allowed this. Germany's had been an export-led recovery, much as Asia later followed to great effect. Growth through trade, sponsored by the US: so different from today's MAGA and Me First.

Subsequently, Zambia and Africa also taught me a great deal. In 1970 I was an exchange student in the heart of Africa. Mumbwa was in the "bush", 100 miles from the nearest large town, the capital Lusaka. Zambia was six years old, emerging out of many decades of British colonialism. Again, school holidays gave me the opportunity to travel, to explore. This time not just around all points of Zambia's compass but also in the White-ruled South during South Africa's Whites-only election in the *apartheid* era: as well as in newly independent but still very dependent Swaziland.

Almost three months prior to university enabled me to get to know the similarly young post-colonial states of Kenya, Tanzania and Malawi in the East. All had their own and different ideas about how to develop: from Kenyatta's more freewheeling capitalism to Nyerere's austere African Socialism to Banda's Church of Scotland-inspired arch conservatism and relations with the White South.

Attracted by a syllabus that included Development Economics and African Politics, I soon changed from studying law at Oxford to Politics, Philosophy and Economics. This proved the perfect background from which later to consider the changing world economic order and how to manage what is already a very difficult transition. It is not going to be like the colonial powers "granting" of freedom as in Africa and Asia. Though that was not given willingly or won without a long struggle, and, in notable cases like Vietnam, Algeria, Angola and Mozambique, without a major war.

Index

About the Author

From a rare perspective, over 45 years Hugh Peyman has watched China re-emerge. After reading Politics, Philosophy and Economics at Oxford in 1973, he co-authored *The Great Uhuru Railway: China's Showpiece in Africa* (Gollancz London 1976). Since 1977 he has lived in Hong Kong, Kuala Lumpur, Singapore, Shanghai and Bali.

Before 35 years of financial markets research, he worked for Reuters and Asia's top economics, politics and business magazine the *Far Eastern Economic Review*, gaining a 360-degree view of Asia and China's global integration. At Merrill Lynch he headed Asian Research from Korea to India for eight years. To do independent long-term research, in 1999 he founded Research-Works. He now writes. *China's Change: The Greatest Show on Earth* (World Scientific Singapore 2018) won the Sharjah International Non-Fiction Prize. Contact: hughpeyman@research-works.com.

Printed in the United States
by Baker & Taylor Publisher Services